I0029119

John Obadiah Westwood, William Tymms

Fac-similes of the miniatures & ornaments of Anglo-Saxon & Irish manuscripts

John Obadiah Westwood, William Tymms

Fac-similes of the miniatures & ornaments of Anglo-Saxon & Irish manuscripts

ISBN/EAN: 9783337118587

Printed in Europe, USA, Canada, Australia, Japan

Cover: Foto ©Andreas Hilbeck / pixelio.de

More available books at **www.hansebooks.com**

FAC-SIMILES

OF THE

MINIATURES & ORNAMENTS

OF

ANGLO-SAXON & IRISH

MANUSCRIPTS

EXECUTED BY

J. O. WESTWOOD. M.A.

DRAWN ON STONE BY W. R. TYMMS.

CHROMO-LITHOGRAPHED BY DAY AND SON. LIMITED

LONDON.

BERNARD QUARITCH. 15 PICCADILLY.

MDCCCLXVIII.

FAC-SIMILES

OF THE

MINIATURES AND ORNAMENTS

OF

ANGLO-SAXON AND IRISH MANUSCRIPTS

"Scribtori vita eterna; Legenti pax perpetua; Videnti felicitas perennis; Habenti possessio cu salute; Amen Do gracias; Ora pro me; Ds tecum."

GOSPELS OF TREVES, fol. i.

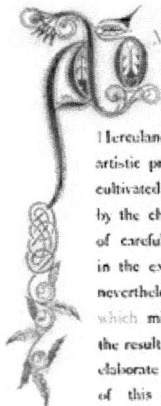

MIRABLE AS ARE THE SCULPTURED PRO-
DUCTIONS OF GREECE AND ROME, AND

exquisite as are the ornamental designs of the wall-paintings of
Herculaneum and Pompeii, it must be admitted that there is an element in the
artistic productions of ruder tribes which is wanting in the works of more highly
cultivated nations, amongst whom the power of representing the human form, either
by the chisel or the pencil, or of depicting human events, is necessarily the result
of careful study and of a highly artificial state of society. This element consists
in the excessive elaboration of ornamental details, often exceedingly minute, but
nevertheless frequently so arranged as to afford fine broad effects in a manner
which might scarcely be supposed possible, and which often, indeed, seem to be
the result of accident rather than of design. India and China in the East, and the
elaborate productions of the South-Sea Islanders, may be referred to as instances
of this power of producing excellent effects from minute but well-arranged
details; and it is precisely this peculiarity which renders the study of the
Manuscripts and other relics of the early Anglo-Saxon and Irish schools so interesting
to the Art-student.

The work now submitted to the public may be regarded as constituting the
first chapter of a History of the Fine Arts in this kingdom, extending from the
Roman occupation of Great Britain to the Norman conquest. To many, this "dark
age" will scarcely be supposed to afford materials for such a history; and indeed,
with the exception of a very few examples given by Strutt, Astle, Shaw, and Humphreys,
scarcely any opportunity had been afforded of judging of the marvellous beauty and
excessive intricacy of Anglo-Saxon and Irish MSS., until the publication of my "Palæographia sacra pictoria" in 1843-5, in which many plates were devoted to these
marvels of Art.

If the earliest Manuscripts of Greece and Italy still in existence be examined
—of which the splendid work of Silvestre contains so many entire-paged examples,—it
will be at once seen that, until the eighth century, it was the custom to write the
whole volume in uniform-sized letters, the first initial being plain, and not at all, or but
very slightly, larger than the rest, the first two or three lines being only distinguished by
being written in red letters; and if the volume was ornamented with drawings, of
which instances are of the greatest rarity, they were illustrations of the subjects of the
text, executed in body-colours, and intercalated into the pages in their proper places,
rarely, if ever, occupying entire pages. On the other hand, the earliest of the fine
MSS. executed in these islands of which we have any knowledge, have the first few
words of the chief divisions of the volumes written of a gigantic size, occupying

entire pages, which are filled with ornamental details; whilst the illuminations also occupy whole pages, and are sometimes entirely composed of intricate ornament alone.

In addition to these peculiarities, the study of these works has incontestably proved that, at a period when the pictorial art may be said to have been almost extinct in Italy and Greece, and indeed scarcely to have existed in other parts of Europe—namely, from the fifth to the end of the eighth century,—a style of Art had been originated, cultivated, and brought to a most marvellous state of perfection in these islands, absolutely distinct from that of any other part of the civilized world, and which, having been carried abroad by numerous Irish and Anglo-Saxon missionaries, was adopted and imitated in the schools founded by Charlemagne, and in the monasteries established or visited by the former, many of which, in after-ages, became the most famous seats of learning.

On this subject, Mr. Digby Wyatt, one of the most accomplished of living artists, observes, that "in delicacy of handling and minute but faultless execution, the whole range of palæography offers nothing comparable to these early Irish MSS., and those produced, in the same style, in England. When in Dublin some years ago, I had the opportunity of studying very carefully the most marvellous of them all, the 'Book of Kells,' some of the ornaments of which I attempted to copy, but broke down in despair. Of this very work, Mr. Westwood examined the pages as I did, for hours together, without ever detecting a false line or irregular interlacement." From this extraordinary volume four entire pages are represented in this work; whilst the libraries of London, Lambeth, Oxford, Cambridge, Durham, Lichfield, Salisbury, Dublin, Paris, Rouen, Boulogne, St. Gall, Milan, Rome, Copenhagen, Stockholm, Utrecht, St. Petersburg, Darmstadt, Carlsruhe, Munich, &c., have been examined and, more or less, laid under contribution for materials.

In a memoir "On the distinctive Character of the Various Styles of Ornamentation employed by the early British, Anglo-Saxon, and Irish Artists," which I published in the 10th volume of the "Journal of the Archæological Institute," in 1853, and in an article on Celtic ornament, published in Owen Jones's "Grammar of Ornament," I have entered at some length on the historical facts bearing on the subject, and have illustrated the various modifications of ornamentation adopted by our native artists, with especial reference to their exclusive employment of each of them. These different kinds of ornament are formed,—

1st. Simply by the use of dots, generally in different coloured inks.

2nd. By simple lines, straight or curved.

3rd. By the step-like angulated pattern.

4th. By the Chinese-like Z pattern.

5th. By interlaced ribbons.

6th. By interlaced zoomorphic patterns ; and

7th. By the various spiral patterns, which are by far the most characteristic of the whole *

I shall therefore in this place confine myself to the question of the origin of these peculiar styles of ornament which are described in the two memoirs above mentioned, and which are so extensively illustrated in the plates of this work.

To suppose that (occurring, as they do, abundantly in manuscripts, stone monuments, ivory carvings, and chasings of the precious metals) these systems of ornamentation had their origin in Byzantium, where nothing analogous in any of these materials, of a contemporary or earlier date, has ever been seen, is, it must be allowed, somewhat illogical. The same observation may be applied also to Rome, from whence it has been affirmed not only that the early artists of these islands derived their inspiration, but that even one of the finest of the Irish crosses had been brought from Italy! During a recent visit to Rome, Ravenna, &c., I especially directed my attention to the solution of this question, if possible, by a careful study of the existing remains of Early Christian Art, some of which, especially the earliest Mosaics, must doubtless have been seen by our Anglo-Saxon and Irish pilgrims, so many of whom are recorded to have made even frequent visits to Rome, as well as to the Holy Places of the East. My search, however, was in vain; and I returned home more than ever convinced that the peculiar styles of our earliest works were elaborated in our own islands, and I now venture to assert that no monument or Art relic of a date previous to the ninth century can be produced in which they, and especially the spiral pattern, are introduced, the execution of which cannot be satisfactorily shown to have been dependent on the teaching of some of our missionaries.

Again, it may be observed that the earliest of the sculptured Christian stones of Wales exhibit the same system of ornamentation, as well as the same style of writing, as the Irish manuscripts, which are, in all probability, of a somewhat more recent date.† This fact, together with the traditions of the early British Church, which are too numerous and too probable to allow us to consider them to be entirely without foundation, appears to be of sufficient importance to throw doubt upon the assertion that the style originated exclusively in Ireland. On the other hand, to affirm as Dr. Rock, from the Roman point of view, has done, that " Britain taught Ireland a peculiar style of scription and ornament," appears by no means capable of proof; whilst his statement, "that although some beautiful samples of our British MSS. were taken over to Ireland, the Irish never

---

* The remarks of the late Mr. Kemble on the exclusive peculiarity of these spiral patterns, contained in his address delivered to the President and members of the Royal Irish Academy, at their meeting, February 9th, 1857, are too important not to be here alluded to. They have been quoted by Mr. Stuart in the 2nd volume of the "Sculptured Stones of Scotland," p. 81.

† The Welsh lapidary inscriptions form a continuous

series from the Roman to the Romano-British and Christian Romano-Anglo-Saxon periods. The Roman inscriptions in Wales, as is also the case with the hundreds of other Roman inscriptions found in other parts of this kingdom, are entirely pagan. Christianity cannot be clearly detected on one of them. On the contrary, the Romano-British inscriptions of Wales are often marked with the cross.

made any progress in the art of illuminating" (Church of our Fathers, i pp. 273, 278)
must be considered as erroneous, and which the plates of this work will sufficiently
disprove. That in both islands these arts followed the introduction of Christianity scarcely
affords a solution of the difficulty, since that event itself, as well as the source from
which it was derived, is still a *quæstio vexata*: although the fact of there being a church
in Britain long previous to the coming of St. Augustine cannot be questioned; whilst
the assertion of Venerable Bede, that the early British Church differed in no
respect from the Irish, sufficiently accounts for the identity in the styles of ornamentation
practised in both parts of the kingdom.

The claims of Scandinavia to be regarded as the originator of the peculiar
Hiberno-Saxon styles merit but few remarks. That there are many carved stones in
different parts of these islands bearing Runic inscriptions, and elaborately ornamented
with the same designs as the MSS., has given rise to the popular idea that these
latter are of Scandinavian origin, and the name of Runic knotwork has been indis-
criminately applied to them, as well as to the uninscribed and truly Irish or Anglo-
Saxon remains. That this is only a popular fallacy will be admitted, when we recollect
that the Northmen did not visit these islands till long after our native Arts had been
brought to perfection; and, on the other hand, that it was from this kingdom that
Scandinavia was christianized, the mother Church of Denmark, at Roeskilde, having been
erected in the eleventh century by Bishop William, an Anglo-Saxon, confessor of Canute
the Great; whilst the Metropolitan Church of Sweden, at Lund, was also founded by
Englishmen in the early part of the eleventh century. Moreover, it is to be observed,
that although the numerous ornamented monumental stones of Scandinavia exhibit interlaced ribbons, often terminating in the heads of lacertine animals, and interlaced patterns
occur to a great extent in the carved woodwork of the earliest Swedish churches, we
never meet with the more characteristic Anglo-Saxon ornaments; namely, the Z-pattern
or the special spiral ornament. Of spiral patterns, indeed, many instances are given in
the plates of the great Danish Collection of Antiquities at Copenhagen, both of the Bronze
and Iron ages, published by Worsaae; but it will be at once observed that in all these
the whorls are consecutive and of equal size, connected together like the letter ω;
whereas in all the most characteristic of the Irish and Anglo-Saxon works, the spirals are
not consecutive, but extend over wider surfaces, so as to form diapers; that the whorls
are invariably of different sizes, and that the spires are connected together by being
arranged like the letter O.

Of the later metal-work ornamentation in which interlaced animals occur, of which
examples are also given by Worsaae, I think I am justified in considering that this
peculiar style of ornament was rather borrowed by the Northmen from the Anglo-
Saxons, or, even if that were not the case, that its origin in this country was entirely
independent of Scandinavia.

There is still, however, a class of Roman Art-work executed in this country with which the early native artists of Britain, at least, must surely have been acquainted, and which may be assumed to have influenced them in originating their peculiarly ornamented volumes, and especially the great decorated pages opposite the commencement of the Gospels. I allude to the Roman tessellated pavements, of which, even still, so many exist in this country. Here we find great masses of ornament arranged in compartments, and in some we even see interlaced ribbon-patterns geometrically arranged; whilst one very peculiar pattern, consisting of a series of interlaced circles, is precisely reproduced on some of the crosses of Cumberland and the Isle of Man; e. g., at Kirk Michael (Cuming, pl. 1, f. 1a) and at Ballaugh (ibid., f. 2b). On studying the various examples of this pattern, it is evident that it is intended to represent two interlinked chains, formed of circles united together by a single bar, alternately interlapping over each other. These are, however, comparatively late monuments; and it must be added that not a single instance of such an ornament has been met with in the MSS. Again, if we carefully compare even the interlacements of the pavements with those of the MSS., we see such a total difference between them, the latter being so intricate, whilst the former are so simple, as to lead us to doubt whether the artists of the MSS. obtained more than a general idea of ornamentation from these pavements, in which we look in vain for the other more characteristic designs of the Hiberno-Saxon works, such as the interlaced zoomorphic patterns, the Chinese-like Z-pattern, or the spiral scrolls. It must, moreover, be borne in mind that the Irish artists could not have had the Roman pavements as their models, since none exist in Ireland, where, indeed the Romans never set their feet.

It is not, however, only the MSS. executed in these islands previous to the tenth century which are so exceedingly characteristic and distinct in their style, since the later Anglo-Saxon artists developed, in the schools of SS. Ethelwold and Dunstan, an equally distinct and national style of ornamentation of a very gorgeous character, in which gold was profusely introduced, and in which conventional foliage is very freely used, but which still, in accordance with the old interlaced feeling of the preceding style, is made to intertwine with the framework of the pictures round which it is applied.

It cannot perhaps be denied that it was from the Frankish schools of Art that the idea of this peculiar style was derived, although it cannot be doubted that its elaboration in this country was carried to such an extent as to earn for it the name of " Opus Anglicum " on the Continent.

If we look at the great MSS. executed in the ninth century in the monasteries of Tours, &c.,—such, for instance, as the Bible at the Basilica of St. Paul beyond the Walls of Rome, or the Bible of Count Vivien, written for Charles le Chauve, now at the Louvre, we find a great variety of classical foliated designs: thus D'Agincourt has given, in his 45th plate of Paintings, not fewer than seventy different patterns

d

of borders from the former volume, executed either for Charlemagne or Charles
the Bald, all of which, save two, are composed of foliage and scrolls quite unlike
anything found in our Hiberno-Saxon books; and that these were derived from classical
models can scarcely be doubted, when the great intercourse between Charlemagne and
Pope Hadrian is remembered. In like manner, the equally great intercourse between
the Frankish and English Courts, consequent on the various royal marriages between
different members of each,* almost necessarily introduced into England the then fashion-
able style of Frankish ornament, whilst it assisted in disseminating on the Continent the
greatly-admired style of the Hiberno-Saxon artists. If we look, however, at the still
existing specimens of Carlovingian or early Capetian works of Art, executed during the
ninth or tenth century, we shall find nothing which can be compared with the grand
ornamental borders of the Æthelwold books, the nearest approach to them being the
ornamental borders of the carved ivory diptychs of the Frankish school, in which
conventional foliage is introduced, and, indeed, forms the main feature.

Since the publication of my "Palæographia sacra pictoria," the character of the
ornamentation of our early Art-works has been investigated or commented upon by
several authors, to whose writings I can here only refer the student.

WILSON. "Prehistoric Annals of Scotland."

KEMBLE. "Address delivered to the President and Members of the Royal Irish Academy, at their meeting, February
9, 1857;" also his "Horæ Ferales," published since his decease, by Mr. Franks.

H. O'NEILL. "The Fine Arts and Civilization of Ireland," 1863; also "The Crosses of Ireland."

PETRIE. In the Appendix to the "Cromlech on Howth."

DIGBY WYATT. "Art of Illuminating."

H. N. HUMPHREYS. "The Illuminated Books of the Middle Ages," and "The Art of Illuminating and Missal Painting."

DENIS (FERD.). "Histoire de l'Ornementation des MSS.," Paris, 1857, large 8vo., 143 pp., with Illustrations, forming
the Appendix to "L'Imitation de Jésus-Christ."

MAZURE (B. CHASSÉS). "Livre de Prières, illustré à l'aide des ornements des manuscrits, classés dans l'ordre
chronologique. Tome ii, Notice historique et Texte expliqué par Ferd. Denis et B. Ch. Mathieu." Paris,
1862, 12mo. A charming volume.

WAAGEN. "Kunstwerke und Kunstler in England und Paris," i. 134, iii. 241; also "Treasures of Art in England;" and
Article in the Kunstblatt, No. 11, 18 March, 1850, translated in the Ulster Journal of Archæology, viii.
p. 306.

KELLER, FERD. "Bilder und Schriftzuge in den Irischer Manuscripten der Schweizerischen Bibliotheken," in Trans.
Zur Antiq. Ges., vol. vii., 1851, translated, with Notes, by Dr. Reeves in Ulster Journal of Archæology,
vol. viii. p. 227.

FRENCH (GILBERT J.). "The Origin and Meaning of the early Interlaced Ornamentation found on Ancient Sculptured
Stones of Scotland," &c., 8vo., 1858. Manchester: Simms †

STUART. "The Sculptured Stones of Scotland," 2 vols. folio, published by the Spalding Club. See especially the
Appendix to vol. ii.

CUMMING (REV. J. G.). "The Runic and other Monumental Remains of the Isle of Man." 4to., 1857.

C. PURTON COOPER. Appendix (A, B, and C) to "Report on the Fœders."

In order to render this work as complete a monograph of Anglo-Saxon and
Irish Art as possible, I have added descriptions of all the ornamented manuscripts
with which I am acquainted, of which I have not been able to give fac-similes, and

---

* Thus Æthelwulf, the father of Alfred, married as
his second wife, Judith, daughter of Charles the Bald.
Alfred himself visited Rome several times, and the
Carlovingian Otho the Great, of Germany, married the
sister of King Athelstan. The Coronation Oath Book and
the Psalter of King Athelstan, both in the British Museum,

are proofs of this intercommunication. The historical details
of both these volumes are given in my "Palæographia sacra."

† Mr. French's theory that the interlaced ornamentation
of these schools originated in the interlaced wickerwork
of the gigantic animals within which the natives immolated
their victims is ingenious, but scarcely tenable.

have, moreover, given an Appendix, containing a series of descriptions and figures of
contemporary objects of Art executed in these islands, in stone, metal, ivory, &c., which
serve to illustrate, in a remarkable manner, the Art of the Manuscripts. I have also in
all cases referred to any published copies from the MSS., &c., in the works of other
authors, whereby the student may the more easily be enabled to examine the designs,
although he may not have access to the originals.

I have purposely excluded from this work those Frankish MSS., ornamented
in the Hiberno-Saxon style, to which the name of Franco-Saxon has been applied.
The grand Bible of St. Denys, of which forty leaves are in the British Museum
(see Humphreys, "Illum. Books," pl. 6), the Gospels No. 257 of the Bibl. Impériale,
Paris (see two fac-similes in "Les Arts somptuaires"), and the Psalter of the Leipsic
Library (Hefner, "Trachtenbuch," pl. 83), are amongst the most beautiful of this class
of MSS.

I have also purposely omitted many Anglo-Saxon MSS. which contain only one
or but very few ornamental initials. Fac-similes of several of these will be found in
the "Nouveau Traité de Diplomatique," and the works of Hickes, Astle, Strutt,
Silvestre, and Shaw, and in my "Palæographia sacra pictoria." I must, however, allude
to the Bodleian eighth century MS. Commentary on the Book of Job (No. 426),
which has furnished the beautiful initial at the commencement of this Introduction,
and which has been selected on account of its peculiarity, arising from the introduction
of conventional foliage, of which scarcely any other examples at this early period can be
found in our MSS.

In almost every instance the fac-similes from the original MSS. for this work
have been executed by myself, with the most scrupulous care, the majority having been
made with the assistance of a magnifying-glass, and the plates have been produced
under my especial direction and constant supervision; so that I may in conclusion
venture to express the hope that my work may be regarded as a humble rival of the
grand but enormously expensive work of Count Bastard on the Miniatures and
Ornaments of early French MSS.

LISTE DES PLANCHES,

AVEC DES RÉFÉRENCES À LEUR DESCRIPTION DANS LE TEXTE.

L'ornementation du titre général est dessinée d'après
divers MSS. qui sont illustrés dans l'ouvrage, à l'exception
des ornements circulaires, ceux-ci étant imités de quelques
fibula contemporaines.

LIST OF PLATES.

WITH REFERENCES TO THEIR DESCRIPTIONS IN THE TEXT.

f

The ornaments of the general Title-page of the work
are designed from various manuscripts illustrated in the
volume, with the exception of the two circular ornaments,
which are copied from contemporary Rizals.

LIST OF MANUSCRIPTS.

NOTE.—The six MSS. to which an * is prefixed are written in Roman uncials, or rustic capitals, but with Anglo-Saxon initials.

APPENDIX.

b

ANGLO-SAXON AND IRISH
MANUSCRIPTS.

THE GOLDEN GOSPELS OF STOCKHOLM.

Plates I. and II.

THIS magnificent volume may justly be placed at the head of those early Anglo-Saxon Manuscripts which have the text written in Roman uncials or capital letters.

The style of the drawings with which it is enriched, the grand initial letters, and the Anglo-Saxon entries, combine to render this volume extremely interesting. It is preserved in the Royal Library of Stockholm, and consists of 192 leaves of vellum, measuring about sixteen inches by twelve and a half inches, and from the tenth leaf inclusive every other folio is of a rich violet or purple colour.* It contains the Gospels according to the version of St. Jerome, but with valuable readings, and is written throughout in fine uncial letters of large size, closely resembling those of the purple Gospels of Perugia,† and the purple Psalter of St. Germain,‡ of which fine fac-similes have been published by Silvestre and Count Auguste de Bastard. The text is written without any space between the words. In the white leaves the letters are written with black or red ink, gold being occasionally used for special words. In the coloured leaves gold is commonly used, occasionally also silver, and also red and white inks. Each page is written in double columns. The text commences, as usual in MSS. of the Vulgate, with the Epistle of St. Jerome to Pope Damasus, commencing " Novum (written Nouvm) opus," &c., the first word being formed of large size, and ornamented capitals, the O being inscribed in the middle of the central stroke of the initial N. This is followed by the Preface of St. Jerome, commencing, " Plures fuisse qui evangelium," &c. On leaf 4 commence the " breves causæ," or summary of St. Matthew's Gospel, beginning " Nativitas jhu xpi; magorum munera; Occultatio ihu; infantes occiduntur," &c. Then follow the Eusebian Canons upon eight pages, inscribed between columns with rounded arches adorned with various ornamental lines and drawings of animals, and with the figures of fourteen saints and martyrs, represented in a profusion of various colours.

On the verso of fol. 9 is the full-length figure of St. Matthew, represented in my first plate, from a fac-simile made for this work by a skilful artist at Stockholm, under the direction of the Rev. W. Ellison, the British Chaplain at Stockholm, to whom I am indebted for a detailed account of the volume.

---

* In the fac-simile, Plate 1, the ground colour of the text, at the foot, has been printed in too chocolate a tint.

† Nouv. Tr. de Dipl. iii. pl. 42, div. ii. This fine

manuscript, which I had the pleasure to examine at Perugia in April, 1866, is written on very thin vellum, quite unlike that used in our purple Anglo-Saxon manuscripts.

‡ Op. cit. iii. pl. 43, div. v.

B

The opposite leaf (fol. 10 r.) contains the commencement of the Gospel of St. Matthew, the opening of the historical portion of the first chapter, "Xpi generatio," &c., forming the principal page in the volume, represented in my second plate, copied from a very elaborate fac-simile made for D. Chambers, Esq., to whom I am indebted for its use for this work, corrected by notes from Mr. Ellison. The Gospel of St. Matthew terminates on fol. 61, and that of St. Mark commences at fol. 63, ending at fol. 93. It will be seen, from my fac-simile at the foot of Plate 1, that the first words of this Gospel are written in the ordinary text of the volume, the initial L being only slightly enlarged and lengthened into a J carried below the line. In this respect I would invite a comparison between this fac-simile and those of the same passage from the two Gospels of St. Augustine, given in my "Palæographia sacra pictoria." The question also arises whether all the four Gospels may not have been originally written in the same manner, and the ornamental page of St. Matthew's historical introduction subsequently added. The Gospel of St. Luke extends from fol. 97 to 149, and the verso of fol. 150 is occupied with a full-length figure of St. John and his eagle under a rounded arch, in the same style as the figure of St. Matthew.

The interest of the volume, so far as the object of the present work is concerned, arises from its agreement with, or variance from, the other early Anglo-Saxon and Irish manuscripts of the Gospels. And first as to the text, which differs from most of the latter in containing the Vulgate instead of the Italic or mixed versions employed in them: on the other hand, the ornamentation of the commencement of the Epistle of Pope Damasus, the Eusebian Canons, and the commencement of the historical instead of the genealogical part of St. Matthew, chapter 1, indicate the work of a native calligrapher. Professor Stephens, who has had repeated opportunities of examining the volume, assumes it to be a "master-piece of ancient Italian art, probably not later than the sixth or seventh century." That the text may have been written by an Italian scribe, or by an Anglo-Saxon who had studied Roman caligraphy, is most probable; but, as in the Psalter of St. Augustine, the introduction of Anglo-Saxon details, even to the extent of whole pages, sufficiently shows that portions of the volume are unmistakably Anglo-Saxon.

If we now turn our attention to the two great miniatures of St. Matthew and St. John (the former represented in Plate 1), we observe a grandeur in the design which no early Italian manuscript of the Gospels possesses, and which, in some respects, might be regarded as Byzantine, were it not for the fact that no Greek manuscript of this early period hitherto described exhibits such representations of the sacred writers. The miniature of St. Matthew before us represents the saint seated on a red cushion upon an ornamental high-backed chair, the framework of which is ornamented with inter-laced ribbon patterns of the genuine Celtic character.* The saint, wearing a pale blue upper, and a red under garment, extending to the feet, has the upper part of the head tonsured (as is also most singularly the case with his angelic symbol). He wears long moustaches and a forked beard. His right hand is engaged in giving the benediction in the Eastern manner, by extending the first and second fingers and closing the third upon the extremity of the thumb (as is also done by the angel). He also holds in his left hand the *roll* of his Gospel, commencing with the words "Liber generationis jhu," whilst the angel holds the *volumen* or square book of the Gospels. The Evangelist is represented as wearing sandals, and his head, as well as that of the other figures

---

* It is interesting to notice that the chief inter-lacement of this chair is exactly reproduced in the border of the garment of one of the small Irish Ecclesiastics in Mr. Petrie's Shrine. *See* Plate 32, fig. 5

in the drawing, is surrounded by a plain golden nimbus. On either side of the Saint, hanging from a rod extending between the capitals of the arch, are two large curtains, such as were used in hot climates to keep out the heat from churches, &c., looped up to the marble columns on either side of the picture.* The capitals of these columns are plain, but each is surmounted by a circle enclosing the half-figure of a saint (beardless, as is also the angel), one of whom holds a roll, and the other a volume. The arch itself is ornamented with a pattern which seems borrowed from mosaic-work, formed of two white undulated lines, the enclosed spaces formed of bars of plain colours gradually increasing in depth of tint and dotted with white spots symmetrically arranged. We shall in vain look for such an ornament in any true Celtic work, but instances somewhat similar occur in early Carlovingian manuscripts, as in the Evangelistiarium of Charlemagne at the Louvre. Another peculiarity to be noticed in this miniature, found also in the Gospels of St. Augustine at Cambridge, is the introduction of plants and foliage represented as growing at the bottom of the picture, of which I was much struck with the recurrence in some of the buildings at Pompeii, where the artist seems to have aimed at giving a *natural* effect to his internal decorations of the apartments.

The miniature of St. John is treated very similarly to that of St. Matthew. The upper part of the arch is marked with thin lines arranged somewhat like scales. The eagle (by no means ill drawn) holds a very large open book in one of his claws. The two circular discs above the capitals are occupied by a spiral pattern† (see Plate 52, fig. 10), especially Anglo-Saxon in character, resembling the enamelled discs which have been occasionally discovered. (*Arch. Journ.*, i. 162; *Journ. of Arch. Ass.*, iii. 282.) The transverse bar is on the contrary ornamented with a classical ornament, and the framework of the chair with a flowing arabesque. This Evangelist is represented as young, without a beard, but with the tonsure like St. Matthew. His right hand is in the act of benediction, in the same manner as St. Matthew; with his left hand he holds an open book. His upper robe is seen on both shoulders, and descends in the middle of his figure between his feet, as well as on his right-hand side. The curtains are marked with several large circles, each surrounded by a row of small dots.

In the execution of these two remarkable miniatures the flesh-tints of the face are gradually shaded, and the colours well preserved; the lips are dark red; the hands and feet are pale flesh-tinted, with strong black outlines; the outlines of the face are hard and black; but in the drapery, dress, and cushion, the folds are indicated by darker lines somewhat graduated off, and not by simple decided black or darker lines of the local colours. If we compare these miniatures with any of those contained in the subsequent plates of this work, whether with those emanating from the pure Irish school, or the remarkable ones contained in the Gospels of Lindisfarne, we shall be convinced that they must have originated in a totally different school. In the Gospels of St. Augustine at Cambridge, however, we find a drawing of St. Luke, so similar in its general design, as well as even in its artistic manipulation, as to prove that a

---

* The rods for the support of these curtains still remain, *in situ*, in a few of the oldest churches in Italy. The heavy flat curtains, sometimes of leather, now in use, and vulgarly called "Baby-crushers," are a modern contrivance.

† I consider that the introduction of this piece of spiral ornamentation, and the interlaced pattern inserted in the framework of the chair of St. Matthew, clearly show that the miniatures were executed in this country, and contemporaneously with, if not by, the identical artist who drew the great initial page of St. Matthew.

close connection must have existed between the artists by which it and those of the Stockholm manuscript were executed. Of this miniature I have published a fac-simile in my "Palæographia sacra pictoria," from which it will be seen, that although differing in several respects, such as the want of the nimbus, the hand not engaged in benediction, the classically ornamented capitals of the columns, and the generally superior effect of the whole design, there is so great a uniformity between the two drawings as to warrant the supposition of both having originated from the same school—of which, I know of no other examples ; if, indeed, we may not suppose the representation of the Evangelists in the Golden Gospels of St. Medard,* and those of the Harleian Library† to have been traditional modifications.

If we look back at the earliest efforts of Christian art as existing in the mosaic pictures of Italy, we find indeed no such seated figures of the Evangelists which might be considered as having served as models of those found in these early manuscripts, although it can scarcely be doubted that the grand central figures of our Saviour might well have served such a purpose; nor can it, I think, be doubted that the latter must have originated in those beautiful productions, the Ivory Consular or Imperial Diptychs, in which the Consul or Emperor is represented seated in the curule chair holding the mappa circensis in his hand as a reward of the victor in the games of the Circus.

The grand page represented in my second plate is quite unique in its character: the alternation of rows of coloured capitals on a gold ground, and golden letters on a white one is very striking. The text (St. Matt. i. 18) is to be read — XPI autem generatio sic erat cum esset disponsata mater eius Maria Ioseph antequa convenirent inventa est in Vtero habens. Although consisting for the most part of well-formed Roman Capitals, we perceive a strange mixture of Anglo-Saxon square and angulated letters, together with some uncials, and with several of the letters conjoined, evidently to save space towards the end of the lines. The great initials XPI although wanting the elegance observable in the same letters in the Gospels of Lindisfarne (of which Mr. Shaw has given an exquisite fac-simile), are very characteristic, and the series of spiral designs with which they are surrounded is very striking;‡ whilst the introduction of gold is of the greatest rarity in the early Anglo-Saxon manuscripts, and is, I believe, entirely wanting in the Irish ones. I have no doubt that the large dogs' heads on gold ground, with which the two right-hand arms of the X are terminated, were originally marked with the eyes, &c., of the face of the quadruped, and that the markings have scaled off, just as we find to be the case in the Psalter of St. Augustine, in which gold is introduced in precisely the same manner, and in which animals are also introduced in the open spaces of the rows of capitals, some of which letters are formed like most of those in the coloured rows of capitals before us, of thin interlaced black lines, the interstices being parti-coloured. I think, therefore, that it will be admitted that this page affords evidence of having been executed in the same school as the Psalter of St. Augustine.

I am indebted to Mr. Ellison for a few of the readings of this manuscript :—

St. Matt. vi 4. Ut sit eleemosyna tua in absconditon et pater tuus qui videt in abscondito reddet tibi; as in the Vulgate.

ii. 11. Panem nostrum quotidianum [Vulg. supersubstantialem] da nobis hodie.

* See fac-similes in Count Bastard's great work.
† No. 2788. See Humphrey's Ill. Books of M. Ages.
‡ In some copies the ground colour of the different compartments of the body of the letter X and the lower space of the letter M in the top line have been left white instead of being coloured dark claret pink.

St. Matt. vi. 14.—Si enim dimiseritis hominibus peccata eorum dimittet vobis pater vester cœlestis delicta vestra: as in the Vulgate.

viii. 17.—Ut adimpleretur quod dictum est per Esaiam Prophetam dicentem ipse infirmitates nostras accepit et ægrotationes [Vulg. nostras] portavit.

xxvii. 48.—Et continuo currens unus ex eis et accepta [Vulg. acceptam] spongia [Vulg. spongiam], implevit aceto et imposuit arundini et dabat ei bibere.

xxvii. 17. agrees with the Vulgate.

Mark i. 6. agrees with the Vulgate.

Mark ii. 1, 2, 3, 4.—Et quum venisset (1) ad Capharnaum et auditum est quod in domo esset, et convenerunt multi ita ut non caperet usque ad januam et loquebatur eis verbum, et venerunt *ferentes ad eum* (2) paralyticum qui a quatuor portabatur, et cum non possent *eum illi offerre* (3) præ turbâ, nudaverunt tectum ubi erat et patifecientes *miserunt* (4) grabatum in quo paralyticus jacebat. For No. 1 the Vulg. has "iterum intravit Capharnaum post dies." In 2, 3, in the Vulgate, there is a difference of order in these two passages. In 4. the Vulgate has submiserunt.

John iii. 5 and 6.—Et respondit Jesus Amen Amen dico tibi, nisi quis renatus fuerit ex aquâ et Spiritu Sancto non potest *vivere* [Vulg. introire] regnum dei: quod natum est *de* [Vulg. ex] carne caro est, et quod natum est *de* [Vulg. ex] spiritu spiritus est.

Matt. i. 16.—Hunc ergo cum vidisset dixit Jesus Domine hic autem quid.

iv. 10. Tunc dixit illi Jesus, vade *retro* Satanas, scriptum est dominum deum tuum adorabis et illi soli servies. The Vulgate wants the word *retro*, but it has *enim* before dominum.

The historical data afforded by the present volume are not less interesting than its artistic details. The Act of Donation inscribed at the upper and lower portions of the page containing the commencement of the historical portion of St. Matthew's Gospel (*see* Plate 2), is as follows:—

✠ In nomine dñi nři ihu xpi. Ic ælfred aldorman 7 perburg min gefera begetan ðas bec æt hæðnū herge mid uncre claene feo ðæt ðonne pæs mid claene golde 7 ðæt pit dodan for godes lufan 7 for uncre saule ðearf.... end forðon ðe pit noldan ðæt ðas halgan beoc lengc in ðære hæðenesse punaden, 7 nu pilað heo gesellan innto cristes circan gode to lofe 7 to pulðre 7 to peorðunga 7 his ðropunga to ðoncunga 7 ðæm godcundan gebroðrige to brucenne ðe in cristes circan dæghpamlice godes lof rærað, to ðæm gerade ðæt heo mon ærcde æghpylce monðe for ælfred 7 for perburge 7 for alhðryðe heora saulum to ecum læcedome. ða hpile ðe god gesegen hæbbe ðæt fulpiht æt ðæsse stope beon mote . . . . Et spilce ic ælfred dux 7 perburg biddað 7 halsiað on godes almæhtiges noman 7 on alra his haligra ðæt nænig mon seo to ðon gedyrstig ðætte ðas halgan beoc aselle oððe aðeode from cristes circan ða hpile ðe fulpiht stondan mote et. . . . .

Portion of this last letter, as well as some other words, possibly including the date, are cut away in the binding; the whole, including the marginal names, being in the same handwriting.

In the margin are inscribed the names Aelfre(d) Werbur(g), and Alhthryth eorum;* the W and th being in the Anglo-Saxon forms.

This document was first published (but inaccurately) by Celsius in his "Bibliothecæ Regiæ Stockholmensis Historia," 1751 (page 181), and again by Rask in his "Angelsaksisk Sproglære," 1817 (page 167), the orthography being altered according to his system, and with a fac-simile of a few of the lines. In Thorpe's translation of Rask's work the text and its translation (at page 439) are given with little change.

In the volume of "Proceedings of His Majesty's Commissioners on the Public Records of the Kingdom, June 1832—August 1833," may be found (at page 42) a copy of this inscription taken from Rask's Anglo-Saxon Grammar, which is not so correct as the copy printed in Mr. Purton Cooper's Appendix B to the Report on the Fœdera, page 165. In the latter work the reader is directed to "see the accompanying fac-simile;" but no such occurs in the copy of that still unpublished Appendix, which I obtained through the good services of the late Sir F. Palgrave.

The following is the translation† of this document as given by Professor Stephens:—

* Rask prints and reads this last word *eorung*, as though it existed in the manuscript, which makes no sense. Stephens suggests that the word is "eorum," and that it was followed by "filia." The last stroke of the m is too plainly shown in my plate.

† *See* another translation in Sybrant's "Rambles in Sweden," p. 187.

✠ In the name of our Lord Jesus Christ I, Aelfred Aldorman [Earl] and Werburg my partner [wife] got this book from a heathen war troop with [in exchange for] of-huth our clean fee [a sum in the personal property of us both which then was, with clean [pure] gold. And that we-two did for God's love and for our souls' behoof, and for that we-two would not that these holy books [writings] should longer abide in heathenesse [heathen hands]. And now will we give it into Christ's Church. God to praise and glory and worship and in thankful remembrance of His passion and for the use of the sacred community [Brotherhood] which in Christ's Church is daily heard to magnify the Lord, to the end that the same may be read each month for Aelfred and for Werburg and for Alhtryð to the eternal health of their souls, so long as God may vouch-fit [may permit] that Baptism [holy rites] may continue at this place. And eke I Aelfred Duke, and Werburg pray and beseech in the name of God Almighty and all his Hallows [Saints] that no one shall dare to give or part these holy books [gospels] from Christ's Church so long as Baptism may there abide.

ALFRED   WERBURG.   ALHÐRYÐ their [daughter]

From this document we learn that this precious volume was rescued by an act of costly sacrifice by an Anglo-Saxon, Earl Ælfred, and his wife, from a Scandinavian heathen-Wiking force, and deposited among the rich treasures of the Metropolitan Church of Canterbury, which, in all the old English Charters, was called Cristes Circe,[*] not as being especially "dedicated to our Saviour, but as being the Mother Church of all England, as its Archbishop has always been the primate of the English Church."[†]

The date of this document is clearly ascertained to have been a little later than the middle of the ninth century, by the will of the same Aldorman Ælfred, who was subsequently raised to the rank of Duke, published by Kemble (Cod. Dipl. Æv. Saxon., ii. p. 120, A.D. 871—889), and who leaves his lands in Surrey, at Horsley, Sanderstead, Westerham, Chertsey, &c., to his wife Werburgh, and *their* daughter Alhthryth, mention being also made of *his* son, "minum sunu," Æthelwald, to whom a small fortune only is left; but "if a male heir of my race should spring forth and be born," then he leaves his whole inheritance to him. In this will we thus see the same names of the testator and his wife and daughter, as mentioned in the entry in the Stockholm Codex; and the "Cristes circan tha hwile the fulwiht sio," is also legatee of portion of his property. The will is attested by, among other witnesses, Ealered, Archbishop (of Canterbury), who is again mentioned in an agreement drawn up by the same Aldorman Ælfred, given by Kemble (Cod. Dipl. ii. p. 96‡) under the name of Ethelred. Thus the identification of our Aldorman Ælfred is very satisfactory, and affords clear evidence that the volume itself was executed prior to the middle of the ninth century, when the act of donation was written on the margin of one of its most important pages.

Another short entry made on the top margin of the first leaf "overlooked by every one," but first published by Professor Stephens, gives us a little further insight into the history of the volume. That so noble a book was written for a royal personage, and that it was enclosed in a costly cover of silver beautifully chased, and enriched with precious stones, can scarcely be doubted; but, as in the case of the Gospels of Lindisfarne, these were doubtless stripped off by the Vikings, who had stolen the book in some of their marauding excursions. Mr. Stephens seems to infer that it was some "rich abbey or cloister, or church or palace, in Italy or France;" that the heathen captors found the volume: but, taking into consideration the facts connected with the production of the volume above referred to, I see no reason why it should ever have been found elsewhere than in England. The entry, however, above referred to (for

* See, for instance, the Grant made by King Canute to Archbishop Æthelnoth, in "Palæogr. sacr. pict." (Gospels of MacDurnan [Pl. 2]).

† Georgii Stephens; "Fortrekning öfver de Grecanista Brittiska och Franzyska Handskrifterna uti Kongl. Biblioth

‡ Stockholm, &c," 1847 [a Copy in the British Museum Library], and in his "Description of Two Leaves of King Waldhere's Lay." Cheapinghaven (Copenhagen), 1860.

‡ See also Kemble's "Saxons in England," i. 299.

careful tracings of which I am indebted to Professor Boheman and Herr Stål of Stockholm) requests the reader to pray for Ceolheardwr, Nicolas and Ealhhun, and Wulfhelm the goldworker. "Orate pro Ceolheardwr Niclas 7 Ealhhun 7 Wulfhelm aurifex."

Hence Mr. Stephens reasonably suggests that the first care of the monks of Canterbury, after the volume was given to the Cathedral, would be to restore the costly cover, which had been probably stolen from it, and (just as in the Gospels of Lindisfarne) the name of the maker of the cover was inscribed in the volume.

But the migrations of the volume, notwithstanding the pious wish of Ælfred and his wife, did not end here, since, at the close of the seventeenth century, the volume (destitute of Wulfhelm's cover) was found at Mantua, where it was purchased by J. G. Sparfwenfeldt, and by him given to the Stockholm Library. The present binding is apparently of the seventeenth century, and may have been executed at Mantua, as it has an Italian look; and it was on this occasion that the "infamous bookbinder," as he is styled by Stephens, cut away part of the Anglo-Saxon inscription, as above described.

FRAGMENT OF THE GOSPELS AT UTRECHT.

A FEW leaves of a very noble manuscript of the Gospels are preserved at the end of the Cottonian Psalter now in the University Library at Utrecht. It is of a folio form, with twenty-eight lines (in double columns) in a page, written in fine solid black uncials, intermediate in size between those of the Golden Gospels of Stockholm and the Psalter of St. Augustine. The first word LIBER of St. Matthew's Gospel is written in plain capitals of gold, the initial L being two inches, and the others nearly an inch high. The gold, as in the Psalter of St. Augustine, has been ornamented with lines of black, which, as well as the gold itself in parts, has scaled off. In the I and partly in the L these black lines exhibit traces of interlacement. The headings of the Lectiones are written in red rustic capitals—INCIP. CAPITULA LEC. SEC. MAT.,—and the capitula in uncials about equal in size, and similar to those used in the text of St. Augustine's Psalter, with the first two letters red. The frontispiece of the Gospels is very striking, although comparatively plain. The words—

INCIP
IN NOMINE DÑI
NI IHU XPI EUANGE
LIA NUMERO IIII
SEC MATTHEUM
SEC MARCUM
SEC LUCAN S...
SEC IOHANNEM

are written in noble uncials, even slightly larger than those of the Stockholm Gospels, within a circle formed of a ribbon about an inch and a quarter wide, on which are represented a series of twenty-six pink scallops or plain festoons interlaced by thirteen blue ones of twice the diameter of the others, and in the open spaces formed by the former is inscribed a prayer for help to the Virgin Mary in the Greek words—

✠ ΑΓΙΑ ΜΑΡΙΑ ΒΟΗΘΗCΟΝ ΤΨ ΓΡΑΨΑΝΤΙ

THE RULE OF ST. BENEDICT, AT OXFORD.

IN the Bodleian Library is preserved, amongst Lord Hatton's MSS., No. 93, Bodl. 4118, a copy of the Rule of St. Benedict, regarded by Astle as a manuscript of the fifth or beginning of the sixth century, reported to have been brought to England by St. Augustine at the end of the sixth century. It is written in fine solid black uncial letters (as large as the Utrecht fragment of the Gospels), of which Astle has given a fac-simile (Origin of Writing, tab. IX.). The manuscript is remarkable, however, for the fine capital letters with which the different chapters commence, which vary in height from one to two inches, the first letter, A, in the book being nearly three inches high. These letters are vermilion, with strong black outlines and surrounded with a marginal row of minute red dots. They are for the most part of the uncial form, but modified by the taste of an Anglo-Saxon calligrapher, as appears in the angulated middle strokes of the A and N, the square C, the long-tailed N, &c. Of these initials Astle has given a complete series in his eighth plate, and, notwithstanding their evident Anglo-Saxon peculiarities, he tells us that this plate "furnishes us with curious examples of the capital letters used *in Italy* in the decline of the Roman Empire" (p. 81). This statement no doubt originated in the tradition that the volume had been brought into England by St. Augustine; but as no real Italian manuscript has ever been seen with such initials, the volume must doubtless be classed amongst the few copied in this country, either by Italian scribes or by most expert Anglo-Saxon copyists, who added the initials in their own style of art.

A red Greek cross is represented at the top of the first initial, A(usculta o fili). The text is written in double columns, with twenty-two lines in a page. The uncials are very broad in their form, with very thin hair-lines. The margins and lines of the columns are ruled with a dry point, and the commencement of the rule respecting "Mensa fratrum edentium" is marked with musical notes of a very early form.

GOSPELS IN THE CAPITULAR LIBRARY OF DURHAM.

ANOTHER remarkable manuscript of nearly the whole of the Gospels is preserved in the Library of the Dean and Chapter of Durham, being No. A ii. 16 of Rud's Catalogue; in the early portion of which the text is written in pure and very elegant Roman uncials, whilst the initials and smaller writing are of Hiberno-Saxon origin. It is of the folio form and size, the leaves measuring about fourteen inches by ten, and written in double columns, with thirty lines in a page. The ordinary uncial letters of the text* are very similar to those of the Psalter of St. Augustine; the small marginal parallel references to the Eusebian Canons are written in Anglo-Saxon minuscules, as is also the heading, Incipit Evangelium secundum, &c., which latter is in red letters. Each sentence of the text commences with an uncial letter about twice the size of those of the text, surrounded with minute red dots.

---

* See Astle, tab. XIV., for fac-simile from St. Matt. xii. 15, 16, and 24.

The commencement of the Gospel of St. Mark is distinguished by having the first word INITIU written of a large size: the first I being eleven inches long and about two-thirds of an inch wide (extending all down the margin of the column): it is divided into five compartments, each filled with an interlaced ribbon pattern delicately executed, forming a great variety of knotted designs of thin white lines on a black ground, the bottom terminating like a J in a large dog's head with a gaping mouth, drawn with much spirit, whilst the top of the letter is surmounted with a kind of capital formed of a human face on an ornamented shield, with a crown composed of interlaced ribbons. The other letters, NITIV, are narrow black Roman capitals edged all round with a slender border of red. The following are specimens of the text from this page:—

"Fuit Johannis* in deserto babtizans et prædicans babtismum penitentiæ in remissionem peccatoris." "Et erat Johannis vestitus pilis camelli et zona pellicia circa lumbos ejus et locustas et mel silvestre ædebat." "Et vox facta est de cœlis tu es filius meus dilectus in te complacui."

The initial letter of the capitula of St. Mark's Gospel is also of large size and Anglo-Saxon design, the top terminating in a dragon's head with a long interlacing tongue, and the bottom of the first stroke greatly elongated and formed into an intricate knot, whilst the text is written in Roman uncials.

This volume is described in a manuscript catalogue, drawn up in A.D. 1395, as "Quatuor Evangelia de Manu Bedæ, ii fol. baptizatus." That some portion of the volume may have been written by Venerable Bede may be possible, as the latter portions of the text exhibit two, if not three, distinct handwritings of a character similar to those of the Durham Cassiodorus, and the Pauline Epistles of Trinity College, Cambridge, and the British Museum (Vitell. C. 8), all ascribed to Bede. This is especially the case with (amongst others) the page containing the 23rd chapter of St. Matthew, which nearly resembles the hand used in the Charter of King Athelbald, A.D. 749 (Astle, tab. xv. f. iii.); whilst other portions (as St. John xi.) are written in a larger Anglo-Saxon hand, very similar to, but rather wider than, that of the Gospels of Lindisfarne. The MS. begins with St. Matthew ii. 13, and extends to xiii. 14. The greater chapters or divisions are not marked, but in the margin are indicated certain lessons for festivals and fasts in later hands, differing from those in the Gospels of Lindisfarne and King Athelstan's Coronation Book. St. Mark's Gospel is prefaced by the ordinary arguments and capitula (of which forty-six are given)—part of chap. xii. and xiii. is wanting. St. Luke begins with chap. i. 57. At chap. xvi. 15, begins a new hand, as though this portion of the volume had been taken from a different manuscript, the larger chapters being marked in the margin from 54 to 76, which completes the Gospel. St. John's Gospel begins at chap. i. 27, in another and different hand; forty-three chapters being marked in the margin, corresponding with the Gospels of Lindisfarne, and ending with our ch. xxi. 8.

Portions of another copy of the Vulgate Gospels, containing parts of SS. Matthew and Mark, are also bound up with A. ii. 16, written in smaller and ruder characters, much resembling the older and ruder of Archbishop Usher's Gospels in Trinity College, Dublin. (Palæogr. Saer. Pict., Irish MSS., Plate 2.) On one of the leaves is drawn a large double Roman capital B, ornamented with Anglo-Saxon interlaced ribbons, within the open spaces of which is inscribed, in Roman letters of the eighth or ninth century, the Lord's Prayer in the Greek language. (C. D. J. in Ecclesiologist, February, 1850.)

* This nominative form of the word Johannes is especially indicative of the Celtic scribe of this volume.

1

THE PSALTER OF ST. AUGUSTINE.

Bibl. Cotton. Vesp. A 1.   *Plate III.*

THE manuscript from which the accompanying fac-similes have been made is one of the most precious relics of old English literature, containing, not only a copy of the Latin Psalter which has been traditionally assigned as one of the manuscripts sent by Pope Gregory to St. Augustine, but also an interlineary Anglo-Saxon translation. It consists of 160 leaves of vellum, measuring nine inches by seven; the text of the Psalms being written in rather large Roman uncial letters,* with twenty-two lines in a page, with the title of each Psalm in Roman rustic capitals in faded red ink. The first leaf of the volume, in its present state, is an interpolated illumination of the twelfth century, with burnished gold background, representing the Saviour seated in glory, with the symbols of the four Evangelists. On the verso of this leaf is a very large and elaborately ornamented B of the same date, being the initial letter of the first Psalm. The ten following leaves contain the Prefaces to the Psalms, the first portion of which, commencing "Omnis scriptura divinitus," is written in tall thin rustic capitals, without enlarged initials or any space left between the words,—closely resembling those of the Florence Virgil written in A.D. 498 (of which peculiar character I believe this to be the only example in any library in the kingdom); whilst the latter portion of the Prefaces, including the Epistles of Damasus, Jerome, &c., " de Origine Psalmorum," with an exposition of "Alleluia," is written in a smaller and rounder rustic character, closely resembling that of the MS. of St. Augustine's " de Civitate Dei" of the fifth or sixth century, given by the Benedictines (N. Tr. de Diplom., iii. p. 92, pl. 37, v. 11, ii.).

Unfortunately, the commencement of the Psalms is wanting,—the twelfth leaf containing the end of the 2nd and the 3rd and 4th Psalms. The remainder of the Psalms extend to the 140th leaf.

The large illumination given in my plate occurs on the verso of fol. 30, following the 25th Psalm (the recto being left blank). As it, however, represents David with his four assistants, Asaph, Eman, Ethan, and Idithun, I consider it to be now misplaced, and that it is the original frontispiece of the Psalter. These four figures are represented playing on trumpets of two different shapes, whilst two attendants hold instruments, which Strutt (who copied the dancing figures in his "Sports and Pastimes") conjectured to be a kind of tabor or drum beaten with a single drumstick. I have no hesitation, however, in considering the two attendants as scribes holding styles, the one to the left with a roll (volumen) in his hand, whilst the other holds an open book (liber), or possibly a set of waxen tablets.

The style of the illumination is coarse, and the colouring heavy; the tints, consisting of thick layers of body-colour in excellent preservation, the shades being produced by deeper strokes, or washes of the local tints, and the lights by broad opaque white, or other pale colours. The silver in this design is greatly tarnished, and the gold in many places peeled off, carrying with it the ornamental design which had been painted

---

* The uncial letters of the text are not exceeded in beauty by any known MS. The nearest approach to them is made by the MS. of St. Prosper of the sixth century. in the Paris Library. (N. Tr. Dipl. Plate 43: and see Plate 44, for others of the seventh century.)

upon it. The drawing, I apprehend, is coeval with the text, and is consequently of great value as one of the earliest specimens of art executed in this country, independent of the illustrations it affords of the dresses and musical instruments of the period. It, however, bears so strong a resemblance both in its design and manipulation to the wall-paintings of Italy, and especially to the drawings of the Codex Genescos of the Cottonian Library, the Vatican Virgil of the fifth century, and the Florence Gospels of St. John Zagba, A.D. 586, and is, at the same time, so entirely unlike any productions of our native artists in these respects, that I can only regard it as work executed either by one of the Roman followers of St. Augustine, or as a precise copy made from a Roman original by a skilled Anglo-Saxon artist, by whom, or by one of his fellow Anglo-Saxon artists, the ornamental arch in which the painting is enclosed was executed. This frame (except the two foliated ornaments in the upper angles of the page) is essentially Celtic in its style, forming a rich specimen of the spiral ornament in the arch, whilst the columns are decorated with the interlaced ribbon pattern, and the basal fascia with the Chinese reversed Z-like pattern—the birds, dogs, and dogs'-heads with elongated spiral tongues and top-knots, completing the series of ornamental styles especially adopted in Anglo-Saxon and Irish work. It is, however, difficult to believe that the artist who painted the miniature executed the ornamental border. Several peculiarities exhibited by this illumination merit further notice—the golden nimbus with which the head of the Psalmist is surrounded, the peculiar form of the silver harp which he is playing, the introduction of gold and silver into the picture—and the design embracing, not only David and his attendants and Scribes, but also the dancing figures. This treatment was adopted and enlarged in illuminations of the Psalter in manuscripts of a more recent date, as in the Cottonian Psalter Tiberius, C. 6, and especially a Psalter in the library of St. John's College, Cambridge, of the twelfth century, in which a whole group of musicians and mountebanks accompany the Royal Psalmist.

This miniature doubtless was originally placed opposite the commencement of the 1st Psalm, which has disappeared, and which was in all probability even more highly ornamented than the beginning of the other principal Psalms. These are,—1st, the 17th (18th) Psalm, "Diligam (mis-spelt Dilegam) te Dñe;" 2nd, the 26th (27th) Psalm, "Dñs inluminatio mea;" 3rd, the 38th (39th) Psalm, "Dixi custodiam;" 4th, the 52nd (53rd) Psalm, "Dixit insipiens;" 5th, the 68th (69th) Psalm, "Salvum me fac;" 6th, the 80th (81st) Psalm, "Exultate Deo;" 7th, the 97th (98th) Psalm, "Cantate Dño;" 8th, the 109th (110th) Psalm, "Dicit Dñs;" and 9th, the 118th (119th) Psalm, "Beati inmaculati." All these are illuminated in a similar manner with a large initial letter, the remainder of the words extending across the page, each differing from the rest in the colour of the stripes on which written, and in the colour and form of the letters.

The heading of the first of the chief Psalms, "Dilegam te Dñe," is copied by Astle (Origin of Writing, pl. ix.); the letters are chiefly of the uncial form, ornamented with interlaced and spiral lines, and rows of red dots. The 2nd, "Dñs inluminatio mea," consists of plain capital letters, alternately of silver and gold, upon a bar formed of five longitudinal stripes of blue, purple, green, purple, and blue. The large initial D is represented at the right-hand side of the middle division of my Plate III., and has the open space purple, on which are delineated two men with long spears. Several of the latter letters are drawn within the others, and the word "mea" is singularly written, the M with three upright strokes united by a top horizontal one, the middle stroke having its lower portion formed into a small capital A, and the right-hand stroke having three very short bars at equal distances apart, to represent the E; the 3rd, "Dixi custodiam," consists of capital letters, the M, however, being formed of three upright strokes and a top cross-bar, and the initial D of the uncial form, having the open space formed of four elaborate spiral ornaments: the 4th, "Dixit insipiens," is also formed of capital letters; the second N is, however, remarkable for having its middle bar angulated four times, and not extending either to the top or bottom of the two upright strokes; the terminal S is also angulated, and the initial D is of the uncial form, with David's encounter with the lion treated in a very quiet way, copied in the middle division of my plate (the upper part has unfortunately been cut away): the 5th, "Salvum me fac," is copied in my "Palæographia sacra pictoria:" the 6th, "Exultate Deo," consists of plain capital letters with a large initial E of the uncial form: the 7th, "Cantate," is copied in the lower; and the 8th, "Dicit Dñs," in the upper part of my plate, the latter on a purple bar, with the initial D of the uncial form made up of a large two-legged animal, of which the head has unfortunately been cut away. The small figure introduced behind the T and D contains a curious representation of the short sword and small round shield of the period; and the ingenious manner in which the small vacant space at the end of the line is filled up, deserves notice: the 9th, "Beati immaculati," entirely consists of small golden capital letters on a bar composed alternately of red and green stripes, with a large capital B.

Each of the other Psalms commences with an illuminated initial letter in the genuine fantastic Celtic style, varying in size from one to three inches in height, and generally ornamented with interlaced or spiral patterns, terminating in a few instances in the heads and legs of nondescript birds or beasts, of which a striking example, composed of an uncial d and s conjoined, is given in the middle of my plate.

Other equally curious examples of the letter d occur on fol. 19 v. 42 r. and 47 v; a letter E, moreover, on fol. 33 r. is curious for having three small squares ornamented respectively with a Maltese cross, a dog, and a bird, being miniature copies of those animals given in the columns of the arch in the frontispiece. Other interesting specimens are given in plates 3 and 4 of the "Art of Illuminating," by Messrs Digby Wyatt and Tymms. The initial letters of the verses are marginal uncials about twice the size of the ordinary text, and alternately coloured red and blue.

The Psalms terminate on the verso of fol. 140, with the words "Gloria Patri, et Filio et Spiritui Sancto, sicut erat in alleluia, alleluia, alleluia," written in a cryptic form, the vowels only being given, and all the consonants suppressed; followed by the inscription

EXPLICIVNT PSALMI DAVID NVMERO CENTVM QVINQVAGINTA

written in large red capitals, the initial E being an uncial, the C square, the G rounded and tailed, the M with the outer strokes leaning outwards, and the first stroke of the A not reaching to the top of the thick second stroke.

The 109th and 141st leaves are very interesting with reference to their palæographical characters, as detailed in my "Palæog. sacr. pict.," and to the origin of the volume itself, and its connexion with Pope Gregory and the apostle of the Anglo-Saxons. The remainder of the volume is occupied by Hymns and Canticles in the hand-writing of the eleventh century.

The evidence upon the last-mentioned question—firstly, on the character of the manuscript itself, and secondly, on the traditional statements which have been made concerning it, merits notice.

1st. We have seen above that not only are several pages of the MS. containing the prefaces, &c. (written in rustic or semi-rustic capitals), referrible to the fifth or sixth century; but the whole of the ordinary text of the Psalter is written in Roman uncials, with which several MSS. of the sixth and seventh centuries may be advantageously compared; indeed, were it not for the illuminated initial letters, the volume would unquestionably be assigned to a Roman scribe. On the other hand, the decorative portion of the volume, extending in fact to every page of the Psalter itself, could only have been executed by an Anglo-Saxon artist; and the question arises, how early is it possible to suppose our native caligraphers capable of executing such a work?

In the second place we find, in a manuscript account of the Bibliotheca Gregoriana of the monastery of St. Augustine at Canterbury, containing an inventory of the " Primitie librorum totius ecclesie anglicane," drawn up in the time of Henry V., the following description of the contents of a Psalter, at that time ornamented on its cover with the effigy of Christ and the four Evangelists.* " First, the preface commencing 'Omnis scriptura divinitus;' 2nd, the Epistles of Damasus and Jerome; 3rd, the treatise ' De Origine Psalmorum,' with the division of the Psalter into four books,—the Exposition of the Alleluia in Hebrew, Chaldaic, Syriac, and Latin, &c.; 4th, the Psalter itself, with the effigy of *SAMUEL*; 5th, Hymns."

From the preceding account it will be seen that the volume in its present state exactly agrees with this description, even to the addition of the Canticles and Hymns at the end of the volume (which are in a later hand); the only point of difference being that the unique illustration of the volume is described as the effigy of Samuel, whereas it is David who is represented in the volume before us. But I apprehend this must have been an error on the part of the describer of the fifteenth century. It would, I believe, be impossible to find a manuscript of the Psalter containing (as its only illumination) the figure of Samuel, whilst the portrait of David occurs perpetually.

Wanley, however, while endeavouring to discover these Gregorian MSS., considered that the volume, to which the above description was applicable, was lost, but that the Cottonian MS. was a copy of the Gregorian Psalter, "because the text is written litteris majoribus Anglo-Saxonicis." On the contrary, I have no doubt that this is the MS. which the monkish describer of the fifteenth century had before his eyes, and that Wanley simply erred in affirming it to be written in large-sized Anglo-Saxon characters, the whole, except the initials, being in fine Roman uncials. At the same time, however, I can but consider that, although written in Roman uncials, this could not, from the character of its ornamentation, have been a Roman MS. sent by Pope Gregory to St. Augustine, but that the monkish chronicler was deceived by the tradition respecting it, and that (as I suggested twenty years ago) the text of the Psalms is a copy of the original MS. sent by Pope Gregory, purposely decorated with all the art of the period, and in the spirit of veneration introduced into the place of the old unornamented Gregorian MS., which, moreover, had probably been defaced from much usage.

Mr. Digby Wyatt also opposes the idea that this was one of the Gregorian volumes, considering it "difficult to believe that ornaments so entirely of the Anglo-Irish school of Lindisfarne could have been executed at Rome during either the sixth, or even the seventh century. Nothing is more probable than that, out of the forty persons who

* The interpolated illumination at present forming the first page of the MS. seems to have been introduced as a memorial of the ornamental cover.

are believed to have constituted Augustine's mission, several should have been skilled, as most ecclesiastics then were, in writing, and in the embellishment of books: and in any school established by St. Augustine for the multiplication of those precious volumes, without which ministrations and teaching in consonance with Roman dogmas could not be carried on in the new churches and monastic institutions founded among the converts, it is most likely that the native scribes, on their conversion, should be employed to write and decorate the holy texts with every ornament excepting those of a pictorial nature. In the execution of these they could scarcely prove themselves as skilful as the followers of St. Augustine would, from their retention of some classical traditions, be likely to be. Thus, and thus only, can we account for the singular combination of semi-antique with Saxon writing, and of Latin body-colour pictures executed almost entirely with the brush, and regularly shadowed (such as David and his attendants in the Vespasian A 1 Psalter), with ornaments of an essentially different character; such as the arch and pilasters which form the framework for the picture of King David. Another argument which weighs greatly in my mind against the probability of such a Psalter as Vespasian A 1 being a prototype, is the fact that the Utrecht and Harleian Psalters [described in the following article] in their pictorial illustrations present us with evident copies in outline of some classic coloured original, just, in fact, of such a manuscript of the Psalms as the celebrated Vatican Roll† is of the Book of Joshua. What more likely than that one of the two venerated Psalters brought from Rome should have been such a manuscript, and should have been the very one copied in the Utrecht Psalter in the rustic capitals of the original, and the later Harleian replica in the current Saxon uncial?"‡

THE UTRECHT PSALTER.

Plate XXIX. (3*).

THIS very remarkable manuscript of the Psalms, now contained in the library of the University of Utrecht, formerly belonged to Sir Robert Cotton, whose remarkable and well-known signature appears on the first page. I have not been able to obtain any information, either documentary or otherwise, when or how it reached Utrecht, although it cannot be doubted that such a volume could hardly have been separated from the remainder of the Cottonian MSS. except by undue means; neither ought there, as it seems to me, to be any question as to the justice of its restoration to the library from which it must have been improperly removed, unless its present location can be satisfactorily accounted for.

It is an excellently preserved vellum manuscript of a large quarto size, and contains the whole of the Psalms, according to the Vulgate, together with the Apocryphal Psalm, "Pusillus eram," the Pater noster, Canticles, Credo, and the Athanasian Creed. The whole are written throughout in triple columns on each page, in Roman rustic capitals very similar in size to those of the celebrated "Virgil" of the Vatican (Nouv. Tr. de Dipl. iii. p. 56, pl. 35, fig. iii. 2), but with

---

† D'Agincourt, "Painting," pl. xxviii. xxix. and xxx.   ‡ Art of Illuminating, pp. 17, 18

as much elegance in the form of the letters as in those of the Paris Prudentius (ibid. fig. viii.) : the headings of the Psalms and the initial letter of each verse are in red uncials, and the first line of each Psalm is written in uncials of a size rather larger than the text. In these respects a date not more recent than the sixth or early part of the seventh century ought to be assigned to the manuscript ; but, as will be seen by the fac-simile in the upper part of my plate, the initial letter of the first Psalm is a large golden uncial B, two and a quarter inches high, having a fine line of red edging to the gold, and a fine parallel blue one, the upper part of the letter formed into a large inter-laced knot of the genuine Anglo-Saxon style, the words "(Bleatus vir qui non abiit" being written in three lines of golden uncials, followed by the ordinary text of the volume written without spaces between the words, and with the long words divided properly into syllables at the end and beginning of the lines.   The upper fac-simile comprises Psalm i. v. 1.

A detailed account of this volume has been published by Herr Kist in the "Archeef voor Kerkelijke Geschcedenis van Nederland," vol. iv. Leyden, 1833, from which we learn that it bears the Cottonian press mark Claudius A. 7.

Herr Jansen, the Conservator of the Antiquarian Museum at Leyden, informed me that a complete fac-simile copy of the whole MS., with all its drawings, had been made some years previously, and that it was in the possession of a gentleman at the Hague.   A short time ago this volume of fac-similes was purchased by the British Museum. (MSS. Add. No. 22, 291.)

Each Psalm is illustrated with an elaborate pen-and-ink drawing, executed with wonderful boldness both of design and execution, running entirely across the page. The various subjects contained in many of these drawings, of which there are as many as 165, are treated in exactly the same manner as in the Harleian Psalter, No. 603, a MS. of the end of the tenth century; in the Cambridge Psalter of Eadwine, a work of the twelfth century; in another early copy of the Psalter, which I am informed is in Lord Ashburnham's library; and in the Paris MS. Suppl. Latin. 1194, date circa A.D. 1250.   I made careful copies of many of these Utrecht drawings, and others were some years ago sent to the British Museum by Herr Guermondt.   I also copied the illustration of Psalm 64 (of which I had previously published the corresponding illustration from the Eadwine Psalter in my "Palæographia sacra," with which it exactly agrees (including the quaint illustration of the passage, "who have whet their tongue like a sword"), except that the figures in the Utrecht Psalter are considerably smaller.

In the illustration of Psalm 150, given in the lower part of my plate, the figure of the organ also agrees exactly with that given by Strutt from the Eadwine Psalter (copied by Mr. T. Wright, Domestic Manners, p. 109).

At the same time there are many entire drawings which are either wanting in the Harleian MS., their places being left blank, or they are only rudely or slightly indicated with a leaden or steel point preparatory to inking in.   From some of these I have also copied various details, beautiful in their execution and quite classical in their style, some of which I published in the Journal of the Archæological Institute for September, 1859 (vol. xvi.).

Hence we are led to believe that this must have been the original from which not only the Harleian but also the later Eadwine Psalters were copied.   One particularity is, however, to be noticed with respect to these drawings.   Spaces were left by the scribe across the whole page, cutting through the triple columns of text, for the insertion of the drawings by the artist, and in several instances the space was not sufficient, the drawings running close to or even upon the line of text below.   From this fact it may be inferred that even the drawings of this Utrecht Psalter were copied from some earlier MS., and that they were not composed expressly to fill up the spaces which had been left for them. Still, however, the artist has exercised much care and ingenuity in adapting his design to the text, as may be observed in the arrangement of the group of angels and their banners in the lower part of my fac-simile. The manner in which the wings of the left-hand angel are thrown up (unlike their position in any of the other angels), and the way in which the banners are treated in the two right-hand figures, so as not to interfere with the word EIVS, deserve notice. Supposing these drawings, then, to be later additions by an Anglo-Saxon artist copying from an early classic series of drawings, we should have no difficulty in referring the text to the latter part of the fifth or sixth century. The initial letter of the first Psalm, however, precludes us from assigning it so early a date, and would bring it to the seventh or eighth at the earliest. As stated above, there are bound up at the end of the volume a few leaves of a grand copy of the Gospels written in large uncial letters, but with the first word, Liber, in large square golden Roman capitals, apparently ornamented just as in the Psalter of St. Augustine, above described. Hence I infer that soon after the settlement of the followers of St. Augustine there must have been established a scriptorium, where some of the most beautiful MSS. were copied from originals in the finest uncial or rustic capitals, but decorated with initials in the Anglo-Saxon or Irish style. Of such MSS. we can now record the five uncial MSS. described above, and the rustic capital Psalter of Utrecht now under description.

The question of the origin and style of the drawings in this MS. merits attention, since the very many representations of dresses, manners, and customs which it exhibits, and which have been copied with the greatest care in the Harleian MS. 603, have been treated by Mr. T. Wright[*] and others[†] as affording illustrations of the habits and customs of our Anglo-Saxon forefathers. Herr Kist, however, justly remarks that the Psalms "illustrantur *Romano habitu*, figuris," adding, however, "et antiquitate Imperatoris Valentiniani tempora videntur attingere." The Baron van Westreenen (whose magnificent library now forms one of the national establishments of the Hague) has corrected this statement as to the extreme antiquity of the volume, with much care and learning, in his " Naspeuringen nopens zekeren Codex Psalmorum in de Utrechtsche Boekerij berustende," door W. H. J. Baron van Westreenen van Tiellandt. Hamel, on the contrary, refers the text and drawings to the sixth century.[‡] An examination of the fac-similes given in the accompanying plate will sufficiently prove that the architecture, dresses, arms, and musical instruments therein represented, are evidently of classical origin. In respect to the latter, it will be noticed, that, in addition to the organ and the classical triangular harp, and heart-shaped lyre, there are representations of a second kind of lyre, elongated trumpets, an oblong drum held by both hands, and beaten with the fingers, like the Indian tom-tom, an instrument something like a reversed violin (evidently stringed, and probably intended for the Anglo-Saxon *fithele*—hence our modern *fiddle*—although it seems to have been played upon by the fingers and not with a bow), and cymbals, each pair fixed on elongated slender supports. Other peculiarities in the drawings before us deserve notice. The square temple approached by steps, with a lamp hanging at the entrance, and with curtains looped up at the sides, in lieu of doors, together also with

---

* "Hist. of Domestic Manners in England." 4to. 1862.
† Charles Knight's "Pictorial Hist. of England," vol. i.
‡ It is a remarkable circumstance, that while the Anglo-Saxon copyist of the classical drawings of the Aratus, published in the *Archæologia*, had suited them to his own times and style, the several copyists of these illustrations of the Psalms in the Harleian MS. 603, and the Eadwine Psalter, rendered them almost stroke for stroke

the small square altar; the alcove, with figures seated in pairs in conversation (copied in the Eadwine Psalter (T. Wright, "Domestic Manners," p. 97): the two kings seated, each with one foot in the stocks, and the two other kings with their hands bound in chains.

In the lower composition the figure of the Saviour, young and beardless, with a cruciferous nimbus, and bearing a banner, and inclosed within an oval aureola floating among the clouds: the classical representation of the winds, and the Adoration of the Angelic Host, are admirably delineated.

Mr. Digby Wyatt, on the other hand, in reference to the pen-and-ink drawings of this volume, considers it possible that in them may be recognized the earliest trace of those peculiar fluttered draperies, elongated proportions, and flourished touches which became such a distinct style in later Anglo-Saxon illuminations. So different is it, both from the Anglo-Hibernian work prevalent in England up to the advent of St. Augustine, and *from the contemporary imitation of the antique* practised by Byzantine, Latin, Lombard, or Frankish illuminators, that the conclusion seems, as it were, forced upon us that it can have been originated in no other way than by setting the already most skilful penman, but altogether ignorant artist, to reproduce, as he best could, the freely-painted miniatures of the books, sacred and profane, imported, as we know, in abundance from Rome during the seventh and eighth centuries, and as stated in the preceding article on the Psalter of St. Augustine. Mr. Digby Wyatt is, moreover, of opinion that the Utrecht Psalter and its Harleian copy were both taken from some popular prototype, possibly one of the Augustinian Psalters already alluded to.* Had Mr. Wyatt, however, attentively studied the Utrecht Psalter itself, especially such of its drawings as the triple Crucifixion and the group of the Fates, he would never have ventured to suggest that its outlines and drawings were the efforts of an unskilful artist: indeed he adds in a note, "that very few artists of the present day could block in the general forms in so peculiar a style, with greater freedom or more complete conveyance of expression by similarly slight indications."†

The illustration of the first Psalm occupies the verso of the first page of the volume, and consists of a large drawing, in the upper part of which the Sun (personified as a male half-length figure holding a flaming torch), the crescent Moon and Stars, amongst the clouds, are represented; beneath the sun, David seated, writing within a circular temple at the dictation of an angel (copied in the upper part of my plate): in the middle, beneath the clouds, two men are standing talking together, and to the right, beneath the moon, is the figure of a king seated between two columns, as in the upper right-hand portion of my facsimile (which is, however, copied from p. 94 v., illustrating the apocryphal Psalm "Pusillus eram," in which groups of warriors are introduced). Below, to the left, is represented a flowing river, with a tree on the bank laden with fruit; a man seated on the ground; a winged head occupies the middle of the lower part of the design, emitting a strong blast from its mouth, directed towards winged demons to the right, who hook a number of figures into the mouth of the infernal regions.

The first Psalm occupies the upper part of the second leaf, on which is also the commencement of the second Psalm and its illustration, consisting of three groups of warriors: to the left they are opposed and beaten to the ground by five angels above, who hurl spears at them at the command of the Almighty, personified in the clouds.

* "Art of Illuminating," p. 24. † Ibid. p. 21, note.

K

The group to the right stand erect, with the hand of the Almighty in the clouds above them.

The illustrations of Psalms iii. and iv. occur on the verso of the second leaf; that of the 3rd represents, on the left side, a group of warriors opposed by an angel at the command of the Deity, seated on the clouds and sheltering a man lying on a bed. The energy of the angel, the weakness of the sick man, the dignity of the figure of the Deity, and the dismay of the warrior at the attack of the angel, constitute a wonderful little composition. To the right is a group of men standing near a tree, with palm-branches in their hands.

The 4th Psalm is illustrated by the figure of a man coming out of a square building or prison, and groups of figures with spears, horses and other animals, with large flagons, barrels, and a sacrifice, near a temple to the right hand.

The illustration to the 5th Psalm represents the hand of God holding a wreath, and an angel crowning with wreaths a group of men holding palm-branches; in the centre a castle, with a group of warriors, and angels thrusting figures into the mouth of hell.

The illustration to the 6th Psalm is an interesting composition. To the left is a wall-enclosed space, with a man standing on the top tower; in front, men killing their fallen enemies, a furnace with figures, and a flying angel among the smoke, Christ holding a balance to angels in the clouds, a group of figures seated in an alcove, a man and horse riding over fallen figures, drawn with great spirit, and three groups of men standing on the side of a mountain, the top of which is surmounted by crosses.

The 58th Psalm is illustrated by a wall-enclosed space to the left, with dogs; above is Christ, with open arms ready to receive David flying from men armed with swords; angels with spears, killing figures beneath; and a dinner-table, with figures seated.

The illustration of the 65th Psalm is a very remarkable composition, executed with the greatest freedom and neatness, the figures being of small size. The hill of Zion occupies a circular space fortified all round with walls and towers; on the summit, the Saviour holding a tall cross in his hands, treads the lion and dragon beneath his feet. To the left is a temple, towards which men are driving a flock of sheep, with various figures, some coming out of square graves. The river of God occupies the lower part of the drawing, which is surrounded by a narrow circle, in which are delineated the signs of the Zodiac, with the sun and moon, represented in the old classical manner, at the sides of the upper part of the composition.

The 102nd Psalm is illustrated by figures of the sun and moon, with Christ and Angels above; beneath is the mouth of hell open, with the damned, above which stands an Angel, holding a cross; to the right David addresses a crowd of figures. The last page represents David seated on a throne, surrounded by warriors with a water-organ; David with sheep, crowned by an angel; and David cutting off the head of Goliath.

The following subjects, forming portions of the larger compositions, are also especially worth notice, either on account of their curious treatment, iconographic peculiarity, or artistic merit:—

Fol. 4. A very spirited lion standing over a fallen man.

Fol. 6. A kind of circular tread-mill, or round-about, pushed round by four men (Messrs. Cahier & Martin mention a similar subject in the Paris MS. Suppl. Latin., No. 1194, where the four men push the machine round, "comme feraient des écoliers qui se piquent au jeu, ou des forçats qui presse l'argousin"): this is given in illustration of Psalm x. 9—"In circuitu impii ambulant."

Fol. 8. The visit of the three Maries to the tomb, which is represented as a small square building, with a circular domed tower, built at the side of a rock. The Angel is seated in front of the tomb, and in an opening at the side of the tomb is seen the upper part of the body of the Saviour, lying half-hidden by the rock. There can be no mistake as to the artist having in this unusual treatment, intended simply to delineate the napkin which had enveloped the head of the Saviour lying apart. This is apparently an illustration of the latter part of the first verse of the 15th Psalm, at the head of which it is placed.

On fol. 12 is a slightly sketched representation of the Cross, from which, on one arm, hangs a double-thonged whip, and on the other the crown of thorns. A spear and a reed, with the sponge at its tip, seem to grow out of the earth. A large candlestick, with a lighted candle, stands on one side of the Cross. At the place of the foot-board is a small monogram, formed of the letters P and V, with a straight cross-bar.

A small but very spirited little figure of a warrior in a Phrygian helmet, holding a sword in his right hand, occurs in fol. 13 v.

Fol. 14 v is the representation of a fountain, with the water discharged from the mouth of a lion, and the flogging of a malefactor, quite similar to the miniature in Harl. MS., No. 603. (Copied by T. Wright, "Domestic Manners," p. 37.)

Fol. 20 v is a very spirited group of horses and oxen, and on fol. 21 r are agricultural representations of reaping, ploughing, sowing grain, and measuring wheat.

Fol. 47 v. A charming little figure of Atlas, illustrating the first part of the 6th verse of Psalm lxxxi.

Fol. 59. A grand representation of the mouth of the infernal regions, with demons tormenting the damned with long forks among the flames (Psalm cii.).

Fol. 73 v. Various domestic scenes, a feast, reaping, vine-cutting, a king and queen seated in an arbour.

Fol. 67. A curious representation of the Crucifixion : Christ with a nimbus, and clothed nearly to the feet, which are apart; a large titulus, and a circle of leaves (scarcely intended for the crown of thorns, but rather of laurel-leaves, as a victor). On one side stand the Virgin Mary and St. John ; on the other, a figure holding a chalice to catch the blood streaming from the side of the Saviour, in one hand ; in the other a tray, with small bun-shaped cakes. A man with a spear attacks the latter person.

Fol. 84 r. An exceedingly delicate and excellently grouped representation of the Three Fates engaged in weaving. A very rude copy of this group is contained in the Eadwine Psalter (copied by T. Wright, "Domestic Manners," p. 108), illustrating the Canticle of Isaiah : "Ego dixi in medio dierum mearum."

Fol. 85 v. The Flagellation and Crucifixion of our Saviour, and the two thieves (one of the earliest representations of the three crosses). On either side of the Saviour stands Longinus with the spear, and the sponge-bearer. The figures are very small, but exceedingly spirited.

Fol. 91 v. A seated king, holding his sword and sceptre (surmounted by a warrior's head), and attended by warriors ; copied in the upper part of my plate; illustrating the Apocryphal Psalm, "Pusillus eram." David and Goliah.

Fol. 18 v, and Fol. 87 v. Very classical representations of Water, with Griffins. In the former, a river-god is seated on a sea-dragon, holding a reversed waterpot.

Fol. 82 v. Two very quaint representations of the Sun and Moon, represented as small busts, upon oval plates, in the hands of gigantic half-figures.

Fol. 17 v. The figures are small and faint, representing a festival, with sports : a bear, held by a string, is lying down at the command of its master ; another man dances to the music of double-pipes, played by a third man, leaning on a staff. (Copied in Harl. MS., 603, and by T. Wright, "Domestic Manners," p. 65.)

Fol. 30 v (Psalm li.).   The figures are large and coarse.   A king is seated, with four attendants, and before him stands a prophet, holding a kind of chopper in his right hand, the left hand elevated towards Christ seated in the clouds.   This curious subject is similarly represented in one of the few illuminations in the small purple Psalter of the Douce collection in the Bodleian Library, as well as in the Psalter of Count Henry, preserved in the Cathedral of Troyes, published by Gaussen.

Psalm lxxii. contains a very spirited representation of the Deity, rising out of the clouds in a chariot drawn by four horses, seen in a front view.

In these drawings it seems evident that there were several different hands employed, the figures in some of the compositions being small and very neat, whilst in others they are much larger and ruder.   The two chief groups in my fac-simile are by the hand which executed the major portion of the designs.

THE GOSPELS OF ST. COLUMBA, OR, THE BOOK OF DURROW.

Plates IV. V. VI. and VII.

THESE four Plates contain a complete series of the illustrations in the Gospels of St. Columba, now in the Library of Trinity College, Dublin, MSS. A. 4. 5: a volume so remarkable, in every respect, as to have induced me to devote a large space to it in this work.

It contains a copy of the four Gospels, and is asserted, in an entry on the fly-leaf of the MS. itself, to have been written by St. Columba in the space of twelve days: "Liber autem hic scriptus est a manu ipsius B. Columbkille per spatium 12 dierum an. 500." It consists of 248 leaves of vellum, 9½ by 6 inches in size, with 25 lines in a page, written in single columns.   At the commencement of the volume, and preceding each of the Gospels, are pages entirely covered with tessellated interlaced ornaments.   Of these, the one represented in Plate 5 occurs on the verso of the first leaf, and is remarkable for the series of oblong spaces filled in with black and white patterns, in which modifications of the diagonal Chinese-like pattern and the step-like pattern are introduced.

The recto of the second leaf, facing the preceding design, contains a drawing of the four Evangelical symbols of the rudest kind (represented in my "Palæographia," at the foot of the second article on Irish Biblical MSS., and recently reproduced then, from by Mr. Ruskin): these are drawn within the angles of a cross, ornamented with ribbons, and enclosed within a tessellated border, formed of quadrangular patterns.

The verso of the third leaf, opposite the beginning of the Preface of St. Jerome, is occupied with the grand spiral design copied in the centre of Plate 7,* of which, unfortunately, one of the borders has been cut away.   This design, although less

---

* Copies of this page, and of the two other illuminated pages contained in my seventh Plate, have been given by Mr. Stuart, in the illustrations to the second volume of his most valuable work on the sculptured stones of Scotland, from a proof of the plate communicated by me for that purpose.

elaborate and minute than similar ones in the Gospels of Lindisfarne, Book of Kells, and Paris Gospels, affords one of the best illustrations of this particular spiral ornament which I have met with in MSS.

The recto of the 13th leaf, at the beginning of St. Matthew's Gospel, is occupied with the curious quadrangular and diagonal tessellation represented in the middle of Plate 6. It will be observed that the pattern is simply formed by angulating the inter-lacements of the ordinary ribbon pattern, leaving plain quadrilobed spaces, such as occur more frequently in the Irish metal-work shrines of a later period. The verso of this leaf contains a long inscription in Irish, respecting St. Columbkille.

The recto of the 77th leaf, at the beginning of St. Mark's Gospel, is occupied with the beautiful design represented in the centre of Plate 4, in which the ingenious treatment of the central of the fifteen circles will be noticed, with its four divisions, in which the black and white step-like pattern of the first leaf is repeated. Although only red, yellow, and green colours are employed, it will, I think, be admitted that this is one of the most harmonious compositions which could be devised.

The verso of folio 117, at the beginning of St. Luke's Gospel, is filled with the elaborate design given in the left-hand portion of Plate 7, the centre of which can scarcely be regarded as representing the double cross of the Greek Church, but must be rather looked on as simply ornamental, and in which the curious manner in which the narrow white edging of the yellow central pattern is, by the help of thin black angulated lines, made to form a series of angular windings, within the eighteen small white spaces, will be noticed. Another feature in this design is the narrow interlaced white ribbon, with a black line running along its centre, at the four angles of the inner square. The verso of fol. 174, at the beginning of St. John's Gospel, is occupied with the rude design of lacertine animals, with an elegant circular pattern inscribed with a Greek cross in the centre, represented at the right-hand side of Plate 7. The elongated jaws and limbs of the nondescript animals are worthy of notice, whilst the idea of a series of such beasts biting each other is carried out in the crests of several of the Irish cambattas, or short crosiers, of a later period. It will be also observed that the central circle resolves itself into a triple combination of interlacements, in a very ingenious and unusual manner.

Each Gospel is also preceded by a symbolical representation of its respective Evangelist, enclosed within an ornamental border, occupying the entire page. These drawings are amongst the rudest and most grotesque delineations of the Sacred Symbols ever executed. That of St. Matthew will be seen to represent a human figure, with the body entirely enveloped in a long plaid-like cloak, in small square divisions, resembling a Roman tessellated pavement (which the native artist could scarcely have seen). The head exhibits no sign of tonsure, the hair being parted down the middle, and cut square over the shoulders; and the beard short. The stockings are also plaid-like; and the shoes have the front, as well as the hind part above the heel, carried up to a point.[*]

The Lion of St. Mark would be a respectable beast, were it not for the harlequin's dress in which it is represented. The dotting-over of the head with red points (as also in

* Mr Wilde, in his Catalogue of the Museum of the Royal Irish Academy, p. 282, has given representations of two shoes, the second of which (fig. 184) is illustrated by the drawing before us. The interlaced ornament of the front of its instep, and the slender angulated lines of the point above its heel, occur in the manuscript before us, the latter especially being found to correspond almost exactly with the manner in which the small white squares in the centre of the design of fol. 117 v [my Plate 7, left-

hand division] are cut up into narrow white angulated ribbons. Mr. Wilde considers that the workmanship of this shoe (fig. 184), as compared with that of his figure 183, "shows the great advance in art which had taken place between the periods when these two specimens of leather-work were made." With the help afforded by manuscripts, I, on the contrary, should consider that the later-made shoe (No. 183) shows a decadence of art, regarding fig. 184 as the older work.

the face of St. Matthew's emblem, and the body of the Calf of St. Luke), is also a curious mode of treatment. The latter animal would also scarcely excite a smile, were it not for the spiral ornaments, extending upwards from the legs, and the coloured boot-like terminations of the latter. The Eagle of St. John has only its hook-like beak and strong claws to recommend it to our favour as a set-off against its globose head and parti-coloured feathers.

The volume contains a copy of the Latin Vulgate of the Gospels, constituting in this respect a remarkable exception to most of the other ancient Irish copies of the Gospels. It commences, accordingly, with the Epistle of St. Jerome to Pope Damasus; followed by a series of explanations of Hebrew names; the Eusebian Canons (not enclosed within ornamented columns), and the "breves causæ," or synopsis of the Gospels. The first twelve leaves of the volume are thus occupied.

The commencement of the Epistle of St. Jerome (Novum opus, &c.), and of the several Gospels, namely, the "Liber generationis," and "Xpi autem generatio" of St. Matthew; the "Initium Evangelii Ihu Xpi" of St. Mark; the "Quoniam quidem multi," and "Fuit in diebus Herodis," of St. Luke; and the "In principio erat verbum et verbum erat apud dm" of St. John, are written in large ornamented letters, occupying, however, only the upper part of each page; the text in the lower part being written in the ordinary handwriting of the volume, which will be seen, from my fac-similes in Plate 6, to be in that character which has been termed Hiberno-Saxon, and which is in fact a compound of the Roman uncials and minuscule letters, modified into a distinct national kind of writing.

These fac-similes consist, first, of the entire page containing the beginning of St. Mark's Gospel, headed by the rubric "Incipit euangeliu saecundum marcu." The large ornamental initial is a compound of the letters I and N; the two narrow conjoined upright ribbons representing the I and the first stroke of the N. This initial is ornamented with the interlaced ribbon and spiral patterns (the only introduction by way of ornament of grotesque animals in the volume, occurring in the page represented in Plate 7; and the only Chinese Z-like pattern, considerably modified, in the black and white oblong portions in the page, represented in the middle of Plate 5).

The initial N of the Epistle of St. Jerome, having an elongated first stroke, is not quite so large as the initials of the Gospels of St. Mark and St. John, and is copied on the right-hand side of the third division of my 6th Plate. The "Liber generationis" is copied in the 2nd Plate of "Irish Biblical MSS." in my "Palæographia."

The "Quoniam quidem multi," and "Fuit in diebus," of St. Luke, are copied by O'Conor ("Scrip. vet. rer. Hibern."); the former, also, together with the initial F of the latter, in my Plate 6, and the initials "IN principio" of St. John, very similar in design to that of St. Mark, in my 6th Plate, are copied in the ninth illuminated page of Mr. Ferguson's "Cromlech on Howth," published by Messrs. Day, in 1861; and portion of the heading (Verbum erat apud dm) in my "Palæographia."

The "Xpi autem generatio" of St. Matthew commences with a large ornamental X, with the ends elongated and formed into scrolls.

The illuminations in this volume, although of a very effective character, want much of the extreme delicacy observable in other early Irish and Anglo-Saxon manuscripts, such as the Book of Kells, the Gospels of Lindisfarne, and the Gospels of the Paris Library, with which last the volume agrees in the initial letters of each Gospel only occupying the upper portion of each page; the text, also, being that of the Vulgate: the emblem of St. Luke, also (a calf), is quite similar in both Gospels; although, as will be seen from a comparison of my fac-similes in Plates 4 and 21, those of St. Matthew and St. Mark are totally different.

With respect to the question of the date of the present volume, the following passage by the late Dr. Petrie will be read with attention:—"Whatever doubt may be felt as to the exact date of the Book of Kells, no doubt whatever can be entertained as to the age of the Book of Durrow, the writing of which is also ascribed to St. Columba, and in which there are illuminations of the same style of art, though inferior in beauty of execution; for in this manuscript we find the usual request of the Irish scribe, for a prayer from the reader, expressed in the following words:—

"Rogo beatitudinem tuam, sancte præsbiter Patrici, ut quicunque hunc libellum manu tenuerit meminerit Columbæ scriptoris, qui hoc scripsi ipsemet evangelium per XII dierum spatium, gratia Domini nostri;" i.e. "I pray thy blessedness, O holy presbyter Patrick, that whosoever shall take this book into his hands may remember the writer, Columba, who have myself written this Gospel in the space of twelve days, by the grace of our Lord." Below which is written, in a cotemporary hand, "Ora pro me, frater mi; Dominus tecum sit."

The volume was originally enclosed within a silver-mounted ancient Cumhdach* or shrine, made for it by the orders of Flann, King of Ireland, who reigned A.D. 879—916, but which has long been lost. Most probably this loss took place in A.D. 1007, when the volume was stolen, in the time of the Coarb Ferdomhnach.

Its absence is, however, the less to be deplored, as a record of the inscription which it bore is entered in the handwriting of the famous Roderic O'Flaherty, on the fly-leaf of the manuscript:—" Inscriptio Hibernicis literis incisa cruci argenteæ in operimento hujus libri in transversa crucis parte, nomen artificis indicat; et in longitudine tribus lineis a sinistra et totidem dextra ut sequitur: ✠ Oroit acus bendacht Cholumbchille do flann mace mail sechnaill do righ erenn las a ndernad a cumdach so; hoc est Latine: ✠ Oratio et benedictio S. Columbæ cille, sit Flannio filio Malachiæ regi Hiberniæ qui hanc (operimenti) structuram fieri fecit.† Flannius hic rex Hiberniæ decessit 8 Kal. Maii et die Sabbati, ut in MS. Cod. Hib. quod Chronicon Scotorum dicitur, anno æræ Christianæ vulgaris 916. Hanc inscriptionem et interpretationem interpretatus est Ro. Flaherty, 19 Jun. 1677." Thus it appears that the book was venerable in age and a reliquary at the end of the ninth century.

Mr. Digby Wyatt also, after carefully comparing the present volume with the Book of Kells, states that he "remained strongly impressed with the superior antiquity of the former to the latter. The one may have been St. Columba's property, and the other illuminated in his honour after his death, as was the case with the Gospels of St. Cuthbert (or of Lindisfarne);" adding, with reference to the artistic treatment of the drawings, that "in none of them were shadows represented otherwise than by apparent inlayings under the eyes and beside the nose; and yet, at the same time, the ornaments were most intricate, and often very beautiful both in form and colour."‡ Dr. Reeves also, in his "Life of St. Columba" (p. 276), considers that the volume approaches, if it does not reach, the age of Columba.

Of the connection of this volume with Durrogh or Durrow, in King's County, where was a monastery dedicated to St. Columba, and of the fame of the saint himself as a scribe, the following passages from an article by Dr. J. H. Todd§ may be quoted.

---

* See Article on the Irish Cumhdachs in the Appendix.

† More literally, ✠ Oratio et benedictio Columbæ cillæ, pro Flannio filio Malachodalii, pro rege Hiberniæ per quem factum est ri operimenti hoc. (Reeves's "Life

of St. Columba," p. 392, note W.)

‡ "Art of Illuminating," p. 16.

§ "Irish Ecclesiastical Journal," iv. p. 27, 29th September, 1847.

"Archbishop James Ussher, who was bishop of Meath from 1621 to 1624, states that 'amongst the records (*ἀναξικα*) of the monastery of Durrow, was preserved a very ancient manuscript of the Gospels, which the monks used to say had belonged to Columba himself, out of which, and another of no less antiquity, also ascribed to the same Columba (and held sacred by the inhabitants of Meath, in the town called Kelles, or Kenlis),* I have collected, for my own use, two books of various readings by a diligent collation of them with the Latin Vulgate.'"†

The monastery and church of Durrow were founded by St. Columba. A sculptured cross, still called St. Columkille's cross, stands in the churchyard of Durrow; and near it is St. Columkille's well.—(Reeves's "Life of St. Columba," p. 276.)

Dr. Todd proceeds :—" St. Columba was a celebrated scribe, and from his early youth devoted himself to the work of multiplying copies of the Psalms and Gospels, and other portions of the Scriptures.   He was born December 7th, A.D. 519; so that the manuscripts written by him are among the most ancient now extant in Europe.   There is a curious legend of him on record, which proves his early taste for transcribing the Scriptures, and is on many accounts interesting.   It is given at length in the curious life of St. Columba, written in Irish by Magnus O'Donnell, chief of Tirconnell, and translated into Latin by Colgan.   The learned Dr. Keating also, in his 'History of Ireland,' notices this legend, and quotes as his authority for it the black book of St. Molagga, a chronicle now, I fear, no longer in existence."   He then transcribes the abridged account of the legend given by the Rev. R. King in his "Primer of the Church of Ireland," 3rd edit., p. 79.   "St. Columba, it is said, being on a visit with St. Finnian of Moville, obtained from him a loan of some part of the Holy Scriptures {Keating, from the Book of St. Molagga, says that it was a copy of the Gospels], which, being greatly pleased with it, he began to transcribe from beginning to end, without Finnian's knowledge; and used to stay in the church of the place where he was [Druim-finn, in the county Louth], after service by day and night, for the purpose of carrying on the writing without being interrupted or observed.   The copy was nearly finished when Finnian, having occasion for his manuscript, sent a messenger to get it from the saint, who discovered the proceeding, and made Finnian also acquainted with it.   Upon this the latter became highly displeased, and told Columba that he had no right to have copied privately, and without his consent, a book that belonged to him; he also demanded the copy for himself, as having been in some sort the produce and offspring of his own book [Mac Leabhair, the son of the book, as Keating calls it].   St. Columba replied that he would leave the matter to the arbitration of Diermit, then King of all Ireland, to whose judgment the case was accordingly referred.   He decided in favour of Finnian, giving sentence in a remarkable form of Irish words, which afterwards became proverbial among the people; ' Le gach voin a voinin, agus le gach leabhar a leabhran;' *i.e.*, 'To every cow belongs its calf; so likewise to every book its copy.'   The sequel of the story, although extremely curious and interesting, is not to our present purpose; neither is it necessary for me to discuss how far the legend is true, or founded on truth.   Even though we should suppose it to be a pure fiction, it will suffice to prove two things: the great value that was set on copies of the Scriptures in that age, or at least in the age when the story was invented; and, secondly, that Columba was popularly known as a zealous transcriber of the Scriptures."

Adamnan, one of the most ancient biographers of St. Columba, also mentions a book of weekly hymns (Hymnorum liber septimaniorum), and other numerous books, in

---

* Here evidently referring to "The Book of Kells."   † "Primord." p. 691. Dublin ed. 1639.

the autograph of Columba, that were extant in his time. (Vit. Columbæ, lib. ii., cc. 7, 8.)
And O'Donnell, in his life of the saint already referred to, says. "He left behind him
three hundred volumes of the Gospels, or other sacred books, written with his own hand;
many of which, in gold and silver covers, adorned with gems, like the most precious relics,
are preserved by posterity, and held in the highest veneration to the present day [this
was written in 1520]; but the rest, wars and the injury of time have destroyed." [*]

The volume itself was preserved at Durrow down to the time of the Reformation,
when it was given to the Library of Trinity College, Dublin, by Dr. Henry Jones,
Bishop of Meath, A.D. 1584, in whose bishopric the church of Durrow was situated
(Petrie, *ut supra*), and who was Vice-Chancellor of the College.

THE BOOK OF KELLS

Plates VIII. IX. X. XI.

IRELAND may justly be proud of the Book of Kells,—a volume traditionally
asserted to have belonged to St. Columba, and unquestionably the most elaborately
executed MS. of so early a date now in existence; far excelling, in the gigantic size of
the letters at the commencement of each Gospel, the excessive minuteness of the ornamental details crowded into whole pages, the number of its very peculiar decorations, the
fineness of the writing, and the endless variety of its initial capital letters, the famous
Gospels of Lindisfarne, in the Cottonian Library. But this manuscript is still more valuable
on account of the various pictorial representations of different scenes in the life of our
Saviour, delineated in the genuine Irish style, of which several of the manuscripts of St.
Gall, and a very few others, offer analogous examples, and of which the present volume
and my "Palæographia sacra pictoria" offer a complete series of fac-similes.

This fine volume was long ago enshrined in a golden cumhdach, or cover, and
narrowly escaped destruction in A.D. 1006, when the volume was stolen. The Irish
passage, referring to this circumstance, in the "Annals of the Four Masters," is quoted
in my "Palæographia;" and Dr. Todd[†] thus cites the ancient chronicle called the
"Annals of Ulster," in which the same fact is recorded :—" A.D. 1006. The large
Gospel of Columbkille [‡] was sacrilegiously stolen in the night, out of the western erdom
[perhaps what we should now call the sacristy or vestry-room] of the great Church of
Kennansa [the old Irish name of Kells]. This was the chief relic of the West of the

* Colgan, "Trias Thaum," p. 438.
† "Irish Eccl. Journ.," iv. p. 37.
‡ The corresponding word, Chúdaimeille, is rendered
"Columba: Ecclesiarum" by Dr. O'Conor. Columba was,
however, baptised by the presbyter Cruihnechan, under the
name of Colum, to which the addition of *cille*, signifying
of the Church (not churches), was subsequently made in
reference to his diligent attendance at the church of his
youthful sojourn. (Reeves, p. lxx.) Bede rightly derives
"Columcelli à cellà et Columba" (H. E., v. 9). So O'Donnell,
as translated by Colgan, "Additamento *ille* quod *cella*

usu ecclesiam significat, partim ab Ecclesia *felici* omine
sortitorum quorú *volvbant* pra: gaudio, elevatis in *eodem*
monibus ditere, *hæc advenit* Columba de cella." (Act. SS.,
pp. 641-6.) And in the Leabhar Brenc it is stated (as translated into English) that he was called *Columcelle*, because
of his frequently coming from the cell in which he read
his Psalms, to meet the neighbouring children; and what
they used to say among themselves was, "Has our little
Colum come to-day from the cell?" i.e., from Tulach-
Dubhglaise in Tir-Logadech in Cinell *oonáill*.—(Reeves,
p. lxx, note u.)

World, on account of the *human cover*.* This Gospel was found after twenty nights and two months, 'with its gold stolen off, and a sod over it.'" (And see Petrie on this passage, in the "Round Towers," p. 436.)

Here we find the name of Columba (Columbkille) in conjunction with a *large* copy of the Gospels; and it is certain that the volume before us is the great Gospel of Columbkille, to which the foregoing record of the Four Masters refers. It is, as Dr. Todd justly remarks, of an unusually large size, written in very large letters, at a period when it was customary to write in a very small hand; it belonged to the church of Kells, as is evident from the curious charters, relative to the clergy of Kells, which it contains; and it continued among the treasures of that church down to the time of Archbishop Ussher, by whom it was saved from destruction, and who was bishop of Meath from 1621 to 1624. After his death, when his library was granted by King Charles II. to the University of Dublin, this precious volume, with other inestimable treasures, was found amongst his books, and has ever since remained in the safe custody of its present possessors, who, on account of its containing a royal charter of one of the kings of Ireland, deemed it not unfitting to allow Queen Victoria and her royal consort to inscribe their names in the volume, on the occasion of their visit to Ireland.

St. Columba, who was born in December, A.D. 519, died on Whitsun-eve, A.D. 595; so that the Book of Kells, if written by him or ever in his possession, was upwards of 400 years old when its precious cover was stolen, and is now of the antiquity of thirteen hundred years. Mr. Digby Wyatt, as we have seen in the preceding article, considers that this volume was written after the death of St. Columba, in his honour, as was the case with the "Gospels of Lindisfarne," written in honour of St. Cuthbert, shortly after his death; but Dr. Todd, whose acquaintance with Irish MSS. is unrivalled, regards the volume as "a valuable monument of the piety and zeal of the Irish Church of the sixth century, even though we should be disposed to question the tradition that it is in the handwriting of Columba; which, however, I must say I see no reason to doubt, as the volume is undoubtedly a manuscript of that age" (*ut supra*, p. 38).

Dr. Todd, moreover, refers to a legend recorded in the "Annals of Ulster," from which we learn that St. Columba was the possessor of a celebrated copy of the Gospels not written by himself, but given to him (as the legend says) by an Angel, and therefore called the "Gospel of the Angel." This volume was, however, found with two other "noble relics," according to the legend, in the tomb of St. Patrick, when his remains were translated by Columbkille into a shrine. The latter part of the legend is omitted (purposely, as it would seem) by O'Donnell in his "Life of Columba" (lib. i. c. ult.); but he also gives sufficient to show that, at least at the time when the legend was invented (if not before), a singular copy of the Gospels, as also a chalice and a bell,† were said to have been in the possession first of St. Patrick and then of Columba.

In the account of this volume in my "Palæographia," I have considered it as most probable that Giraldus Cambrensis had it before him when, at the close of the twelfth century, he wrote (as quoted in my former description, and as translated by Dr. Todd), "Of all the wonders of KILDARE, I found nothing more wonderful than that marvellous book, written in the time of the Virgin [St.] Brigid, and, as they say, at the *dictation of*

---

* The "Four Masters" state, according to O'Conor, that the date of the volume was owing to the veneration paid to it as an oath-book. "Præcipua reliquia occidentalis mundi ob porumenta perstandis hoc vita contra perjores hominum," and O'Donovan and Petrie translate the word *decada* by the word *cingulos*, which Dr. Todd renders *domum*

† This bell is called the Bell of St. Patrick's Testament by the "Four Masters," and evidence exists in support of the opinion that the "Bell of St. Patrick," of whose splendid outer covering two portions are represented in my Plate 50, figs. 1 and 2, was the one here referred to.

an Angel." [Hence, possibly, the origin of the name of the Gospel of the Angel above referred to, as applied to the Kildare rather than the Kells Gospels.] "The book contains the Concordance [*i.e.* the Eusebian tables or canons] of the Evangelists, according to Jerome, every page of which is filled with divers figures, most accurately marked out with various colours. Here you behold a majestic face, divinely drawn, [in the original, 'Majestatis Vultum divinitus impressum,' which I prefer to translate, the face of the Divine Majesty, considering it to refer to a portrait of the Saviour,] there the mystical forms of the Evangelists, each having sometimes six, sometimes four, and sometimes two wings; here an eagle, there a calf; there again a human face, or a lion, and other figures, of infinite variety, so closely wrought together, that if you looked carelessly at them, they would seem rather like a uniform blot than an exquisite interweaving of figures, exhibiting no skill or art, where all is skill and perfection of art. But if you look closely, with all the acuteness of sight that you can command, and examine the inmost secrets of that wondrous art, you will discover such subtle, such fine and closely-wrought lines, twisted and interwoven in such intricate knots, and adorned with such fresh and brilliant colours, that you will readily acknowledge the whole to have been *the result of angelic* rather than human *skill*. The more frequently I behold it, the more diligently I examine it, the more numerous are the beauties I discover in it, the more I am lost in renewed admiration of it. Neither could Apelles himself execute the like; and indeed they seem rather to have been formed and painted by a hand not mortal." ("Topogr. Hibern. distinct.," ii. c. 38.)

And, to quote only another art-critic of the highest fame, Dr. Waagen, the conservator of the Royal Museum of Berlin, who has especially made ancient illuminated manuscripts a profound study, says of these Irish and Hiberno-Saxon works: "The ornamental pages, borders, and initial letters, exhibit such a rich variety of beautiful and peculiar designs, so admirable a taste in the arrangement of the colours, and such an uncommon perfection of finish, that one feels absolutely struck with amazement."

The very numerous illuminations of this volume render it a complete storehouse of artistic interest. Foremost, and quite unique of their kind, are three pictures, representing scenes of the life of the Saviour; namely:—1st, the representation of the Virgin and Child; 2nd, the Temptation of Jesus Christ; and 3rd, the Seizure of Christ by the Jews.

The verso of fol. 7 is entirely occupied with an illumination representing the Virgin seated, holding the infant Saviour in her lap (copied in the first plate of the article on this MS. in my "Palæographia"),* but which is enclosed in a frame-like border an inch and a quarter wide, composed of a great number of interlaced lacertine animals, of various colours; the angles of the frame are, moreover, ornamented with additional designs (as in my Plate 10), that at the upper angle of the left side being an intricate interlacement of thin white ribbons on a sienna ground, and that at the lower angle of the same side like the centre portion of my Plate 12. Each of the two angles on the right side is filled with a design, composed of a pitcher, holding two branches, with large trefoil leaves, as in the upper part of the central group in my Plate 51, fig. 1. Moreover, a small square space is taken out of the right-hand border (at the back of the lower angel), in which the heads of six persons are represented, similar to those in the lower part of my Plate 11, with their backs turned towards the central miniature. It is difficult to comprehend the object of this group of heads, of which I know no other instance in miniatures of the Virgin and Child.

---

* In the original the whole ground of the space enclosing the miniature of the Virgin and Child is coloured burnt sienna. It is left white in most of the copies of my "Palæographia."

The Virgin Mother is here represented seated on a low-bottomed chair of elegant design, represented in profile, with a high straight back, reaching as high as the ears of the Virgin, and terminating at its upper part in a red dog's head, with a tongue of enormous length, twisted in various complicated folds round the top of the chair; being partly coloured blue and partly yellow. The seat is concave, and the whole space between the front and hind legs is decorated with a charming pattern, apparently representing richly ornamented bars or tapestry-work; the open spaces being coloured pink and green, and bearing alternately white crosses and red circles. The Virgin is drawn of a large size, as was often done, by way of showing veneration, in drawing the sacred persons by early artists. As usual with figures of females also, at this early period, the head is covered with drapery, and surrounded by a purple circular nimbus, bearing three pale-yellow Maltese crosses, and several groups of three white dots arranged in a triangle; the nimbus being edged with a narrow band of pearls, on a sienna ground. The wings of the two upper angels are represented as crossing portion of the nimbus, and being coloured green and blue. Dr. Todd has mistaken them for part of the nimbus itself. It is remarkable that neither the infant Jesus, nor the four Angels occupying the corners of the design, have any nimbus or glory surrounding their heads.* The feet in all the figures are bare and ill drawn.

The upper robe of the Virgin is reddish-purple, bearing a number of small white dots, arranged by threes, forming triangles; and on her right shoulder the dress bears a lozenge-shaped spot, edged with white; of which Dr. Todd expresses himself as ignorant of the meaning. I simply regard it as an ornament, intended to break the large uniform purple space in this part of the design. The lower robe of the Virgin is lilac, edged with yellow. The upper robe of the Child is green, and the lower yellow, with red dots arranged in triangles. The two Angels occupying the upper angles of the design, appear to be intended for females, having the head covered with a yellow cap, like the Virgin. Each holds a rod, with a circular disk at the top, coloured green, with a brown edging, and bearing a small Maltese cross. Two other Angels occupy the two lower angles of the picture; one holding in both hands a rod, on the top of which is a circular disk, enclosing a twelve-leaved rosette; whilst the other has in his hand an instrument consisting of a short stem, separating itself into two convoluted branches, each terminating in a large trefoil or shamrock leaf, analogous to one of the sceptres held by St. Luke in the "Book of St. Chad." (See my plate of the Gospels of St. Chad, in " Pal. sacr. pict.")†

The Virgin, moreover, is represented with a narrow interlaced ribbon of a golden

* Dr. Todd says that this "is singularly in accordance with the doctrine of the School divines, which represents the aureola, as they term it, as peculiar to certain saints, and indicative of their victory over the world, the flesh, and the devil. It would therefore be improper, according to this notion of it, to represent our Lord, or an Angel, with the aureola, an error into which many modern painters have nevertheless repeatedly fallen. But the theory of the School theologians, that the aureola of a virgin is white [Virginis siquidem in capite aliquam coronulam albam, Martyre rubeam, et Doctores virides gestabant.' Joh. Anglus, Flores Theol., p. 398.], has not been adopted in the ancient picture before us; for the glory round the Blessed Virgin's head is there represented in several colours, yellow, purple, green, and white." The above attribution of the aureola (by which term I apprehend Dr. Todd alludes to the circular nimbus round the head, and not the whole oval glory, more definitively termed the aureola, with which the entire body of a sacred person is enveloped, and which is occasionally termed the vesica piscis) only to certain saints may be theoretically correct, but it is entirely refuted by the practice of artists from the earliest period, and is not confined to "modern painters," who have given a nimbus to the head of the Saviour, as well as to that of the other persons of the Trinity, &c.

The attribution also of certain colours to the nimbus of certain personages is also entirely refuted by the like practice of painters of all ages. The reader who may be induced to work out this question for himself, may consult Didron's "Iconographie Chrétienne," and Mrs. Jameson's volumes on "Sacred and Legendary Art."

† Dr. Petrie showed me an ancient Irish relic, which appeared to me possibly to be the handle of one of these instruments. Can it be intended for the "flabellum muscarium," used in the early Church " ad muscas a sacrificio abigendas " ?

colour round the neck. Can this have been intended for portion of a torque, or is it simply introduced for the sake of ornament? The two semicircular open spaces at the sides of the drawing are filled in with grotesquely interlaced human figures, and a similar space at the top with interlaced lacertine animals.

The drawing representing (as I apprehend) the Temptation of the Saviour occurs on fol. 202 v. and is copied in my Plate 11. Here the bust of the Saviour is represented at the summit of an elaborately ornamented conical design, which I suppose represents a "pinnacle of the temple," rather than the "exceeding high mountain." The head of the Saviour is surrounded by a cruciferous nimbus, like that of the Virgin in the above-described drawing, and He appears to hold a roll in his left hand. Two very rudely-designed Angels hover above His head, and two others occupy the upper angles of the picture, the interstices of the latter being filled in with foliage and branches springing from vases; that on the right hand being in an unusual position. The strangely emaciated black figure of the Tempter (destitute of tail, but with hoof-like feet), and the crowd of heads at the side and bottom of the design, as also the bust within a frame, holding two rosette-bearing rods, merit particular notice.

The third of these designs occurs on fol. 114 r, and represents, as I apprehend, the seizure of Christ by the Jews (St. Matth. xxvi. 50). The chief portion of this design is copied in outline in the middle of my 51st Plate. Here the Saviour is represented destitute of a nimbus, with curling hair and straight beard, whilst the Jews are distinguished by being drawn of considerably smaller size, and wearing short hair, black pointed beards, and moustaches. They have seized the arms of the Saviour. All the feet are here represented as naked. The scene is indicated by branches, with foliage, in the upper part of the drawing, and by the words "Et (h)ymno dicto exierunt in montem Oliveti." (St. Matth. xxiv. 30.) The whole is enclosed in the original between two highly-decorated columns, supporting a rounded arch, the crown of which terminates in two large dogs' heads.

Mr. Petrie thus comments on this picture:—" Here the Saviour is drawn at the moment when, having risen from His last Supper with His followers, He turns to walk forth to His Passion and Death. There is no sense of heroism, no proud endurance in His form, but there is of sorrow and sinking. And there is deep tenderness in the way two of His followers are painted as coming to His side, and placing their arms beneath His arms, as if they would support and reassure Him, while he utters the words, ',All ye shall be ashamed of me this night.' The three figures are passing forth beneath an arch, the ornament on which seems miraculous in the delicacy of its detail, and through whose branches, arching over the group, may be read the words of the first text quoted, while the second is written on the back of the picture." It is surprising that Mr. Petrie, who was so thoroughly acquainted with the details of the great sculptured crosses of Ireland, should have failed to perceive the intention of the drawing before us. Although obscure, I have no doubt that the lowest compartment of the west side of the south-east cross, Monasterboice, (O'Neill's Crosses, Pl. 14, where the two Jews are armed with swords and wear long moustaches,) the upper compartment of the west side of the north cross, Clonmacnoise, (O'Neill, Pl. 23, where the head of the middle figure has a circular nimbus, and the two side figures are armed with long spears,) and the upper compartment of the stem of the Arboe cross, west side (O'Neill, Pl. 32), represent the same subject, namely, the Seizure of Christ by the Jews. Sometimes also the two side figures are represented on the Irish crosses with dogs' heads, in allusion to Psalm xxii. 16.

The volume comprises also three full-length figures, intended for portraits of the

Evangelists. On fol. 28 v is St. Matthew, opposite the commencement of his Gospel. This figure (copied in my 10th Plate) appears to be standing, but the two ends of the blue cushion, dotted with white in triangles, seen at the sides of the figure below the elbows, indicate a seat; the curly flaxen hair, the short stiff beard, the misplaced ears, the book held by the *covered* left hand, whilst the right hand appears to be in the act of benediction, with the first and second fingers extended in the Roman manner, the feet evidently wearing sandals, the two peacocks* standing on plants in vases beneath the large arch, the three Angels with a fourth figure apparently destitute of wings, and bearing a branching foliated rod, together with the whole general design of the drawing, and the excessive elaboration of the interlaced details, render this picture one of the greatest interest.

On fol. 32 v is a full-length portrait misplaced, but evidently intended for St. Mark or St. Luke, whose portraits do not occur before either of their respective Gospels, and which is inscribed in a modern hand, "Jesus Christus," upon an erasure. This figure, which is destitute of any attribute of the Saviour, is similar in design to that of St. Matthew, and appears also to be standing; but the ends of the ornamental cushion appear at the sides of the columns supporting the rounded arch, above the head of the figure, which is surrounded by a circular nimbus, of which the disk is ornamented with red and blue triangles, and parti-coloured dots, also arranged in triangles. The right hand is hidden beneath the outer garment, but the left hand, uncovered, holds the book of the Gospels; the seat is ornamented with the heads of animals and birds, and the whole is enclosed in a splendidly ornamental border formed of lacertine animals.

The third of the figures of the Evangelists occurs opposite the beginning of St. John's Gospel, on fol. 291 v. It is a splendid page, the upper portion of the figure being copied in my "Palæographia" (Book of Kells, p. 5). Here the Evangelist is seated on an ornamental cushion, with the head adorned with a magnificent nimbus, of which the outer circle (omitted in my figure above referred to) consists of a series of interlaced animals, with three large circular disks, ornamented with a star-like design: the figure holds the book elevated in his left hand, with a pen of large size in his right. The folds of the hair illustrate, as Mr. Petrie informed me, the ancient habit of the Irish. The feet are shod with sandals. The ink-pot is placed near the right foot. The whole of the design is, like the others, enclosed within a highly decorated border.

The page (fol. 33 v) opposite the commencement of the historical portion of St. Matthew's Gospel (ch. i. ver. 18), is entirely occupied with an elaborately tessellated page, enclosing a cruciform design of a character similar to, but far more intricate than, any in the Gospels of Lindisfarne, St. Columba, or St. Chad. I suppose each Gospel was preceded by a similarly ornamented leaf, which has disappeared.

---

* Mr. Petrie, mistaking the figure of St. Matthew for Christ himself, thus speaks of this picture (" Cromlech on Howth," p. 78): " The peacock, the bird of Juno, was an ancient pagan symbol, and used to signify the deification of an Empress, as we find from many of the old Roman coins and medals. The early Christians, accustomed to this interpretation, adopted it as a general emblem of the mortal exchanged for the immortal existence ; and with this signification the peacock is seen, with mystical toil, on the walls and ceilings of catacombs, the tombs of the Martyrs, and many of the sarcophagi in Rome, down to the fourth and fifth century, *when we find it placed at each side of the head of Christ*, standing amidst a garland of trefoil in the frontispiece of the *Book of Kells*" (With the exception of the inaccurate statement at the end of this quotation, the whole is copied, without acknowledgment, from Mrs. Jameson's "Sacred and Legendary Art," p. 15.) The curious fancy of the early Christians, that the flesh of the peacock was incorruptible when dead (" quis enim nisi Deus creator omnium dedit carni pavonis mortui ne putresceret," says St. Augustine, De Civ. Dei, xxi. c. 4), was a more probable ground of the adoption of this bird as a Christian symbol ; but in the Syriac Gospels of St. John of Zagba, sixth century, in the Laurentian Library of Florence, two of these birds are introduced in one of the paintings, evidently as simple ornaments, without any symbolism (D'Agincourt, Painting, tab. xxvii. fig. 3, and see Munter, " Sinnbilder und Kunstvorstellungen der alten Christen," i. p. 92) ; and such, I believe, is also the case in the Irish miniature before us.

Three full pages also are devoted to the illustration of the Evangelical symbols; namely, the verso of leaf 27, at the beginning of St. Matthew's Gospel, where they are singularly delineated and ornamented, and enclosed within broad elaborate square borders. They occur again on fol. 129 v, opposite the beginning of St. Mark, in a beautifully designed page; and a third time on fol. 290 v, at the beginning of St. John's Gospel, copied in my 9th Plate. The singular manner in which these figures are treated deserves careful attention, and has much more resemblance to Assyrian or Egyptian designs than to ordinary Western work. In the first of these pages the Angel is represented winged, and with a nimbus around the head, bearing a long rod, with a beautiful Greek cross at its upper end.

The symbols themselves in the second of these drawings are copied in the second plate from the "Book of Kells" in my "Palæographia;" each is, however, enclosed in an oblong frame (as represented in outline in my 53rd Plate, fig. 7), and the whole within a highly ornamented border. In this series, the Angel is attended by a supplemental Angel, of which the head and wings occupy the upper, and the spread tail the lower part of the first small frame; that containing the Lion of St. Mark, copied in my 53rd Plate; is accompanied by the symbols of St. Luke and St. John; the Calf of St. Luke has the Lion and Eagle in the angles, and the Eagle of St. John has the Calf and Lion. Each frame also contains figures of two rods, terminating in rosettes, the pendent objects somewhat like fuchsia-flowers, being probably intended for small bells, and which are replaced in two of the frames by four small groups of rounded plates, arranged in pendent triangles, probably intended to produce a sound when the instrument represented was shaken by the hand.

In my 9th Plate it will be seen that the symbol of St. Matthew is represented with four wings, with a short beard, without any nimbus round the head, and as holding a book in each hand. It may be proper to add that it is the Lion of St. Mark which occupies the left, and the Eagle of St. John the right side of the design, which, in its elaborate details and elegant arrangement, is unequalled in Celtic art.

Besides the above-described illustrations, the text itself is far more extensively decorated than in any other now existing copy of the Gospels. Not only are the pages containing the commencement of each Gospel, namely, the "Liber Generationis" (fol. 29 r) and the "Xpi autem generatio" (fol. 34 r) of St. Matthew, the "Initium Evangelii" of St. Mark (fol. 132 r), the "Quoniam quidem" of St. Luke (fol. 188 r), and the "In principio" of St. John (fol. 292 r), entirely filled with these words (the initials being of a gigantic size, and ornamented with the utmost prodigality of ornamental design); but the Eusebian Canons occupying several pages at the beginning of the book; the commencement of the "breves causæ," or headings of the chapters, commencing on fol. 8 r, with the words "Nativitas Xpi in Bethlem Iudæ, magi munera offerunt et infantes interficiuntur, regressio"[*] (written in rows of angular and lacertine letters of different sizes, separated by highly ornamented bars); as well as various detached passages of the Passion; as, "Tune dicit illis Jesus omnes," fol. 114 v; "Tune crucifixerant," fol. 174 r; "Erat autem hora tertia," fol. 183 r; the end of St. Mark's Gospel, fol. 187 v; "Ihs autem plenus," fol. 203 r; and "Una autem Sabbati," fol. 285 r,—are all written of a large size, each occupying a separate page, and being beautifully decorated.

In the pages of the Eusebian Canons the figures of the Evangelical symbols are introduced beneath arches, in the upper part of the designs, and in the pages at the commencement of the Gospels human figures are also introduced, often in a

* The initial N in this passage is copied in page 7 of the "Cromlech on Howth," and the remainder of the word, (Nativitas, formed of curious lacertine letters, in the second plate of my "Palæographia."

K

very fantastical manner. In the pages of the "Liber Generationis" a figure nearly half the height of the design, holding a book, occupies the bottom left-hand portion of the page.

An excellent idea of one of the less elaborately designed pages is conveyed in the illuminated title-page of the "Cromlech on Howth,"[*] being a partial adaptation of the page illustrating the words "Tunc crucifixerant," &c., mentioned above.

The page containing the last few words of the Gospel of St. Mark is one of the most remarkable in the volume. On either side the page is margined by the slender body of a nondescript animal (having its interior filled up with birds, with interlacing tails and top-knots), with the head and mane of a lion, and with the tail and hind legs strangely bent and intertwined. Each has only one fore leg, which is, however, of wonderful length, and is angulated in such a manner, in conjunction with the corresponding leg of the opposite animal, as to form the letter X, occupying the whole of the centre of the page. On either side, within the triangular space between the body and this leg, is respectively introduced an Angel, inscribed "Angelus dñi." One of these animals (omitting the long fore leg) forms the margin of the sixth page of the "Cromlech on Howth."

Another artistic peculiarity of the "Book of Kells" arises from the decoration of the initial letters of each of the sentences or verses, so that each page presents us with several of these letters, varying in size and design; as well as from the introduction of coloured representations of men, animals, birds, horses, dogs, &c., placed without any reference to the text, but simply to fill up any vacant space at the end of a line. Of these peculiarities, portion of the Beatitudes, copied in the second plate from the "Book of Kells" in my "Palæographia," and the 8th Plate of this work (from fol. 200 of the MS.), offers excellent examples, the latter being portion of the genealogy of Christ, from the beginning of St. Luke's Gospel (ch. iii. ver. 23).

The elegant design at the head of my plate has been transposed from the end of the genealogy to the beginning; and it will be observed that the right-hand division is intended to represent two branches with leaves and flowers, arising out of a blue-and-white vase, not dissimilar in shape to that in the hand of the upper figure at the right-hand side of the page (introduced from page 201). The introduction of natural foliage in this MS. is another of its great peculiarities; whilst the intricate intertwining of the branches is eminently characteristic of the Celtic spirit, which compelled even the human figure to submit to the most impossible contortions. In the series of initials in my plate (being the letter Q often repeated), the round part of the first is formed of a monstrous animal with a green neck, a long curved body, half formed of minute white ribbons on a black ground, and half plain yellow, with one of the hind legs red and the other yellow; the second portion of the Q being formed of a human head, a thin body with a pretty interlaced pattern, forming a series of lozenges, a very long and thin yellow thigh, and naked shanks and feet, one of which is seized by the beak of the bird forming the centre of the fourth letter Q.

The figure at the bottom of the right side of the page is valuable as a representation of an Irish warrior of the sixth century, armed with the small round shield (as in

---

[*] The marginal designs, and larger initials, in this beautiful work, are, with one exception, copied from the "Book of Kells;" it is, however, to be regretted that the more intricate and minute details, which in fact constitute the great peculiarity of the original work, have not been rendered with scrupulous precision. It hardly need be added that the smaller initials at the beginning of each line of the Poem and the text itself, are intended for Gothic black-letter of the fourteenth century.

the Psalter of St. Augustine.—*see* Plate 3) and a long spear. The two figures on this page, as well as two small equestrian figures from pages 89 and 255, are copied and described in Mr. Wilde's "Catalogue of the Antiquities of the Royal Irish Academy" (pp. 299, 300).

Ten of the smaller initial letters at the beginning of the verses are copied in my "Palæographia;" and others have been published by Dr. Todd in the "Irish Ecclesiastical Journal," No. 76. A few others of great elegance, or singular quaintness, may be referred to.

In page 297 v (Pater noster) is a grotesque little figure of a man in a sitting position, with one of his legs thrown upwards, forming a figure like the letter K. In p. 130 is a small circle, within which three men are contorted, with their legs and arms singularly interlaced.

In p. 291 v is a curious series of lozenge-shaped designs, the central one formed of eight lacertine animals, all the noses of which converge to the centre. Dogs well drawn are represented on p. 40, and in the open spaces of a fine letter Z in the early part of the volume; and again in p. 48, in conjunction with an elegant bit of arabesque, formed of trefoils and a hare awkwardly sitting on its hind legs, and regarding the dog with great indifference. On the same page a cat sits very demurely, whilst a rat runs off with a small pat of cheese. A butterfly, or more probably, from the markings on the body, a death's-head moth (*Sphinx atropos*), is represented in p. 63; a cock and two hens, of blue and green colours, appear in p. 67; a man on horseback, in a green cloak edged with red, in p. 89; a strangely distorted man strangling an eagle in p. 96; whilst in p. 134 is a singular little composition of two cats, seated with their tails between their legs, each holding in its fore paws the tail of a mouse; the two mice, careless of their proximity to the cats, being engaged in devouring a circular cake marked with a cross (the consecrated wafer?); two other mice are quietly seated on the backs of the cats, whilst below is a black rat devouring a fish. Some of these groups of animals are copied in the "Cromlech on Howth," p. 30, but not with sufficient attention to the minute details.

The palæographical details of this volume are described in my "Palæographia," whilst the curious charters inscribed on its blank pages have been printed by the Irish Archæological Society, in the first volume of their "Miscellany," in the original Irish, with a translation and notes by Mr. O'Donovan, and which are believed to be the only specimens which time has spared to us of legal deeds composed in the Irish language prior to the Anglo-Norman invasion.

THE GOSPELS OF LINDISFARNE.

Plates XII. and XIII.

THIS noble manuscript, known sometimes as the Durham Book (from having been long preserved in the Cathedral of Durham), or the Gospels of St. Cuthbert (in whose honour it was written and illuminated), forms the glory of the Cottonian Library, preserved in the British Museum, where it is marked Nero D IV, and is certainly the most elaborately ornamented of all the Anglo-Saxon manuscripts; it has, moreover, the advantage of being quite entire, and containing its own evidence of its origin and date. It is of the same size as the Book of Kells, and somewhat smaller than the Gospels of Mac Regol; consisting of 258 leaves of thick vellum, measuring 13½ inches by 9½. It contains the four Gospels, written in double columns, according to the Latin Vulgate, with an interlineary Anglo-Saxon gloss, preceded by the Epistle of St. Jerome to Pope Damasus (Novum opus, &c.), the Eusebian Canons or tables of parallel passages, arguments or abstracts of each Gospel, similar to the short headings prefixed to the chapters of the Gospels in English Bibles, and capitula of the lessons ordered to be read on Sundays and festivals in the Church; the whole written in a beautifully clear, large, rounded hand, and most exquisitely ornamented with drawings, illuminated initials, some occupying entire pages, and tessellated designs, the entire volume being in an extraordinarily perfect state of preservation, although now nearly 1200 years old.

The colonization, about A.D. 635, of the afterwards famous island Lindisfarne, from the still more famous island Iona (which had been given to St. Columba and his Irish associates, by the King of Dalriada, in Scotland, about the middle of the sixth century), will enable us to understand the complete resemblance existing between the artistic and palæographic peculiarities of the Book of Kells and the volume now under consideration; since, notwithstanding the mission of the Scoto-Irish missionaries came to an end after an existence of only thirty years, it is evident that Eata and his pupil Cuthbert, coming to Lindisfarne from Melrose in 664, found most of the monks still strongly favourable to the Scoto-Irish traditions. The manuscript now under consideration was written at Lindisfarne at the end of the seventh or very beginning of the eighth century, as we learn from a short Anglo-Saxon entry at the end of St. Matthew's Gospel, and a longer one at the end of the volume, in the same handwriting as the interlineary Anglo-Saxon gloss.[*]

These, together with the account given by Simeon, precentor of Durham at the end of the eleventh century, prove that the volume was written by Eadfrith (a monk of Lindisfarne, and who became its bishop, and held the see from A.D. 698 to 721), in honour of God and St. Cuthbert (who died in 687); that the illuminations were executed by Æthilwald, who was a contemporary monk with Bishop Eadfrith, and who succeeded him in the bishopric of the island, which he held till his decease in 737, according to the Saxon Chronicle, or in 740 according to the supplemental notes to Bede; that a splendid gilt cover, adorned with precious stones, was made for the book by Billfrith

* The two Anglo-Saxon entries above referred to are extremely interesting, and are thus translated by Mr. Waring ("Prolog. Lindisf. and Rushworth Gospels," part 4, p. xliv): the first being "Thou, O living God, bear in mind Eadfrith, and Æthelwald, and Billfrith, and Aldred the sinner. These four, with God's help, were employed upon [or busied about] this book;" and the second, "Eadfrith, bishop over the church of Lindisfarne, first wrote this book in honour of God and St. Cuthbert, and all the company of saints in the island; and Æthilwald, bishop of Lindisfarne, made an outer cover and adorned it, as he was well able; and Billfrith the anchorite, he wrought the metal-work of the ornaments on the outside thereof, and decked it with gold and with gems, overlaid also with silver and unalloyed metal; and Aldred, an unworthy and most miserable priest, by the help of God and St. Cuthbert, over-glossed the same in English, and domiciled himself with the three parts: Matthew, this part for God and St. Cuthbert; Mark, this part for the bishop; and Luke, this part for the brotherhood; with eight oras of silver [as an offering on entrance; and St. John's part for himself, i.e. for his soul; and [depositing] four silver oræ with God and St. Cuthbert, that he may find acceptance in Heaven, through the mercy of God; good fortune and peace on earth, promotion and dignity, wisdom and prudence, through the merits of St. Cuthbert, Eadfrith, Æthilwald, Billfrith, and Aldred have wrought and adorned this book of the Gospels, for those of God and St. Cuthbert." The words applied to Æthilwald's share in the work, "geðryðe and geloclike," appear to me to refer to the illuminations of the volume. The Anglo-Saxon ðryðan, to finish or make perfect, and the old Friesic, Swedish, and German word fold, a painting, strongly favour this idea. Moreover, Billfrith is stated to have made the metal covering, and it is well known that it was the custom for the scribes of such manuscripts to leave spaces for the illuminator subsequently to fill in and complete the work. Thus we may add Bishop Æthilwald (Aethelwald, Aethelwald, or Oethlvald, as his name is variously written), to the list of famous art-worker Church dignitaries, of whom St. Eloi and Dunstan were examples.

the anchorite, and that Aldred, an "indignus et miserrimus presbyter," added the inter-lineary Anglo-Saxon gloss and notes. It does not appear, indeed, at what date Aldred the glosser lived; but a bishop of that name presided over the see of Durham from 946 to 968. If the two were identical, the gloss would probably have been written before the former of these two dates, whilst Aldred was a presbyter; and Mr. T. Wright ("Anglo-Saxon Lit." p. 427) conjectures that it was during the first half of the tenth century that this gloss was written,* as the same name is attached to an Anglo-Saxon gloss in the Durham Ritual, published by the Surtees Society, with a note relating to Bishop Alfsige, who flourished during the latter half of the tenth century. Sir Frederick Madden says, "It is quite certain that the second hand in red [in the gloss] in the Durham Book [Lindisfarne Gospels] is the same that has glossed the collection of Collects and Prayers known as the Durham Ritual." ("Letters of Eminent Literary Men," published by Sir H. Ellis, p. 267.)

I, however, found the same name twice inscribed in the fine fragment of the uncial Gospels in the Durham Library (No. A. n. 17), with the title "Boge messe preost God preost Aldred god biscop;" but written in a very rude hand, quite unlike that of the gloss in the Lindisfarne Gospels. We can, however, scarcely conceive these entries to have been written by the bishop himself.

The palæographical peculiarities of this volume having been described in my "Palæographia," I shall here confine the following remarks to its artistic details, of which the figures of the Evangelists are the most important. These, indeed, are completely unique in their style, being as unlike the contemporary Irish miniatures as they differ from the paintings of the finest Carlovingian manuscripts, of which so many have been published by Count Bastard. The figures are of large size, occupying, together with the symbolic animals, the greater part of the respective pages on which they are delineated, with but a very narrow and plain framework, slightly produced, and ornamented at the angles with interlaced lines.

The figure of St. Matthew is copied in Plate 13. The scribe wears long straight grey hair, falling on the shoulders, with a long straight moustache and beard. He is clad in a dark purple under-garment, with orange edging seen at the neck, wrists, and at the bottom of the skirt: strong black lines on the arm indicate the folds. The large outer garment is of a verdigris-green colour, laid on quite flat, and relieved with red lines, to indicate the folds. The feet are marked with lines, to indicate sandals, and rest on a flat carpet or footstool. The figure is seated on a large red cushion, resting on an ornamentally-painted stool, or settle without any back, and is engaged in writing, apparently with a reed pen (as there is no indication of the web of a feather pen) in a large open volume. The head is surrounded by a large plain yellow nimbus, with a red border, on the upper part of which rests the upper part of the body of the symbolical Angel, blowing a long Anglo-Saxon trumpet, and also holding a square volume in his left hand, and with a nimbus round the head. The most remarkable feature in the miniature, however, is the introduction of a large red curtain, suspended on a rod by rings occupying all the upper right-hand side of the drawing, looped up at the side, allowing space for the introduction of a head, surrounded also by a

---

* Hunterick, in the Preface to his "Reconstruction of the Cotton Gloss," gives several reasons for assigning it to the first half of the twelfth century. These appear to be satisfactorily answered by Mr. Waring, in his valuable Prolegomena to the four volumes of these Gospels issued by the Surtees Society, p. viii. In the note at the end of the volume Aldred had written and partially erased the pronoun "ic," I, before his own name. No one looking at the fac-simile of the beginning and termination of this entry which I have published in my "Palæographia," could come to the conclusion that the entry had been written in the twelfth or even in the eleventh century.

plain nimbus, with short grey curly hair and long moustache and beard curled at the tip, and with the right hand covered by the purple garment, holding a green-backed book. After much consideration I am inclined to believe that this figure (of which no similar instance has hitherto been published in any of the many representations of the Evangelists), is intended for the Holy Ghost, dictating the Gospel to the Evangelist.[*] I was fortunate in finding a copy of this miniature at Copenhagen (see Plate 41). In the upper part of the drawing the words "Imago hominis" are introduced, and below, instead of the Latin Sanctus Mattheus, we find the Greek "O AGIOS MATTHEUS," written in large angulated Anglo-Saxon capitals.

The figure of St. Mark is rather larger than that of St. Matthew, and is turned towards the left. He is represented as headless, and is engaged in writing upon a square flat tablet, placed on a circular writing-desk before him, holding at the same time a closed book in his left hand. Over his head (surrounded with a plain nimbus) is the symbolical Lion, winged, holding a book between its fore paws, and blowing a trumpet, more curved than that of St. Matthew's Angel. The inscriptions, "Imago leonis" and "O AGIUS MARCUS," prove that the artist was better acquainted with Latin than Greek.

The figure of St. Luke, inscribed "O AGIOS LUCAS," is very similar to that of St. Matthew, except that the head bears a strong resemblance to that of the side figure in the miniature of the latter; and that the scribe is engaged in writing on a long scroll (volumen). His symbolical Calf (with short horns), inscribed "Imago vituli," however, bears a square book, and a yellow nimbus round his head; the Evangelist himself wears a pale pink under-garment, with green folds, and a long outer blue or lavender one, with red folds. The cushion on which he is seated is red, covered with circles of small yellow dots surrounding a larger central one.

St. John, with the inscription "O AGIOS IOHANNES," is represented young and beardless, with short curly hair, and is drawn full-faced towards the spectator, holding a long scroll on his knees with the right hand, whilst his left rests with extended fingers on his breast. His Eagle, the inscription misspelt "Imago aequilae," bears a small square book in his talons. The ornamental bench on which he is seated is destitute of a back, but a large bolster-like cushion rests on it.

In addition to the remarkable style of the drawing of these figures, and that of the colouring of the draperies, we may also notice the green shading over the eyes and along the sides of the noses as peculiar, after the Byzantine manner.

Dr. Waagen, who has probably more carefully studied the miniatures of early manuscripts than any other author, observes that these miniatures are very different from the *contemporary*[†] Byzantine and Italian paintings, as well as from those of the monarchy of the Franks of the eighth and ninth centuries ; for in all these the character of ancient art, in which the four Evangelists were originally represented, is very clearly retained in the design and treatment : these paintings, on the contrary, have a very barbarous appearance, but are executed, in their way, with the greatest mechanical skill. Nothing remains of the Byzantine models but the attitudes, the fashion of the dress, and

---

* Mr. J. B. Waring, in some artistic notes on these Gospels supplied to his brother, inserted in his "Palæogmena," speaks of this figure as representing "God himself in the act of dictation to the Apostle, a representation which would never have been tolerated in the Eastern Church. It is most unusual to find God the Father represented under the human form in early Western manuscripts, although we know that in after-ages this violation of the express command of the Deity became common in the pictorial and carved art of Mediæval Europe."

† It is rather with the early Mosaic pictures of Italy than with the later (by a century) miniatures of the Carlovingian school, that our miniatures should be compared.

the form of the seats. Instead of the broad antique execution with the pencil or water-colours, in which the shadows, lights, and middle tints were given, all the outlines here are very delicately traced with the pen, and only the local colours put on; so that the shadows are entirely wanting, with the exception of the sockets of the eyes and along the nose. The faces are quite inanimate, like a piece of caligraphy; the folds of the drapery are marked with a very different local colour from that of the drapery itself. Besides this, there is no meaning except in the principal folds of the garments; in the smaller ones the strokes are quite arbitrary and mechanical. Among the colours, which are often laid on very thick, only the red and blue are, properly speaking, opaque; but all the colours are as brilliant as if the paintings had been finished only yesterday. Gold, on the contrary, is used in very small portions. (" Arts and Artists in England," i. 137.)

Mr. J. B. Waring, who has also carefully studied the remains of early Christian art, says of these figures that they " are of the Roman school, roughly drawn and executed, in comparison with the Byzantine figure illuminations with which we are acquainted; they are also distinguished by greater freedom of action and boldness of treatment, than is to be seen in the stiff and severe models of the Byzantine school; only in the draperies do we recognise its influence, with their peculiar plaits, in minute, unnatural, and regularly-disposed lines. These figure subjects are of especial interest, as they probably exhibit the highest state in which pictorial art, founded on very late and debased Roman models, had attained in England about the middle of the eighth century. We meet, then, in this volume with a conjunction of Eastern and Western art curiously combined, each distinct in character, and both destined in a very short time to give place to the Anglo-Saxon school, in which both were blended, interspersed, and finally merged, forming another distinct style." (" Proleg. Lindis. Gosp.," iv. p. xliii.)

Engravings of these four figures of the Evangelists were published by Strutt in his " Manners and Customs," vol. i., and reduced rude copies of them in Miss Twining's " Symbols of Christian Art," pl. 47.

Another remarkable characteristic of the Lindisfarne Gospels consists in the five entire pages covered with most elaborate and intricate designs, generally arranged so as to form a large cruciform pattern in the middle of the page. These occur—1st on the verso of leaf 1, opposite the commencement of St. Jerome's Epistle to Pope Damasus,—" Novum opus, &c.;" 2nd, on the verso of leaf 25, opposite to the beginning of St. Matthew's Gospel (" Liber generationis"), on the recto of leaf 26; 3rd, on the verso of leaf 93, opposite the beginning of St. Mark's Gospel,—" Initium Evangelii," &c.; 4th, on the verso of leaf 137, opposite the beginning of St. Luke,—" Quoniam quidem;" and 5th, on the verso of leaf 209, opposite the beginning of St. John's Gospel,—" In principio." The five pages containing the commencement of these five portions of the volume, opposite the tessellated pages, were finished with equally elaborate intricacy and beauty of colour-ing, and it seems probable that the object of decorating the blank pages opposite to the commencement of each Gospel, was, that when the volume was placed upright and open on the altar, facing the people (not laid flat nor held up closed), a grand display of colour and design should be visible, naturally inducing an idea of reverence to the sacred text. The placing, at the present day, of an illuminated text of the commencement of St. John's Gospel, on the altar of Roman Catholic churches, seems a relic of such a custom, of which a series of early illustrations occurs in the Baptistery of Ravenna (San Giovanni in fonte; Ciampini, i. tab. 70).

None of these grand tessellated pages have hitherto been published, but one is now copied in my 12th Plate. It is interesting as being the page which furnished the design for the new silver chased and jewelled cover for the front of the volume, made at the expense of the late Bishop of Durham. Another of the pages, in which the design exhibits a still more defined cruciform treatment, is composed of nearly 150 different lacertine animals and birds, most elaborately intertwined, with long tails and top-knots. In this design the creatures composing the cruciform part of the design are coloured green and red, on a chocolate ground; whilst those in the open parts of the design are pale pink and blue, with green and red tails, upon a black ground. The effect of the minute coloured tracery is exceedingly rich and oriental. In making a careful fac-simile of this page for this work, I detected only one or two irregularities in the immense number of interlacements of the design, which, fearing it would be too elaborate for chromo-lithography, I was obliged to omit from my series of plates.

The commencement of the Epistle of St. Jerome, together with that both of the genealogical ("Liber generationis") and historical part ("Xpi autem generatio") of St. Matthew's Gospel, and the commencement of each of the three other Gospels respectively, occupies, as stated above, an entire page, written in large curiously-formed capital letters, the initial letters of each being of gigantic dimensions, and most elegantly ornamented with an endless variety of patterns, in which the interlaced ribbons, spiral lines, and intertwined lacertine birds and beasts, are everywhere introduced,[*] the intervening spaces being profusely ornamented with red dots, arranged in a great variety of patterns. The page commencing the Epistle of St. Jerome, the genealogical portion of St. Matthew (ch. i. ver. 1),—"Liber generationis," and that of the beginning of St. Mark, have not been published. Of the last of these I had also prepared a fac-simile for the present work. The page at the beginning of the historical part of St. Matthew's Gospel (omitting the lower portion), was published by Mr. Shaw, in his "Illuminated Ornaments," whence it has been copied in the first volume of the Surtees publication of the text of these Gospels. The beginning of St. Luke's Gospel is copied by Strutt, as well as by Astle ("Origin of Writing," pl. xiv.), and partially by Humphreys, in his "History of Writing." The latter gentleman has also published a fac-simile of the page at the beginning of St. John's Gospel, in his work on the "Illuminated Manuscripts of the Middle Ages." The initial N of the Epistle of St. Jerome has the first stroke elongated down the left margin of the page, and the middle connecting stroke is composed of two large spiral ornaments. The initial L (iber generationis) is large, and of the rounded or uncial form; the i formed into a long j, crossing the lower part of the L; and the b, also large, and of the rounded form (as in the Paris Gospels published by Silvestre, and other manuscripts); and the initials INI(tium) and INP(rincipio) of the two other Gospels are conjoined together as in most of the early Anglo-Saxon and Irish Gospels, the first stroke being nearly eleven inches long. The other letters in these ornamental pages vary from half to one inch and a half in height; they are greatly diversified in their forms (exhibiting great fancy in the scribe), scarcely any two being alike. An extensive series of them is given by Astle, in his second plate xiv. Besides these large initial pages, the first word of the various Prefaces, Arguments, and Capitula of the different Gospels is also written of a comparatively large size, with the initial letter of a still larger size, ornamented like the great initials;[†] but the text of these Gospels is continued

---

[*] These, together with the Chinese-like Z pattern, and the step-like pattern, constitute the only kind of ornament throughout the volume, with the exception of two or three minute rosettes in one of the tessellated pages.

[†] The M(attheus) conjoined is given by Humphreys

in his "Illuminated Books," the M(arcus) in my "Palæographia," the "Fuit in diebus" by Astle, and the P(lures) by Shaw, in his "Dresses and Decorations," as the initial of the Introduction to the first volume.

throughout in double columns, without any illuminated capitals to the several divisions or verses (unlike the Book of Kells in this respect, except the " Fuit in diebus," St. Luke i. 5 which was generally written of a large size in the early Gospels) : the first letter of each verse being only slightly rather larger than the text, and coloured with patches of red, green, or yellow, in the open spaces.

The tables of the Eusebian Canons, which in these early copies of the Gospels afforded so great a scope for the ingenuity of the artist, in this volume occupy eight leaves (fol. 9—16). They are inscribed within columns, highly ornamented in the same style as the initial letters, supporting rounded arches, and which, from the beauty of their execution, are very deserving of being engraved, although much less elaborate than those in the " Book of Kells," and having no representation of the Evangelical symbols, which are there profusely introduced.

THE BIBLIA GREGORIANA. MS. REG. 1. E. 6 (British Museum).

Plates XIV. XV., and purple Title-page.

IN its present state, this noble manuscript contains only the four Gospels, with the Epistle " Beato Papæ Damaso Hieronimus," Capitula, and Eusebian Canons ; but from the numeration of the quaternions of eight leaves each (lxxx. to lxxxviii.), it is evident that in its original state it contained the whole of the Bible, as the Old Testament occupies seven or eight times the amount of space required for the Gospels. This curious circumstance, overlooked by all other writers, has led me to the conclusion that this MS. is no other than the remains of the so-called BIBLIA GREGORIANA, described by Thomas Elmham, a monk of the abbey of St. Augustine, in the time of Henry V., in a manuscript history of the monastery of St. Augustine and the Church of Christ at Canterbury, to which the MS. itself belonged, as appears from the inscription at the beginning of the volume,—" Liber Sancti Augustini Cantuariensis."

The monastic historian (whose work is contained in the library of Trinity College, Cambridge) thus describes the volume, his description perfectly agreeing with the fragment before us :—" Imprimis habetur in librario, BIBLIA GREGORIANA ; in duobus voluminibus : quorum primum habet rubricam in primo folio de capitulis libri Genesis, secundum volumen incipit prologo beati Jeronimi super Ysaiam prophetam. In principio vero librorum in eisdem voluminibus inseruntur quædam folia, quorum aliqua purpurei, aliqua rosei sunt coloris, quæ contra lucem extensa mirabilem reflexionem ostendunt." The agreement of this latter statement with the volume before us will at once be admitted by all who have noticed the beautiful effect of the purple leaves on being held up to the light. The second title-page of this work is arranged after one of these leaves. Of all the Augustine MSS. (the "primitie librorum totius ecclesie Anglicane," as they are called by the annalist above mentioned), Wanley observes that the "Biblia Gregoriana, duobus voluminibus scripta, agmen ducunt ;" adding that these volumes were in existence no long time previous to his researches; since, in the apologetic petition of the Catholic laity, presented to King James I. in July, 1604, they were expressly described in these words:— "The very original Bible, the self-same numero, which S. Gregory sent in with our Apostle S. Augustine, being as yet preserved by God's special providence."

It may, however, be objected that the numeration of the quaternions indicates a continuous text, forming only a single volume; and that the manuscript itself is an Anglo-Saxon production, and certainly not an Italian one. Against the former objection I may suggest, that although the quaternions are numbered continuously,* the work, when complete, might have been bound in two volumes; the Prophecies of Isaiah (which formed the beginning of the second volume of the "Biblia Gregoriana") being about the middle of the Old and New Testaments united. Against the latter objection I can only reply that the noble size and appearance of the two volumes might easily have induced a monkish writer in the fifteenth century to have erroneously identified these two volumes with the description or tradition of the copy of the Bible, which Bede informs us was sent by Pope Gregory to St. Augustine.

At present, the volume comprises only 77 leaves, measuring 18 inches by 14, the text being written on both sides in double columns, each containing 42 lines, several of the leaves containing the illuminations and their descriptions being stained of a very dark purple colour. Both Casley and Astle concur in referring the text (of which fac-similes are given by those two authors, and also in my "Palæographia") to the seventh century, whilst Sir Frederick Madden refers it "unquestionably to the eighth century."

The first leaf is stained dark purple, on the verso of which is inscribed, in capital letters an inch high, "HAEC EST SPECIOSA QUADRIGA LUCIFLUA AIAE SPS GRATIA PER OS AGNI DI INLUSTRATA IN QUO QUATTUOR PROCERES CONSONA VOCE MAGNALIA DICA(NT.) These form eight lines, written alternately in gold and silver (the second title-page of the present volume being arranged in the same manner, with copies of the letters, so as to afford a complete idea of one of these original purple pages). I have not the least doubt that in the original state of the volume, the above words were intended to apply to an illumination on an opposite purple leaf, containing the symbolical representations of the four Evangelists, no longer in the volume. Various specimens of these fine capital letters are given by Casley, the Benedictines, Astle, and Shaw in his "Alphabets."

The tables of the Eusebian Canons occupy five pages, extending to the verso of fol. 6, commencing on leaf 4 (preceding which, and following the present third leaf, are small portions of two leaves, one of a dark purple colour, which has been apparently cut away close to the binding). The Canons are inscribed within narrow columns a foot high, supporting rounded arches, most elaborately ornamented with knots and scrolls, forming intricate patterns in numerous compartments, and with singular dragon-like monsters, the whole margined with rows of red dots. An excellent fac-simile of portions of one of these pages is given in Mr. Shaw's Book of Alphabets. The seventh leaf commences with St. Matthew i. 19; so that it is evident that several pages have been abstracted, some of which were most probably purple and illuminated, containing the portrait of St. Matthew and the commencement of his Gospel.

The Gospel of St. Matthew ends on fol. 28. Fol. 29 is occupied with the Capitula of St. Mark's Gospel. Fol. 30 is stained of a dark purple colour, on the recto of which is the inscription (evidently referring to a miniature of the Baptism of Christ now no

---

* The famous "Codex Alexandrinus," although bound in four volumes, has the quaternions numbered consecutively.

longer in the volume) " HIC HIS BAPTIZATUS EST AB JOHANNE IN JORDANE COELIS APERTIS SPŪ SCŌ IN SPECIE COLUMBA DESCENDENTE SUP EVM VOCEQ: PATERNA FILIUS ALTI-THRONI VOCITATUS," in large capitals, as above described.

The verso of this purple leaf is occupied with the figure of St. Mark, copied in my Plate 15, in which great care has been taken to represent the very peculiar treatment of the original drawing, the colours of which are opaque, and laid on very thick and glossy, as though mixed with some kind of varnish. The under-garment is of a dull apple-green, and the upper one white, in which latter the only attempt to represent the folds is effected by a number of dark-brown or black lines without any shading: on the under-robe, the lights are formed by a paler yellow body-colour, but still with the folds indicated by dark lines. The feet are naked (indications of the strings of a sandal very slightly appearing on the right foot). Both hands and feet are greatly attenuated and sprawling, the naked flesh being represented by an opaque very pale salmon-colour, relieved by opaque white, laid on in stripes, giving the flesh almost a tattooed appearance. Shading has been attempted by the use of dull-green, laid on the yellow back-ground and by a dark-claret margin to the red seat, which is, however, carried all round the legs and feet. Dashes of opaque white colour on the red seat are probably intended to represent marble.

The quatrefoil, containing the Lion of St. Mark, drawn with considerable spirit, is very unusual if not unique in this manuscript. The hand of God extended from a cloud giving a scroll to the Evangelist, and the black inkpot on the left side of the figure, are striking peculiarities. The drawing is indeed altogether unlike that of any other Anglo-Saxon MS., although the attenuated forms and exaggerated positions of the limbs recall to mind the little figures of the Utrecht Psalter and its Harleian copy. Special notice must also be drawn to the minuteness of the folds of the drapery, and to the unnatural manner in which the under-garment is thrown upwards at the bottom on both sides of the drawing, in the fluttering manner of the later Anglo-Saxon MSS. The frame-work of the picture will be seen to have been left in an unfinished state; and not only are the seven ornamental rosettes treated in a very unusual style, but five of the compartments of the framework are decorated with conventional foliage, of which no other Anglo-Saxon manuscript previous to the 10th century affords an example, but which is repeatedly found in the borders of Carlovingian ivories. These foliated patterns will be seen to be formed entirely by filling in the plain coloured ground with black-work, leaving the foliage unshaded. They were evidently executed by a rude hand, and are totally unlike the delicate and elaborate details of the Eusebian Canons. This singular miniature is drawn on the reverse of the leaf, containing on the other side the large inscription relating to the Baptism of Christ; but the reverse of the two purple leaves containing the two other large inscriptions concerning the Evangelical symbols, and the Visit of the Angel to Zachariah, *remain blank.* I am thence led to infer that the miniature before us is a later addition, possibly of the tenth century, at which time the volume must have been partially despoiled of its portraits of the Evangelists, as the present state of the volume at the commencement of St. Luke's Gospel shows that each Gospel was preceded by four purple leaves. Another leaf, containing the first three verses of St. Mark's Gospel, has also been abstracted.

Two other purple leaves, of which traces remain, have also been cut out close to the binding at the end of St. Mark's Gospel. These doubtless contained the portrait of St. Luke and a representation of the visit of the Angel Gabriel to Zachariah, as the recto of fol. 44 is occupied by another inscription in large capitals :— " HIC GABRIEL ANGELUS ZACHARIÆ SACERDOTI IN TEMPLO DNI APPARUIT ALMUMQ. PRAECURSORE MAGNI REGIS EI NASCI-TURUM PRÆDIXIT."

The recto of the 43rd leaf is copied in my 14th Plate. It contains, within a magnificent arch, the first two words of St. Luke's Gospel, "Quiam quidem," written in fantastical silver and golden letters, the initial Q being of gold, and of a large size, orna-mented with interlaced knots and dragons' heads, marginal with silver spots. The arch itself rests upon two columns, ornamented with three interlaced compartments, the fourth being, however, an elegant foliated arabesque. In the centre of each column is a purple porphyry-like circle, whilst the base also evidently represents marble mosaic-work, in a manner of which I have seen no other instance in these MSS. Above the Ox of St. Luke with outspread wings, and resting on blue, lilac, and orange clouds, is a circle containing a miniature which Casley considered to be that of St. Luke himself, but which appears to me to be intended for God the Father (as it is most probable that a portrait of St. Luke, as well as of each of the other Evangelists, occupied entire pages, as does that of St. Mark). This miniature represents an aged man, with flowing hair and a short beard, holding a book in his covered left hand, whilst his right hand, with two disproportionately long fingers extended, is in the act of giving the benediction. Two ornamental rosettes, formed of solid yellow paint on the green ground, serve to fill up the space below the wings of the Ox in a very unusual manner.

The arch itself is ornamented with four compartments, in two of which scrolls with foliage and green and yellow dogs' heads (in the place of flowers) are introduced, whilst the other two spaces are occupied by curious angulated ribbon-patterns, terminating at one end in dogs' heads, and the other in scrolls. These ribbons, although drawn on triangular red, black, and yellow compartments, are continuous, the ribbon being pointed green on the red, red on the black, and yellow on the red ground; the terminal dog's head and scroll being either alternately yellow or green on red grounds. The verso of this 43rd leaf is blank, and as the following commences with the "Fuit in diebus" (ch. i. ver. 5), it is evident that the page containing the remainder of the first and three following verses has also disappeared. The whole of the purple and illuminated leaves at the beginning of St. John's Gospel have also disappeared.

With four of these purple leaves at the beginning of each Gospel, containing— 1st, a portrait of the Evangelist; 2nd, a historical scene recorded in each Gospel; 3rd, a descriptive page of large-sized capitals; and 4th, the initials of the Gospel;—and, as we are, I think, further warranted in believing, also with similar leaves, "in principio librorum eisdem voluminibus"—(at least in the great books, such as Genesis, Exodus, the Psalms, the Acts, and the Apocalypse),—we can easily conceive that the two volumes of this glorious Bible might well be referred to in the phrases "imprimis in librario,——agmen ducunt."

BOOK OF PRAYERS OF BISHOP ÆTHELWALD.

Plate XXIV.

THE fine quarto MS., measuring 9½ inches by 7 inches, which has supplied these fac-similes, is preserved in the University Library of Cambridge (No. L. I. I. 10), amongst Bishop Moore's MSS., presented to the University by King George I., and is especially interesting from its containing certain verses and entries which enable us to determine that the volume was written for Bishop Æthelwald, with whose name we are already familiar in connection with his share in the ornamentation of the Gospels of Lindisfarne, to the real date of which this volume bears, therefore, most important testimony. For many years it belonged to Cerne Abbey, in Dorsetshire.

The volume is divided into four parts, of which the first is, in respect to its ornamental details, of the most interest; consisting of the chapters containing the account of the Passion of our Lord from each of the four Evangelists, preceded on the recto of folio 1 of the original MS., by an Anglo-Saxon exhortation to prayer, in the original hand of the text of the Passion, and which is about the earliest specimen of the Anglo-Saxon language existing. It has been published with a translation by Mr. Paley, in his notes on the MSS. at Cambridge, in the "Home and Foreign Review," No. ii. p. 482.

Each Evangelist with his symbol occupies the page facing his respective Gospel, drawn in a remarkable manner, quite unlike that of the drawings in the Gospels of Lindisfarne. In my two fac-similes I have copied the pages of St. Matthew and his Angel, and St. John with his Eagle; with, however, the substitution of the bust of St. Luke (to show the pen and inkpot of the Scribe), in lieu of that of St. Matthew, who is drawn like St. John, except that the third and fourth fingers of the right hand are bent down; thus representing the Evangelist as in the act of benediction in the Latin manner. The dress of the four Evangelists is identical (except in colour). St. Matthew in the original wears a blue upper garment over the shoulders, with a brick-red under-robe. St. Mark agrees with St. John, as copied in my plate; whilst St. Luke (introduced in my plate, as above stated, in lieu of St. Matthew) has a purple upper and a blue under-garment. An attempt at shading the folds of the dresses is made by thin black lines forming the edges of narrow dashes of colour, distinct from that of the ground colour of the dress, without any attempt to soften down the lines, just as in the Gospels of Lindisfarne.

The Angel of St. Matthew and the Eagle of St. John are better drawn than in the majority of these early designs. The winged Lion of St. Mark is represented sideways, seated on his hind legs and tail, and holding the book of the Gospels in his fore paws; he is coloured brick-red, with blue mane and feet, and with a blue-and-white-barred tail, whilst the Bull of St. Luke is an unwieldy claret-coloured animal standing sideways, on its hind legs, holding a red book with its fore legs; a large yellow nimbus, edged with red, surrounds its head, and a large pair of wings complete the symbol, which is very similar to the Bull in the Royal MS. I. E. 6, copied in my Plate 14.

Each symbol has a yellow nimbus, and is enclosed within a yellow arch, having in that of St. John rude capitals, like those employed in Saxon Architecture, formed of grotesque heads and foliage; whilst in that of St. Matthew the space on either side above the plain boss-like capital is filled in with the spiral pattern carefully drawn. The capitals on either side of the Bull of St. Luke are quite plain, but those of St. Mark represent a conventional kind of bud arising out of a cup-like capital. The inscriptions of the figure of St. Matthew and his symbol are to be read—"✚ HIC MATHEUS IN HUMANITATE ✚ HIC MATHEUS IN ANGELICA ASSPECTU VIDE- TUR;"—St. Mark, "✚ HIC MARCUS IN HUMANITATE HIC MARCUS IMAGINEM TENET LEONIS;"—St. Luke, "✚ HIC LUCAS IN HUMANI- TATE HIC LUCAS FORMAM ACCEPIT VITULI;"—and St. John, "✚ HIC IOHANNIS [sic] IN HUMANITATE HIC IOHANNIS VERTIT FRONTEM IN AQUILAM." These inscriptions are written in moderate-sized ornamented angulated capitals.

St. Mark holds the sacred volume with his naked left hand, but in the others (except in that of the Scribe) the Evangelists and the Angel have the left hand holding the book covered; the Angel is dressed in the same manner as the Evangelists, with sandals on the feet. The open spaces in these miniatures are filled up with triangular patches of small claret-red dots arranged in triangles.

The text of this part of the volume furnishes us with a variety of writing, each elegant in its kind. The heading of the fac-simile in the left portion of my plate is to be read, "PAS(SIO) DNI NI IHU XPI SECVNDUM MATHEUM. ET factum est cum consummasset Ihs sermones hos omnes dixit discipu(lis)." (St. Matth. xxvi. 1.) The title is written in the angulated capitals used in the miniatures; the beautiful initial "Et" has the outlines formed of gold, with red edging and dots; the cross stroke of the t being formed by the wing of the detached dragon. The large letters completing this line and the interlacing lines of red dots resemble the treatment on several of the great initial pages in the Gospels of Lindisfarne. The fourth line is written in characters resembling those of the same volume, but larger and finer; whilst the fifth line is written in letters quite like those of the Royal MS., 2 A, 20, in the British Museum. (Astle, tab. 18, fig. 1, referred to the eighth century.) The last line of this first page from St. Matthew, and the remainder of the text of this and the three other Gospels, are, however, written in the character of the lower line of the right-hand division of my plate.

The lower division of the right-hand portion of my plate contains the commence- ment of one of the other portions of the volume, consisting of various prayers written by the same hand as the Gospels, the one before us, from fol. 43 r, being a very curious metrical hymn or charm, commencing with an invocation to the Trinity, which, we are informed, was repeated by Loding three times every day:—"Hanc lurica loding cantavit ter in omne die." It commences, "SUFFRAGARE TRINITATI* unitas, unitatis miserere trinitas, suffragare quaesso mihi posito ma(t)ris magni velut in periculo, Ut non secum trahat me mortalitas hujus anni neque mundi vanitas, Et hoc idem peto a subdi- mlibus cælestis militiæ virtutibus)," &c. The peculiar character of the ornamentation of the large initial S, and the manner in which the tails of several of the capitals are drawn out, and terminated in flattened snake-like heads, in this fac-simile and throughout the remainder of the volume, is very unusual; the best example of it occurring in one of the oldest known copies of Bede's "Historia Ecclesiastica," in the Cottonian Library (Tiberius C. 2), which appears to me to have been executed in the same school as the ornaments before us.

---

* It has been suggested that this word is to be read "trinitatis," the final s being supposed to be formed by the green ornament at the upper angle of the frame

This singular Lorica* occupies three pages and a half, and is glossed throughout with Anglo-Saxon, which is considered to have been supplied by two hands, at the end of the tenth and in the eleventh centuries. But the volume possesses a great value from the fact that it belonged to, if it were not expressly written for, Bishop Æthelwald, in the first half of the eighth century.† On the recto of fol. 21 (the verso of which is occupied by the portrait of St. Luke, the Passion from St. Mark ending on the verso of leaf 20) appears the following acrostic dedication to the Bishop:—

A eterna dô donante munera servemesilo zad	1
L isanç laborib' divinis merces in xpo puritu	2
D onam dignam dabit in exlis sedemq' scm scmp beati	3
E i beata præmia ubi scti plaudent coram xpo i æthri	4
L audei atq' dm eminentum sup sidera cæli cum sci	5
V bi uisent fac sine claritet cum beatis et iusti	6
A b angelis conlaudatus pater cu filio filias cu spu sc	7
L atus sit cora iudici vero ubi epulant cu conatu	8
D o inuisibili sui gloria et honor cui numen in alti	9
E n omnipotenti dô libellum hanc ad laudem scribere feci	10
P atrum æternum possidendo via vitæ æternæ saleti	11
I n domum gredi dei cu fiducia huic volumini oraul text	12
S olum dm cantis carminib' indesinenter diligentes pulset	13
C opiosa præla corporetet calor culmino cu agminibus sci	14
O mnis homo operis mercedem mitet tamen mea placula del	15
P ater immensæ maiestatis misericordit relaxa culpi	16
U t cu dno possit miserior orare cu ceraphin atq' seraphi	17
S ine fine modulare sallore scs scs scs dns ds exbaot	18

This acrostic is written in varied-coloured inks, lines 1, 9, 15, 18 being reddish-chocolate; 2, 4, 8, 10, 12, 16 are purple; 3, 6, 11, 14 are greenish-blue; and 5, 7, 13, 17 are minium. The word "zadi" in the first line may probably be intended for that of the scribe; and if so, as Mr. Paley suggests, it resembles the later Byzantine-Greek names Tzetza and Tzetzes. It has also been suggested by Mr. Paley that the handwriting of this acrostic, "though similar to the rest in its general character, seems to be not identical; whence it might be very fairly inferred that the book itself is even still more ancient." On careful inspection, the chief difference appears to consist in the terminal stroke of the m and n, which are never slightly hooked upwards at the bottom in the acrostic, as they are throughout the text; otherwise, the two hands are exactly similar. The capital letters forming the acrostic are also exactly like those of the illuminated pages,

* So called because it was probably worn as a phylactery or amulet, to protect the person like a cuirass (lorica). Its bibliographical history is curious. Davis first published a few of the verses from a Vienna MS. of the fifteenth century (Catal. Codd. Theol. Vindob., i. p. 203); but Mone first published it entire in 1853, in his "Hymni Latini Medii Ævi," i. p. 367, from the Darmstadt MS. 2106, stated to be of the end of the eighth century, without any attempt to explain the many strange words contained in it, of which the following are specimens:—"Deus impenetrabili tutela undique me defende potentia mei gibrae pennas omnes libera tuta pelta protegente singula. Ut non tetri dæmones in latera mea librent ut solent iacula gygram cephalom cum lariis et totas gotham liganam Sonnas atque michinas cladam eruum madurum talios lathma cauglum asque tienus foliomax, &c."

Mone's text was copied by Hagal in his "Thesaurus Hymnologicus," p. 141, in 1855, with a conjectural interpretation of the strange phrases, which he thought were cabalistic medical ones but in a subsequent page (764).

he reprinted the whole from the Vienna MS. VI. c. 28, No. 11857, with another series of conjectural readings by Leo, who fancied the words were Irish. In 1860 Mr. Whitley Stokes again printed the Hymn, with an Irish gloss from an Irish MS. of the latter end of the fourteenth century, in his volume of Irish Glosses, printed by the Irish Archæological and Celtic Society, and has clearly shown that the strange words are of Syriac, Hebrew, and Greek origin, and are employed for the different parts of the body. In the copy which he used it is stated that "Gillas hanc loricam fecit." Lastly, Mr. Cockayne has printed the text and gloss from the Cambridge MS. together with another Anglo-Saxon gloss which he discovered in the Harleian MS. 585, fol. 152-156, in his volume on "Saxon Leechdoms," pref., p. lxvi.

† As stated in the description of the Gospels of Lindisfarne, Æthelwald was the immediate successor of Eadfrith in the see of Durham in 721, which he held till 740.

2 A

and the coloured inks identical; so that I cannot regard the whole otherwise than as contemporary.

Again, in the latter part of the book, consisting of hymns, &c., the sixth, commencing on p. 87 v, is a versicularius or versorius, comprising the commencing verses of all the Psalms, headed in red letters, which are now greatly defaced, but quite legible with a magnifying-glass, — "hoc argumentum forsoru (*i.e.* versorum) oethelwald episcopus decerpsit." This is followed by a very curious "*descensus ad inferos*," and contains a dialogue of our Lord in limbo with Adam and Eve, which Mr. Paley has printed.

The extracts from the Gospels are followed by a beautiful Latin prayer, in a somewhat later Anglo-Saxon hand, published by Mr. Paley, together with other Prayers in the hand of the Gospels, including a poetical Latin version of the Pater noster, commencing —

> "Sublevto genitor residens in vertice cali
> Nominis, oramus, venerablo sanctifoctor,
> In nobis, Pater alte, tui tranquillaque mundo
> Adveniat ——"

Then follows another series of Prayers, forming a morning office, of which one very similar is included in Alcuin's works. To these succeed forty-five short prayers (from fol. 52 to 83), some rhythmical, and mostly unpublished, several of which are stated to have been composed by Alchfrid, an anchorite. In hymn No. 17 (fol. 66 r) is a remarkable rhythmical composition (known from other sources) commencing —

Seu Sator	Nunc in æthra	Quando eclox	Præce posco
Suffragator	Firma petra	Currit velox	Pro ut nosco
Legum lator	A quo creta	Cujes numen	Cacli arce
Largus dator	Cuncta freta	Crevit lumen	Xpc parce
Jure pollens	Quae aplestra	Simul solum	Et gi acls
Es qui potens	Ferunt flustra	Supra polum	Dire iæfx &c

THE CETHAR LEABHAR, OR GARLAND OF HOWTH.

THIS remarkable and very early MS. of the Gospels formerly belonged to Archbishop Ussher, and is now preserved in the library of Trinity College, Dublin, having originally belonged to the church of Inis Meic Nessain, now Ireland's Eye, founded in the seventh century by the sons of Nessan, a descendant of Cethair Mor, king of Ireland. A fac-simile of part of the text is given on the 2nd plate of Irish Biblical MSS., fig. 3, in my "Palæographia sacra." The first three words of the Gospel of St. Matthew, "XPI AUTEM GENE-ratio," and the "Initium evangelii" of St. Mark, are illuminated, of a large size (each occupying an entire page, as in the Gospels of St. Chad and Mac Regol, &c.).

The first of these two pages is arranged in a very unusual manner. The page is divided down the centre by a straight bar, on each side of which, occupying the central part of the design, is an oblong space containing the representation of a human figure. The left-hand figure is bearded, with long flowing hair, holding the arms extended,

with a book in the left hand, and the right hand open.   I presume this represents
St. Matthew himself.   The right-hand figure is beardless, holding a book in the left hand,
and a short sword, resting in its ornamental scabbard, on his shoulder, held in the right
hand.   I presume this to represent the symbol of St. Matthew.   The style of the dress of
both figures is like those of the Gospels of St. Chad and Mac Regol.   Each figure has
the legs bent, as though intended to be represented kneeling, and each is surmounted by a
square containing the upper part of the body, head, and wings of an angel.   The Xp̄i,
of the usual ornamental character, occupies the top left-hand corner, whilst the au-te-m-ge-ne,
in large angulated capitals, occupy, in as many lines as here divided, the right-hand
side of the page, the bottom and left-hand side being filled with dragon patterns.   The
three first letters, " INI(tium Eua," of St. Mark are of a gigantic size (9 inches by 5),
conjoined as usual, with the tops and bottoms formed into large knots of interlaced
ribbons.   The middle stroke is nearly horizontal, so that there is space above for a strange
bust of the Winged Lion, and below for a full-length figure of St. Mark standing, holding
the Book of his Gospel, with both hands against his breast.   The margins of the page
are filled with interlaced ribbon patterns.   The whole is large and coarse in its execution,
and has been much rubbed.

From the style of the writing and the peculiarities of the text, this copy of the
Gospels is considered to be older than any of the other Irish Gospels described in this
work.

THE GOSPELS OF SAINTS LUKE AND JOHN, OF THE
UNIVERSITY LIBRARY, CAMBRIDGE.

THIS fine quarto manuscript, in its present condition, comprises only portions of the
Gospels of Saints Luke and John, the numeration of the quaternions indicating
that those of Saints Matthew and Mark have been abstracted, and that they, with
St. Luke's Gospel, occupied 189 leaves, the 190th and 191st, containing the ornamental
pages at the beginning of St. John's Gospel, having also been cut out, leaving the narrow
strip of the leaves near the binding.   The writing is in the fine large round hand used in
the Gospels of Lindisfarne and of Durham (No. A. II. 17), of which this, in its entire state,
must have been a strong rival.   The writing extends across the page, the space occupied by
the writing being one inch narrower than in the last-named Gospels.   The slip remaining
of the 190th leaf shows that the recto had been ornamented ; there remaining near the
bottom of the page, portion of an ornamental base of a column, ornamented with classical
foliage in a style quite unlike that of any other copy of the Gospels written in this fine
hand.   Moreover, the sharp eyes of Mr. Bradshaw detected in the lower part of the recto
of the 192nd folio the impressed marks of portion of the large ornamental J, terminating in
a dog's head, formed by sketching the letter on the recto of the now lost 191st page with
a hard point.   There are no marginal references to the parallel passages ; the verses are
continuous, and do not commence separate lines, the initial of each being distinguished
by red dots ; and the prefaces are written in a much narrower character ; that of St. John,
commencing with a J about two inches and a half high, terminating in the curious little
flourishes found also in the Durham Gospels, A. II. 17, and also in the Book of Dear.

THE GOSPELS OF THE LIBRARY OF DURHAM CATHEDRAL.

No. A. II. 17.

THIS manuscript in its original condition must have been one of the most splendid copies of the Gospels ever written. It may be referred to the early part of the eighth century. It measures about 13 inches by 10, and is written in a beautiful rounded Hiberno-Saxon minuscule character, intermediate in size between the texts of the Gospels of Kells and Lindisfarne. Unfortunately various portions of each of the Gospels are wanting, including all the grand initial pages, except that of St. John; part of the Gospels of Saints Matthew and Mark being bound up in A. II. 22. The text is written across the whole page, and is not divided into short paragraphs, but into the Eusebian sections, each comprising several of the verses of our printed Bibles, and commencing with an enlarged capital, surrounded with red dots, and with the open spaces coloured with green and yellow patches. These occur indifferently in any portion, and not only at the beginning, of the lines.

The book in its present state commences with St. John's Gospel, the first page being occupied with our first verse, written in large angulated Hiberno-Saxon capitals; amongst which the Greek form of the P (π) occurs. The initials INPR are of very large size and elegantly ornamented, the colours employed being green, lilac, yellow, and red. On the verso of this leaf the text of the Gospel is carried into the beginning of our 14th verse, the words "FVIT HOMO MISUS (*sic*) A DO" being written in the same large angular letters an inch and a quarter high, as the first page; the open spaces of the letters filled in with patches of green and yellow paint, or red dots; the initial F, 4½ inches high, having the top and bottom of the first stroke terminated in elegant interlaced lines, finishing in the monstrous head of an animal and ornamented with the same colours as the other letters, with marginal rows of red dots. These illuminated letters are of bold design and excellent execution. The initial words also of the various Prefaces and Capitula of the different Gospels are illuminated. The name Iohannes is invariably spelt Iohannis; and the tops of the pages of St. Luke's Gospel are inscribed "Secundum Lucanum," a mark of great antiquity, and which also occurs once in the Gospels of Lindisfarne. The passage containing the account of the Baptism of Christ (St. Luke iii. 22, 23) is marked throughout with small musical notes.

On the verso of the 34th leaf is drawn a representation of the Crucifixion in a wonderfully barbarous style. The cross itself is painted red, with a green border; it is dilated at the ends, the upper portion being almost as long as the lower; the upper part of the arms of the Saviour being consequently, as it were, pinioned close to the body, the forearms extending straight outwards from the elbow. The figure is clothed from the neck to the feet, which are fastened with two nails to the lower part of the cross; the dress is formed of a great number of yellow, purple, green, brown (possibly originally red) folds, which are angulated and bent in a very strange manner. On either side of the head of the Saviour is a four-winged Angel, drawn like a great bird, with many-coloured feathers, and with the words "INITIUM ET FINIS" above their head; the Greek letters α and ω being inscribed in red ink, and of a large size, on each side of the head of the Saviour.   Upon the upper part of the cross, above the head of the Saviour, is inscribed, in what were small golden capitals, "HIC EST IHS REX IUDÆORUM."   Longinus, as we learn from the name inscribed over his head, pierces the right side of the Saviour with his spear, whilst his companion, whose name is unfortunately obliterated, applies the sponge on a long reed, to the mouth of the Saviour.   The drawing is surrounded by an inscription in red letters on the Passion of Our Lord, commencing: "Scito quis et qualis est qui talia cuius titulus cui nulla est inventa passus p. nobis pp. hoc culpa," &c.

One of the pages of this part of the volume contains a very rudely long subsequently written passage —" Boge messe preost God preost mantat" (probably for mancat). The same rude hand has repeated the latter inscription on fol. 106, with the addition of the name "Aldred God biscop" and the name Aldred again repeated.   Aldred succeeded Sexhelm as Bishop of Durham in A.D. 946.   The leaves 103 to 111 are portions of a copy of the Gospels of the fifth or sixth century, written in grand Roman uncials above described (p. 8).

THE LATIN GOSPELS OF SS. JOHN AND LUKE AT C. C. C., CAMBRIDGE, No. CXCVII.

A FINE but unfortunately mutilated copy of the Latin Gospels, containing fragments of St. John and St. Luke, written in large Hiberno-Saxon characters similar to those of the Gospels of Mac Regol, is preserved in the Library of Corpus Christi College, Cambridge.   This volume has been traditionally regarded as one of the books sent by Pope Gregory to St. Augustine, as appears from the following inscription written by the celebrated Matthew Parker, Archbishop of Canterbury, on one of the illuminated pages :— " Fragmentum quatuor Evangeliorum. Hic liber olim missus a Gregorio Papa ad Augustinum Archiep': sed nuper sic mutilatus."   The volume is, however, unquestionably a production of the Irish or Hiberno-Saxon school, belonging to the same class as the Gospels of Mac Regol and St. Chad, as may be seen from the fac-simile of four lines published by Astle, tab. xv. fig. 11; as well as from the more extended illustrations occupying four pages, given by the Rev. James Goodwin in his " Evangelia Augustini Gregoriana," in the second volume of the publications of the Cambridge Antiquarian Society, 1847.

The fac-simile given by Astle of the ordinary text of the volume is more carefully executed than Mr. Godwin's; but the latter is more correct in reading the words " de lumine" instead of the "decumino" of Astle's plate, or the " de Lumino" of his text, p. 85.

The text is written entirely across the page, each of the Eusebian sections commencing a fresh line with an enlarged capital, surrounded with red dots and with patches of yellow and green colours.

The initial page of St. John's Gospel is entirely occupied by the first four words, written "I N Principio erat verbum," in large black angulated Hiberno-Saxon letters an inch and a half high, the INP being of a gigantic size, and occupying the greater part of the page, the strokes of the I and P being formed of elongated panels composed of interlaced birds and beasts, whilst the N has the strokes ornamented with interlaced ribbons, the upper and lower ends of the letters forming large patches of ornaments entirely formed of the spiral pattern. A comparative poverty is given to the design by the principal strokes of these three capitals being scarcely more than half an inch wide, the middle stroke of the N being angulated like an upright Z.

Facing the initial page is a representation of the Eagle of St. John, inscribed " Imago aquilae," drawn of a large size, with considerable skill, and by no means wanting in spirit. The figure occupies the centre of a frame with a plain blank border (probably left unfinished), from three of the angles of which, as well as from the middle of each side, extend five large crosses, with the upper ends extending towards the body of the eagle, and evidently introduced with the object of filling up the blank portions of the drawing, just in the same manner as in the miniature of the Lion in the Paris Gospels. According to Casley and Nasmith, the Gospels of St. Matthew and St. Mark, which originally formed part of this volume, were subsequently separated, and formed part of the Cottonian MS., Otho, C. 5 (next described), which was greatly injured in the Cottonian fire.

THE COTTONIAN MS., OTHO, C. 5.

A MONGST the many fine MSS. which were either destroyed or greatly injured by the Cottonian fire in October, 1731, was a volume thus marked, which contained the Gospels of Saints Matthew and Mark, marked in the subsequent Cottonian Catalogue, " Desiderantur," and which is stated by Astle to have then perished. This statement is, however, incorrect, as the volume was only partially burnt and greatly scorched; and sixty leaves having being preserved, they were carefully mounted and rebound about twenty years ago, by the care of Sir F. Madden, the then keeper of the MSS. at the British Museum.

Fortunately a fac-simile of portion of the book had previously to the disaster been made, "at the expense of Edward, Earl of Oxford," which was published by Astle, tab. xv. 1, from which it appears that the text was written in large rounded Hiberno-Saxon characters, very similar to those of the Lichfield and Mac Regol Gospels, and especially to those of C. C. C., Cambridge; whence probably Casley, followed by Nasmith, affirmed that they originally formed part of the latter volume, and that thence they had been "supposed to have belonged to Austin the monk." That they were written by an Irish or Hiberno-Saxon scribe is certain, probably at the end of the seventh or early part of the eighth century, if not even in St. Augustine's days. Astle's fac-simile comprises four lines of the ordinary text and one line, containing the words " Cata Marcum," written in large angulated capitals, resembling those of my purple title-page, but of a yellow colour, with the open spaces of the letters coloured green, all the strokes with marginal rows of red dots. It will be observed that the Greek word "Cata" is used instead of the ordinary Latin "Secundum." The initial C is, moreover, of large size (2 inches high), and is further ornamented with spiral lines and a bird's head.

The action of the fire has, however, had the effect of shrivelling up the parchment of what remains of the volume, so that the writing now appears scarcely more than half the original size, as may be seen in the fac-simile published by Casley (Cat. Roy. MSS. pl. 12, 4, and copied in the Nouv. Tr. de Dipl. pl. 55, viii. 2). Astle's fac-similes of this, as well as his other fac-similes from the finest of our Irish and Hiberno-Saxon MSS. have been copied by M. Silvestre without any acknowledgment; but never having seen the originals, he has printed them in faded brown ink, whereas the ink in these volumes is as black as if written only yesterday. We learn, moreover, from Smith's account of the Cottonian Library, published in 1696, that the volume contained a drawing of the Evangelical symbol of St. Matthew,—"imagine hominis," and of that of St. Mark,— "imago leonis," at the head of each of these two Gospels. Fragments of the latter drawing still remain, showing the Lion to have been drawn in a rampant position, like that of the Paris Gospels, and to have been painted red, covered with yellow tufts of hairs. The following page also contains portion of the illuminated commencement of St. Mark, the INI being conjoined as usual, and ornamented with red and yellow interlaced ribbons and dragons.

THE COTTONIAN GOSPELS, OTHO, B. 9, must have been especially interesting, as it contained not only figures of the four Evangelists, but also numerous Anglo-Saxon memoranda, including one stating that the volume had been given by King Athelstan to St. Cuthbert's shrine, together with a miniature, representing St. Cuthbert seated, his head encircled by a crown, as well as a nimbus, holding in his left hand a book, and giving his blessing with the right. Before him was the King upon his knees, offering the book to the Saint in his right hand, whilst his left held the sceptre, with a Latin inscription, "to Saint Cuthberht, Eathelstan, the very pious King of the English, presents this Gospel;" a prefixed note adding that the miniature had been caused to be painted in honour of St. Cuthbrecht by the blessed Evernenficus. A few fragments only of this volume escaped the ravages of the Cottonian fire; among which is the page at the commencement of St. Mark's Gospel, ornamented (the text also being written) in the same style as the Coronation Oath-book of the Anglo-Saxon kings, illustrated in my "Palæographia," the strokes of the large initial letters terminating in dogs' heads, with foliage springing from the mouth. The volume was, therefore, probably of Germanic origin.

[THE COTTONIAN RULE OF ST. BENEDICT, OTHO, B. 1, which contained a portrait of St. Benedict seated, expounding his Rule to a company of monks, was entirely destroyed in the Cottonian fire.]

THE ST. PETERSBURG GOSPELS (olim ST. GERMAIN DES PRÉS, No. 108)

Plate XXV

THE Benedictines, in their great work, the "Nouveau Traité de Diplomatique," obtained their finest fac-similes of Anglo-Saxon writing from a copy of the Gospels, evidently of Irish origin, at that time contained in the noble monastic library St. Germain des Prés, No. 108 (vol. ii. pp. 214, 215, pl. 18, 1st division; vol. iii. pp. 226, 227, &c., pl. 47, 55).

At the period of the French Revolution, when the library was ransacked and its contents dispersed, the volume of the Gospels in question disappeared. I have, however, had the pleasure of ascertaining that it found its way to Russia, and that it is now lodged in the Imperial Library of St. Petersburg, and, by the kindness of the Baron Osten-Sacken and M. Wladimir Stassoff, I am enabled to publish a fac-simile of the most remarkable page in the volume. The general text of the four Gospels is written in double columns, divided into verses always commencing with a line, the initial letters of each verse being daubed with patches of various colours, and often surrounded with red dots. Each Gospel has the first page filled with the first few words written in gigantic letters; the simplest of the four pages being the commencement of St. John's Gospel, having been copied in fac-simile, but in a reduced size, in the French work above referred to. The following is the description of the MS. and its illuminations given by the Benedictines :—

"Toutes les lettres du frontispiece de S. Jean sont ponctuées à points rouges, excepté les entrelassemens intermédiaires des deux premières alternativement à points rouges et noirs. Nous avons fait blasonner le fond des lettres, conformément aux couleurs du MS. Cette planche a paru un chef-d'œuvre aux connaisseurs. La première partie surtout fait au burin du graveur un honneur bien mérité.

"A la tête de chaque évangile, toujours au folio recto du même MS., les premières pages sont encore plus décorées, sans jamais s'écarter du goût anglo-saxon. Celle que nous avons fait graver est la plus simple et la moins chargée d'ornemens. Les lignes du frontispiece de S. Luc n'ont pas tout-à-fait un poutre, mais elles sont séparées par six bandes de points noirs et rouges, avec de pareils entrelassemens des mêmes couleurs servant de massif à ces bandes. Celles du commencement de S. Marc sont semblables, mais plus étroites. Les lettres s'y distinguent par leur épaisseur et par leur grande variété de couleurs; c'est le seul endroit où le pourpre soit admis. Le frontispiece de Saint Matthieu (copié en my 25th Plate) est le plus singulier de tous. Il n'a que quatre lignes; mais sans parler des premières lettres de la première ligne, les deux dernières ont deux poutes [and a half] de hauteur avec une épaisseur proportionée. Les lettres avec maigres des trois autres lignes sont souvent très-entrelassées les unes dans les autres. Elles s'élèvent à un poute et demi de hauteur. Nous passons sous silence les douze portiques ou colonnades très caseux byzantiques, placés à la tête de ce MS. Les deux premiers sont à cinq colones ou pilastres. Les treillages et les dragons à Anglo-saxons leur tiennent lieu de massif. Le bleue, le noir, le rouge, le pourpre, le jaune, et le bleu sont les seules couleurs qu'on y fasse contraster.

From the above description it will appear that there are no figures of the Evangelists, nor any great tessellated cruciform pages in the volume.

The initial letters in my plate can only be contrasted with those of the Book of Kells in respect to their gigantic size. The remarkable spiral and Z-like patterns are, however, in the Gospels before us, almost absent, and are replaced by a greater number of grotesque animals, one of large size occupying, in a very unusual manner, the open space of the great initial L.

M. Stassoff has communicated to me the following short notice of the MS. and its contents:—

"Il est composé de 213 demi-feuilles (ou bien 426 pages) en état de parfaite conservation, le tout dans une excellente et belle reliure française du XVII° siècle, sur la feuille, première recto se trouve un grand N cerf pour les mots 'Nostra ossa.' À droite en haut on lit 'Prologus quatuor Evangeliorum.' Feuilles 12 à 17 verso 'Canones Evangelici,' où les uns sont composés de colonnes avec ornementation anglo-saxonne extrêmement variée avec figures d'animaux, d'oiseaux, d'enlacements, de travaux divers, etc. de la plus grande beauté.

"Feuille 18 recto - Le commencement de l'évangile de St. Matthieu. (C'est la feuille dont je vous ai envoyé la copie), c'est je crois la plus belle feuille du manuscrit, la plus compliquée et la plus ornée.

"Feuille 78 recto. Le commencement de l'évangile de St. Marc (autre dessin, les couleurs sont le rouge, le vert, et le jaune seulement page entière dessinée.

"Feuille 119 recto. —Commencement de l'évangile de St. Luc. Dessins différents des précédents, couleurs rouge, jaune et bleu page entière dessinée.

"Feuille 177 recto.—Idem St. Jean, lettres petites page entière dessinée. Dans le courant du texte des évangiles mêmes il y a des petites lettres initiales jolies, mais sans beaucoup de valeur. Dans tout le volume il n'y a pas de miniature proprement dite."

The Benedictines give the eighth or ninth century as that of the volume, which is evidently a copy of the Vulgate. If the latter date be allowed, I should certainly not be inclined to fix it later than the middle of the ninth century.

THE GOSPELS OF MAC REGOL.

Plate XVI.

THE Manuscript from whence the accompanying plate has been copied is preserved in the Bodleian Library (D. 24. No. 3946), and is justly regarded as one of the most precious of our national monuments. It is of a large quarto size, measuring 14 inches by 11, and consists of 169 leaves, containing the four Gospels in Latin, written and ornamented in the same general manner as the Gospels of Lindisfarne and St. Chad, of which, although less elaborately ornamented, it is a fitting companion. The text, moreover, is accompanied throughout by an Anglo-Saxon interlineary translation; whence, and from the volume having been presented to the Bodleian Library by "that very painstaking gentleman John Rushworth, barrister of Lincoln's Inn" (as stated by Wanley, who characteristically omitted to add that he was Deputy Clerk of the House of Commons during the Long Parliament), it is often cited as the Codex Rushworthianus, or Rushworth Gloss. It has recently been edited with great care, and collated with the Lindisfarne texts, by the Rev. Joseph Stevenson and Mr. George Waring, and published by the Surtees Society, in four 8vo. volumes, 1854—1867.

The manuscript, as usual in Irish copies of the Gospels not written in the Vulgate version, does not contain the Epistle of St. Jerome, nor the ordinary Canons, marginal References, Prefaces, &c., the Gospel of St. Matthew commencing on the first leaf: hence it is not probable, contrary to the suggestion of Wanley and others, that the early sheets of the volume containing these Canons, &c., have been abstracted.

A full description of this volume, with copies of the great initial Q, and the curious angulated letters forming the first five words of St. Luke's Gospel, together with specimens of the text of the book, have been given in my "Palæographia." Astle also devoted an entire page to its palæographic peculiarities in his "Origin of Writing," pl. 16.

The artistic distinctions of the volume are to be found in the figures of the

Evangelists, each with its ornamental frame occupying an entire page, and in the great initials at the beginning of each Gospel, also occupying the entire page. Of the former only three remain, the miniature of St. Matthew being no longer found in the Book.

On the recto of fol. 51 is a rude pen-and-ink drawing of St. Mark without colours, and on the verso of the leaf, another figure of this Evangelist drawn in the true Hibernian style, with a winged lion hovering over his head, the body coloured like a harlequin's dress. The Evangelist is clothed and bearded in the same manner as St. John, but his hair resembles a flaxen wig, with wavy red stripes. He holds a closed book in both hands. St. Luke is represented on the verso of fol. 84, seated upon a striped cushion, the upper angles of the back of which are surmounted by eagles' heads; his hair is thick, and consists of several rows of yellow, red, and purple lunate curls; his beard is long and forked, each division terminating in a point. On his knees he holds an open volume, inscribed, " lu cas," with his left hand, his right holding a pen, which he is in the act of dipping into the inkstand, which is supported on a long slender footstalk, which fits into a little knob at the side of the chair. A winged purple calf, with the neck and wings covered with red, yellow, green, and purple patches, is represented over the head of the Evangelist. The entire page containing the figure of the fourth Evangelist is copied in my 16th Plate. Here the Saint appears to wear a sort of close-fitting yellow cap, open at the top, showing the short hairs at the top of the head, resembling those of the short beard; or possibly the yellow colour may be intended to represent the hair, and the upper space the tonsure according to the Roman method; or lastly, the yellow colour may represent the tonsure of the British method, and the small upper portion hair. The name of the Evangelist is here spelled Iohannis, as usual in many early Hiberno-Saxon MSS. He holds a long roll in his left hand, on which he is occupied in writing, holding the pen in his right hand. Here, as in St. Luke, the pen is destitute of any web to indicate its being formed of a quill. A many-coloured eagle, with enormous claws, hovers over the head of the Saint, the open space below the head of the bird being filled in with a dog's head awkwardly introduced.

The entire design and drawing of these figures is quite puerile, whilst the borders are in the ordinary complicated Irish style. The latter are, however, much more coarsely drawn than in the Books of Kells or Lindisfarne. In the page before us, a peculiar treatment of the Chinese-like Z-pattern will be seen, forming large diapered spaces, occupying the upper left and the lower right-hand compartments of the frame, and having the ends of the strokes dilated into triangles, coloured either red or yellow; the latter colour forming large lozenge-shaped spaces, sometimes with the four middle triangles coloured red. The two narrow spaces on either side of the Evangelist, filled with fine lines, are also another curious modification of the same Z-like pattern.

The few words at the commencement of each Gospel occupy an entire page, and are written in large angulated letters, except the initial, which is of a gigantic size; the whole being enclosed within framework patterns resembling those surrounding the Evangelists. In the page at the beginning of St. Matthew, the Lib(er) are conjoined, the L and b being of the rounded form, and the j extending between them to the bottom of the page. In the pages at the beginning of St. Mark and St. John the letters INI(tium) and INP(rincipio) are also conjoined, and respectively occupy nearly half the entire page. The commencement of the historical part of St. Matthew's Gospel does not form a separate illuminated page, but the xpi, written xp̄i, is enlarged, and occupies a space about three inches and a half by two. In these pages the execution of the ornamental details is by no means so careful or elaborate as in the Books of Kells or Lindisfarne, especially the spiral line-patterns, which are neither so precisely traced nor are the centres

of the coils so much diversified. In some of the compartments of the ornamental
borders grotesque human figures with their limbs intertwined are introduced, as in the
Book of Kells; and in one of these pages is the bust of a man with a marvellously
elongated beard and pig-tail, playing on a small tube held to his mouth, his thumb
quaintly touching the tip of his nose.

The colours used in this MS. are only red, yellow, purple, and green, which have
a glazed appearance. Some kind of gum must evidently have been mixed with the
colours, which has prevented them from scaling off, notwithstanding their having been
laid on in thick patches.

The last two pages of St. John's Gospel are surrounded by a narrow ornamental
border in compartments, and the last page of the volume (which, although greatly
defaced, I have succeeded, with the assistance of the Rev. H. O. Coxe, in deciphering),
is also illuminated, being divided by ornamental frames into six square compartments,
in which are inscribed the following laudatory verses on the Evangelists, together with
the name and intercessory request of the Scribe, and in which it is remarkable that the
symbols and attributes of Saints Mark and John are interchanged.*

Matheus insti- tuit virtutum tramite moras bene vivendi jus to dedit ordine leges:	Lucas uberius descripsit pro elia xpi iure sa- crato vitulus quia vatum moe nia fatur:-
Marcus amat terras inter cælū q: volare et vehy- mens aquila stric to secat omnia lab su:-	Iohannis fremit ore leo similisq: rudenti intonat intonate terme pandens misteria vite
Macregol dipin †exit hoc euange lium:- Quicum que legerit	Et intellegerit istam narratio nem orat pro macreguil scripto ri

<hr>

* In Schannat's account of the Gospels of St. Boni
face these verses are thus given:—

  Matheus instituit virtutum tramite moras
  Et bene vivendi justo dedit ordine leges:
  Marcus amat terras inter cælumque volantem,
  Joannes aquilam sancto regit omnia lapsu,
  Lucas uberius descripsit proelia Christi.

And again (altering the third and following lines):—

  Marcus amat terras inter cælumque volans:
  Et vehemens aquila stricto secat omnia lapsu,
  Jure secat vitulus qui halitus mœnia patris
  Lucas uberius describit proelia Christi.

In the Gospels of Beneventum (British Mus. MS. Add.
No. 5463. fol. 76 v.) the verses are condensed thus:—

Primus Matheus nam hominum generaliter implet.
Marcus Leonis vocem rugiens intonans mihi.
Jure Lucas tenet sacerdoti simul, more juvenci,
Johannes instar aquilae volans in principio intonans
  verbo[m].

† I believe the c at the beginning of this line is
only the ornamental curl of the thin stroke of the s.
Mr. George Waring has printed these lines at the end
of the fourth volume of the Surtees publication, with
several variations, which on examination I find to have
arisen from his mistaking some of the letters on the
other side of the leaf, and which are partially visible in
consequence of its semi-transparency, as belonging to the
text of these verses. The very defaced state of the
writing is an abundant excuse for such mis-reading.

Of the origin and date of this volume, it is to be observed that Astle, overlooking the Irish name of the scribe, asserts this MS. to have been written in England in the latter end of the seventh, and the interlineary gloss in the tenth century;
and Wanley states that it was the property of the Venerable Bede, "which may be the
case, as it seems older than the Cotton MS." (Nero, D IV.). Dr. O'Conor, however,
succeeded in detecting in the Irish Annals of the year 820, the decease of a scribe of
this name:—" Mac Riagoil nepos Magleni, *Scriba* et Episcopus Abbas Birur (hodie
Birr in Comitatu Regio in Hibernia), periit." (Script. Rer. Hibern., i. ccxxxi.)

The volume may, on this authority, be therefore assumed to have been written
towards the end of the eighth, or early part of the ninth century.

THE GOSPELS OF ST. CHAD.

Plate XXIII.

THE Capitular Library of Lichfield possesses a copy of the Latin Gospels very
similar in size and general character to those of Mac Regol, but which presents
several peculiar features of its own, of which the chief consists in a number of entries
written in the margins of the leaves in Latin and Anglo-Saxon, as well as others in the
ancient British language untinctured by the latter tongue, which have been considered
by Lhuyd and other Welsh scholars to be more ancient by several centuries than any
other relic of the British (or Welsh) language now in existence. Fac-similes of many of
these are given by the Welsh MSS. Society, in the "Liber Landavensis," and in my
"Palæographia." The account given of this volume by the Benedictines (Nouv. Tr. de
Diplom., iii. p. 86) is entirely erroneous. The text throughout is written in very fine
Anglo-Saxon characters, the lines running across the page; unfortunately the greater portion
of St. Luke, and the whole of St. John's Gospel, are wanting. Like the Gospels of
Mac Regol, the volume commences with that of St. Matthew, the great illuminated
initials of which occupy an entire page, the L and b of the word "Liber generationis
jhu xpi filii David," being of very large size, and of the rounded form, and the i
formed into a j, seven inches long, similar to the same letters given by M. Silvestre
from the Paris Gospels. The other letters of these words are an inch high, and of the
curious angulated form usual in these large volumes.

The commencement of the historical part of this Gospel, "Xpi autem generatio"
is similarly illuminated, precisely as in the Gospels of Lindisfarne, of which Mr. Shaw
has published a fac-simile. The beginning of each of the Gospels of SS. Mark and
Luke are illuminated in the same manner as the two pages above described, the
"INI"(tium) of the former being conjoined into a gigantic figure, the first stroke
extending the whole length of the page; as is also the case with the q of the first
word, "quoniam," of St. Luke in the latter page. The body of the letter is, however,
of the oblong quadrangular form, the tail being elongated and angulated in the middle.
The right-hand margin of the page is occupied by a framework composed of interlaced
birds, and terminates at the top in animals' heads.

The Gospels of SS. Mark and Luke are also preceded by full-length figures of the Evangelists, that of St. Mark being copied in my 23rd Plate, the drawing of which will be seen to be of the rudest character, and in the same peculiar style as those in the Gospels of Mac Regol. The Evangelist is represented as holding a book with both naked hands upon his breast, and as clad in garments of many folds and colours, without the slightest attempt at shading, with the under-garment embroidered at the wrist. The hair is short, divided in the middle, with four short curls on each side, and the beard is represented as short and stiff. The head is surrounded by a plain yellow nimbus with a white border, over which is extended the symbolical Lion, rudely delineated without wings, holding a book in the fore paws. The chair, or seat, in front of which the figure is standing (for there appears to be no attempt to indicate the action of sitting on the purple cushion, of which the ends are seen on each side of the figure), is of a singular form, the sides being composed of strange giraffe-looking animals, with long interlaced tails, terminated by curious ornamental knots, and with the upper parts on each side not unlike the chair on which the Virgin is seated in the Book of Kells. At the left side of the seat is fixed the inkpot supported on a long slender stem.

The portrait of St. Luke, of which fac-similes are given in Hickes's "Thesaurus" and in my "Palæographia," occupies the verso of folio 109, and represents the Saint standing within a kind of rostrum, the narrow sides of which terminate above in dogs' heads. The hair of the Saint is long and flowing, the curls interlaced, and alternately red and whitish; the beard is short and stiff; the head is surrounded by a purple nimbus decorated with three crosses formed of red dots. In either hand he holds a sceptre, extending over the shoulder, similar to those held by the Angels in the miniature of the Virgin and Child in the Book of Kells. One of these is terminated by a cross bearing a red eight-leaved rosette in the centre, whilst the other is terminated by two elongated interlaced and foliated branches, the precise nature of which is doubtful; but the figure upon the jewel of King Alfred in the Ashmolean Museum at Oxford bears two somewhat similar ornaments. Over the head of the Saint is a rudely-drawn winged calf. The feet of both the Evangelists are represented as naked.

The 110th leaf of the volume (facing the portrait of St. Luke) is occupied with the drawings of the Evangelical symbols represented in my 23rd Plate. I have no doubt this leaf was originally at the beginning of the book, in accordance with the usual practice. I need only to allude to the extraordinary rudeness of these drawings, and to the curious effect produced by the circles of red and black dots with which all the figures are decorated. The contrast between the execution of these drawings and the design upon the reverse of the same leaf is most striking; the latter page being occupied by one of the elaborate cruciform designs facing the commencement of the Gospels, found only in the most splendid of these volumes.

This design, in minuteness and intricacy of detail, and at the same time in richness of colouring, is equal to the most elaborate of those in the Gospels of Lindisfarne, to one of which, above described, containing nearly 150 different lacertine animals and birds singularly interlaced together, it bears a striking resemblance, the cruciform pattern being formed by a series of square spaces enclosed by claret-purple bars connected together. I regret that I have not been able to publish this page, of which I had prepared a drawing for this work. Similar designs, in the original condition of the volume, doubtless occurred opposite to each of the grand ornamented pages at the beginning of the different Gospels.

There is an ancient tradition* that this volume was written by St. Gildas; and in

---

* Harwood, "History of Lichfield," p. 107, and O'Conor, "Scrip. Vet. Hibern.," i. p. cxcvii.

the opinion of Lhuyd the MS. was in his days 1100 years old, and some of the entries in the margins of the book are at least 1000 years old. It certainly possesses all the characteristics of the ancient Irish school, which we know was identical with that of the Early British Church, especially in Wales. This will account for the connection of the volume with Llandaff and St. Teilo, as recorded in the marginal entries, whilst other entries record events which occurred at Lichfield, of which St. Chad, or Ceadda, was the first bishop, in the seventh century; whence the name "TEXTUS SANCTI CEADDÆ," under which the volume has been known. St. Chad, although a Northumbrian, was educated in Ireland, in the school of St. Finan, as stated by Bede (i. 403). It is not impossible that the volume may have been in the handwriting of the Saint himself; and hence its popular designation.

Further accounts of the volume may be consulted in the "Thesaurus" of Hickes, the "Bibliotheca Stowensis," and "Rerum Hiberniearum Scriptores" of O'Conor.

THE LATIN GOSPELS OF THE IMPERIAL LIBRARY, PARIS.

Plate XXI.

THE date of the fine Latin Gospels, No. 693 in the Paris Library, from which I have copied the accompanying figures in Plate 21, has been the subject of some controversy; Messrs. Silvestre and Champollion having assigned it to the tenth century, whilst "attempts have been made to refer it to the eighth century, and even to a period still nearer to the days of St. Jerome, it having been even asserted that the MS. was copied from the *original* Latin text of St. Jerome."

The similarity in several respects of its artistic details with the Gospels of St. Columba and the Gospels of Corpus Christi College, Cambridge, and the fact that it contains the version of St. Jerome, instead of the mixed Italic version usually found in Irish MSS., induce me to refer it to the eighth century, or first half of the ninth century. The text is written throughout in letters of large size in double columns. The few words at the commencement of each Gospel, ordinarily occupying an entire page, here only fill the upper half of the first column of the first page in each; but the ornamentation of these initials is exceedingly delicate and intricate—indeed, the spiral pattern is more elaborate and modified in a more remarkable manner than in any other MS. with which I am acquainted. The first page of the text has been copied in fac-simile by M. Silvestre, with the utmost care, the initial L. of the rounded form being four inches high; the b is also rounded, whilst the i, formed like a j, is elongated between these two letters; the remainder of the two words LIBER GENERATIONIS being formed chiefly of angulated letters about an inch high.

The "XPI (autem generatio sic erat") of the commencement of the historical part of St. Matthew's Gospel are formed exactly as in the Gospels of Lindisfarne (although greatly reduced in size). An excellent fac-simile of this heading is given by Lacroix and

Seré in their fine work on the Arts of the Middle Ages. M. Matthieu, also, in his beautiful little Book of Prayers has given a page excellently adapted from the initials of this MS. The "INItium Evangelii" of St. Mark, the "QUOniam quidem multi" of St. Luke, and the "INPrincipio erat verbum" of St. John, are equally elaborate, agreeing in size with the two headings in St. Matthew.

The manuscript is, however, more remarkable for the four pictures of the Evangelical symbols, each placed at the head of the respective Gospel to which it belongs. Of these, those of St. Matthew and St. Mark are represented in my 21st Plate, whilst the four of a reduced size are given in Lacroix and Seré's work above referred to. The quaint figure of St. Matthew's symbol, inscribed IMAGO HOMINIS, holding the open book of his Gospel,—inscribed "liber generationis jhu xpi," with both hands naked against his breast, will provoke a smile, his garments being represented in a most singular manner; the yellow hair, strangely indicated by rows of small black dots, and the crown of the head plainly exhibit the Roman tonsure. The feet are naked, the yellow portion of the middle garment ornamented with a very unusual scroll-like line, being repetitions of the letter S, which also appears in a simpler form in the border of the dress above the feet. The star in the centre of the figure, above the swollen knees, is quite unique in these figures of the Evangelists, and the red bars on either side of the figure are intended for a seat, on which the figure may be supposed to be sitting.

The "Imago Leonis" is of a gigantic size, represented in a rampant form, and with the mane extending in tufts all over the body; it is, nevertheless, better drawn than in the other MSS. of this early date. The lines in this figure are drawn with the greatest precision and delicacy. The framework has evidently been left incomplete.

The Eagle is also of a gigantic size, but very tamely drawn; and the Calf is almost a fac-simile of that represented in my 5th Plate.

No particulars have been recorded by Silvestre and Champollion of the origin of this volume (which does not appear to have been known to the Benedictine authors of the "Nouveau Traité"). It is to this manuscript that the Count Bastard thus alludes, in his elaborate memoir in the "Bull. Com. de la Langue, Hist. et des Arts de la France," iv. (1857), p. 728 :—

"Toutefois je rapporterai simplement que, dans les beaux Evangiles de Saint Willibrord, en caractères anglo-saxons, et venus d'Epternach, la figure de l'homme, ou compagnon de Saint Luc [Matthew], à l'apparence générale d'une pagode hindoue ; le lion de Saint Marc rappelle les lions de Persépolis ; le veau de Saint Luc fait songer au bœuf apis ; et l'aigle de Saint Jean est semblable à la colombe des pyramides. L'île sacrée, qui fait le berceau de l'île des saints, la Samothrace des mers de l'Ouest, avait-elle religieusement conservé des types anciennes, qu'elle fit servir ensuite au christianisme ? C'est ce que je ne rechercherai pas davantage. Je me borne à énoncer le fait : de nouveaux Vallancey en tireront leurs conclusions."

Dr. Waagen also states ("Kunstwerke und Kunstler in England," 2nd edit.) that this volume is positively attested to have belonged to St. Willibrord (who died in 739), and that it is Irish work, and the oldest specimen of the style in existence.

THE GOSPELS (FORMERLY) OF ST. GATIEN, TOURS.

THE monastic library of St. Gatien at Tours possessed, previous to the French Revolution, a MS. of the Gospels, written in Hiberno-Saxon characters, of which fac-similes were given by the Benedictines in the "Nouv. Tr. de Diplomatique," vol. iii. pp. 86, 383, 384; pl. 37, IV. n. and pl. 55, VI. v. This volume, however, was traditionally regarded as being in the handwriting of St. Hilary of Poictiers (who is recorded to have written a copy of the Gospels), but who died in A.D. 388; but the real scribe has inscribed his name at the end of the volume, at the beginning of a singular note, in which Greek words are barbarized, as in the Prayer Book of Bishop Æthelwold (being probably spelt as pronounced), and written in Latin characters.

"Ego Holcundus mihi Trinitas misereatur amen. Precor vos omnes Xpiani ut pro me commemem Deum deprecimini peccatore ut ne demergat in pyri flago Inraito sed fiam cum binis exercitibus in bapho ubi habitant thesaurdes et coemeterodes his vates et cornui thauera senes et XX. ter et sex his discipuli ut vobiscum omnium Christum salvatorem exorent diem extlemon eparagon ce poescon ceaton in hoc enim tota agiograpa pastricater Emanubel. Amen."

Mention is also made of the discovery of the relics of St. Innocent, one of the martyrs of the Theban legion, who assisted at the council of Chalons-sur-Saone in A.D. 650, which will bring the text to a period not earlier than the middle of the seventh century.

The fac-simile of the commencement of the Gospel of St. Matthew shows a large ill-formed rounded L, three and a half inches high, both ends terminating in a large ornament formed of interlaced lines, with the intervening spaces filled with various colours, the whole surrounded with double rows of red dots; the remainder of the words "Liber generationis" being written in rudely-formed capitals, about an inch high, the open spaces and intervals between the letters being also filled with patches of different colours.

The verso of the leaf preceding the commencement of each of the Gospels is filled with a design formed of interlaced lines, arranged in a most "bizarre" manner, and painted in red, yellow, and green colours, and terminating in the heads and beaks of birds, serpents, dogs, &c.; thus forming a series of tessellated pages such as occur in the Gospels of Lindisfarne and St. Chad, but doubtless far more rude in design, judging from the fac-simile given of the beginning of St. Matthew by the Benedictines.

Anxious to see this curious volume and to obtain fac-similes of some of these drawings, I went from Paris to Tours, but found, to my annoyance, that neither this volume nor any of the other curious early books used by the Benedictines, were to be found in the public library, to which the remains of the monastic library had been carried, nor could I there or elsewhere obtain any clue to their destination.

LORD ASHBURNHAM'S GOSPELS.

IN a series of facsimiles of illuminated MSS., privately printed and distributed by Lord Ashburnham (the present possessor of the late Duke of Buckingham's collection formerly at Stow, and the purchaser of M. Libri's first collection of MSS. sold by private contract), and of which a set was presented by his Lordship to the Bodleian Library, occurs a page containing a facsimile of the beginning of St. Mark's Gospel, " INITIUM EUANGELII DNI NOSTRI IHU XPI FILII DI," written in large angulated Hiberno-Saxon capitals an inch and a quarter high, forming three lines, with the open spaces and intervals between the letters coloured red, yellow, and green, the upper and lower margins, as well as the right side and the two spaces between the lines, filled with broad borders composed of rude interlaced ribbon patterns, and monstrous birds similarly coloured ; the great initials IN being about eight inches high, terminating above and below in large very rudely-executed designs, formed of interlaced lines, with red and yellow patches in the intervening spaces, the whole surrounded with double rows of red dots. No such volume is described by O'Conor in his account of the Stow MSS.

It appears, however, from the privately printed Catalogues of the MSS. at Ashburnham Place (of which also copies exist in the Bodleian Library), that a volume answering to the above description was amongst the MSS. purchased by private contract from M. Libri, being his No. 14 : "Corpus Evangeliorum, VI ou VII cent. En tête de chacun des quatre évangiles se trouve une grande page peinte en arabesque ornée des figures d'animaux, &c., et des caractères d'une forme bizarre. Voyez le fac-simile No. 14." [*] This description thus corresponds most closely with the lost Tours volume, as described by the Benedictines.

It is true that the beginning of St. Matthew's Gospel, "Liber generationis," in the Tours book, is represented as only occupying a single line ; but I infer that, as in the Gospel of Mael Brith Mac Durnan, the beginning of the historical part of that Gospel, " Xpi autem generatio" (ch. i. ver. 18), was regarded as its real commencement, and occupied an entire page, whilst the preceding genealogical part was treated simply as a prologue.

THE HEREFORD GOSPELS.

THE Cathedral Library of Hereford possesses a copy of the Antehieronymian Latin Gospels of the eighth or first half of the ninth century, measuring 9 inches by 7, written in an excellent rounded Hiberno-Saxon hand, evidently by an Irish scribe, who has added the usual "finit. Amen. Do gratias ago," slightly varied, at the end of each

---

* This description is, I presume, a reproduction of M. Libri's descriptive list, and the last reference may be to a fac-simile given by Libri, but which is not contained in the catalogues themselves.

Gospel. The text has a large proportion of readings in common with the Gospels of the University Library of Cambridge, St. Chad's, Mac Regol's, &c.; but is remarkable for the omission of the addition in Matthew xxvii. 49. Characteristic readings occur in Matthew viii. 24; x. 29; xiv. 35; Mark xiii. 18; Luke xxiii. 2; xxiv. 1; John xix. 30; xxi. 6. It is full of the orthographical errors peculiar to the Irish school; e. g., adoliscens, missertus, abeo, peribeo, rappi, sappatum, &c.

The initial words of the Gospel of St. Matthew, "Liber generationis ihu;" Mark, "Initium euangelii;" and John, "In principio," severally occupy entire pages, and are illuminated in a remarkable manner. The "Xpi autem generatio" of St. Matthew i. 18, and the "Quoniam quidem" of St. Luke, are wanting. The great L and b of the Liber are of the rounded form, the i formed into a long j, crossing the lower part of the former letter; the upper part of the L terminates in a bold modification of the spiral pattern, and the open part of the b is filled in with a knotted ribbon of very unusual design. The INI of the "Initium" and the INP of the "INPrincipio" are united together in the usual Hiberno-Saxon manner, the middle bar of the N being modified so as to form an elegant cross-pattern, having in St. Mark four ornamental lozenges at the ends of the arms of the cross, the upper one surmounted by a large plain yellow cross, and another lozenge in the centre. In St. John these five lozenges are replaced by the same number of elegantly-designed circles. In the former the tops and bottoms of the main strokes terminate in bold spiral designs, whilst in the latter they are terminated by the heads and feet of monstrous animals. The main strokes of the letters are filled in with compartments, in which the Z-pattern and interlaced ribbons are introduced. Although the general designs of these pages are very striking and unusual, the details want the delicacy which distinguishes the finer works of this class. The second word of each Gospel is written in very large and ornamental minuscule letters, having the open spaces covered with patches of red, yellow, and purple, which are the only colours used in the volume, and which are in several of the drawings very greatly faded and discoloured.

I have to thank the Rev. F. T. Havergal, the Librarian of the Cathedral Library, for an opportunity of examining and copying the drawings of this very interesting volume.

THE MANUSCRIPTS OF ST. GALL.

Plates XXVI. XXVII. and XXVIII.

THE monastic Library of St. Gall, celebrated throughout the Middle Ages, is still a noble storehouse of the religious literature of the period subsequent to its foundation in the earliest years of the seventh century; including also various important manuscripts even of a still earlier date.

St. Gall, after whom not only the monastery but also the town and canton in which it is situated were named, was born at Bangor, in Ireland, in the middle of the sixth century. He accompanied St. Columbanus, the founder of Luxeuil and Bobbio, into France, in A.D. 585, and at length, in 614, took up his residence in a desert place called Himilinberg, near Lake Constance, which was formally granted to him by King Sigebert, together with the necessary funds for building a cell. Soon afterwards an oratory, with dwellings for twelve brethren, was added by him; and this was the origin of the monastery which in after-ages became one of the most celebrated in Europe, not only for the number of learned men which it produced, but also for the valuable library which it possessed, and for its extensive and powerful dominions. It was suppressed in 1808; but the library and other buildings still exist, where I had recently the pleasure of making a long visit, and carefully examining many of the MSS., which were either carried thither by the founder, or written by his companions or their immediate successors. St. Gall himself died in the middle of the seventh century, at a very advanced age.

Two important documents still exist in the library, dating back to the first half of the ninth century, which throw very considerable light on the history of the monastic buildings and library. The first of these is a large plan of the whole of the monastery, in which every building and outhouse, and even the different trees in the gardens, are precisely drawn, and described in short Latin sentences. This plan is addressed to the Abbot Gozpertus, who began the new Basilica in the year 829, and was succeeded in 841 by the Abbot Grimaldus. The inscription is addressed by the designer, "tibi, dulcissime fili, Gozperte;" from which Mabillon (Ann., ii. p. 571) infers that the person who could thus address the abbot as his son must have been of high dignity, and he supposes that he was no other than the Abbot Eginhardus, who held the office of Prefect of the royal buildings under Charlemagne, and was well skilled in architecture, and who married Imma, the daughter of Charlemagne; but who after his royal master's decease became a monk, and afterwards Abbot of Selgenstadt, where he died in 839. The Emperor himself was so fond of the Monastery of St. Gall, and so familiar with the monks, that the latter "cum non aliter nominarent nisi 'noster karolus.'"—(Ekkehardus, Vit. B. Notker., c. 29. G. p. 277.*)

Although the monastery, as completed by Grimaldus and Hartmotus, varied in several particulars from the plan itself, we learn from it that the library occupied the north-east angle of the great church, adjoining the east end of the north side of the transept, corresponding with the sacristy at the south-east angle. It is inscribed in the plan, "Infra sedes scribentiu; supra bibliotheca;" showing it to have had an upper story for the books, whilst the lower exhibits six windows and seven writing-desks, adjoining the north and east walls.

At the present time the library, far increased in extent, occupies a noble room on the upper story, extending along the whole of the west side of the cloisters on the south side of the church, the scriptorium, where I worked, now occupying an adjoining room on the same story, on the south side of the cloister.

The other document above referred to is an inventory of the "Libri scottice ꝑ scripti," written by Notkerus, a monk of St. Gall, also in the first half of the ninth century, published by Weidmann (Gesch. d. Biblioth. v. St. Gallen, 1841). Gerbertus (Iter Aleman., p. 97), and Keller, in his "Bilder und Schriftzüge in den irischen Manuscripten

---

* This plan was first published by Mabillon, and more recently, as well as far more correctly, by Dr. Ferdinand Keller (Bauriss der Klosters S. Gallen vor Jahr 820. 4to. Zurich, 1844, text and fac-simile of the plan), to whom I am much indebted for matters connected with the ancient

Irish relics still remaining in Switzerland; and subsequently by Willis, in the "Archæological Journal," June, 1848, with a coloured copy of the plan.

† I need hardly observe that in the Middle Ages Ireland was generally termed Scotia.

2 K

der schweizerischen Bibliotheken gesammelt," &c. 4to., with 13 plates from the Transactions of the Antiquarian Society of Zurich.[*]

Many of these books[†] have disappeared from the library, although it is possible that portions of them may exist in the several most interesting volumes of fragments preserved in the library, which form a complete storehouse of palæography.

According to Haenel, there are among these manuscripts not fewer than sixteen volumes of the Venerable Bede's works, one of which, inscribed "*Bedæ famuli Christi de Orthographia*," is believed to have been written by the venerable author himself. (Gerbertus, Iter Aleman., p. 85.) So great was the estimation in which these Irish MSS. were held, that it is recorded by Notker, in the above-mentioned catalogue, that one of them was presented to, and accepted by, Charlemagne, with many thanks ("Carolum M. unum scotice scriptum pro dono gratanter accepisse."—Gerbertus, *ut supra*, p. 97.)

A long account of the present condition of the library and its Anglo-Saxon and Irish manuscripts is given in the Appendix A to Mr. Purton Cooper's "Report on Fœdera," pp. 78—96. Together with the materials for this report, Mr. Cooper obtained a series of thirty-three drawings and fac-similes, which were printed on the same number of quarto coloured plates. These unfortunately have never been published; but on representing to the late Master of the Rolls, Sir John Romilly, and Sir Francis Palgrave, that I was engaged on the present work, they kindly placed a set of the plates in my hands, which I carried with me to St. Gall, in order to compare them with the originals; and I regret to say that, although giving a good general idea of the several subjects, they are by no means satisfactory in their details, the whole being far too rudely executed. Of these, twelve of the illuminated plates are taken from the Codex No. 51—namely, four Evangelists, the ordinary five initial pages, one tessellated page, and two miniatures of the Crucifixion, and the Saviour seated in Glory; two others of St. John, and the title-page of his Gospel from the MS. No. 60;—and three—namely, a portrait of St. Matthew, a cruciform ornamental page, and a page, being the commencement of a Pœnitentiale contained in the volume of Fragments, No. 1395.

A much more careful series of figures and fac-similes from these MSS. is given in thirteen quarto plates by Dr. Ferdinand Keller, in the work above referred to, published in the Zurich Society's Transactions, accompanied by a very careful memoir on Irish art, more especially as exhibited in these MSS., which are described in detail, as well as the other Irish MSS. existing in the other libraries of Switzerland.

[*] The following are the books "Scotice scripti." Metrum Juvenci, in vol. i.; Epistolæ Pauli in vol. i. (a fragment of this is preserved in the vol., No. 1395). Actus Apostolorum in vol. i.; Epistolæ Canonicæ VII., in vol. i.; Tractatus Bedæ in Proverbia Salomonis, in vol. i.; Ezechiel Prophetæ in vol. i.; item Juvenci Metrum in vol. i.; Apocalypsis in vol. i.; item Apocalypsis, in vol. i.; Metrum Sedulii, in vol. i.; De Gradibus Ecclesiasticis, in vol. i.; Arithmetica Boetii, in vol. i.; Missalis, in vol. i. (an Anglo-Saxon Liturgical fragment of this is preserved in No. 1395). Vita Sti Hilarii, in codicillo; Paulus S. Martyrum Marcellini et Petri; Metrum Virgilii, in vol. i.; Ouidii; in alteris; Quaternio I. de Inventione Corporis Sci Stephani; Quaternio I. de Relatione Translationis Sci Galli in novam ecclesiam A.D. 835; Bedæ de Arte Metrica in quaternionibus; Institutio Ecclesiastici Ordinis, in codicillo I.; Liber I. Genesis in quaternionibus; Actus Apostolorum et Apocalypsis, in vol. i. (?). Quaternio I. in Natali Innocentum legendus; Orationes et Sententiæ Variæ in vol. i.; Orationes in quaternionibus; Expositio in Codice Cœlestium, in quaternionibus; item Regina quaternio I.;

item Evangelia II. secundum Johannem, Scotice scripta. Prosperi Epigrammata, in voluminibus duobus, unum fuit Scoticum peculium.

[†] Von Arx, the late librarian of St. Gall, thus alludes to these books:—"Partim Hybernis allati, partim in S. Gallo exarati fuere ii codices Scotici, quorum bibliotheca S. Galli circulo nono viginti numerabat, et adhuc aliquos, v.g. quatuor evangelia, illud S. Joannis, Prisciani grammaticam, et plura fragmenta, cuncta sæculo octavo charactere Scotico (Anglo-Saxonico) scripta possidet." (Annot. Ekkehardi IV. casus S. Galli, in Pertz Mon. Germ. Hist., ii. p. 78.) "Attamen aderant Romano charactere sæculis 5. 6. 7 exarati (idetil, et tum ex residuis fragmentis, v.g. Virgilii, evangelii &c. tum ex meta, antiquum, antiquissimum, vetus, vetus valde, legi non potest, multis codicibus in catalogo bibliothecæ sæculi 9. adjecta, manifestum fit. Sæculo quoque S. Galli avorum libris scribendis jam insudasse, testantur multi ex hoc ævo superstites codices, præcipue epistolæ S. Pauli n. 70, et liber prophetarum n. 44, ac ea quæ Ratpertus de scriptore Waltone habet." (Von Arx, Annot. Ratperti, *ut infra*, ii. p. 66.)

The most important of the Irish manuscripts of St. Gall, in respect to its illuminations, is a quarto volume of the Latin Gospels, No. 51, which, as above stated, contains the four figures of the Evangelists, five large initial pages, the initials of each Gospel occupying the entire page, a highly ornamented cruciform page, and two miniatures.

The Evangelists are very rudely drawn, entirely in the style of those in the Book of St. Chad. They appear to have been executed by two different hands. Saints Matthew and Luke (the former holding a book on his breast, the fingers of the crossed hands being singularly interlaced, having the Angel, and the latter the winged Calf hovering over their heads) are represented as standing in front of chairs, formed of straight bars, ornamented only with rows of dots. Each holds a large book with the two naked hands against the left side of his breast; each also has a large uncoloured circular nimbus, ornamented with concentric rows of red dots. St. Matthew appears to have a yellow cap on his head, elevated to a point, and ornamented with what look like fishes' scales. St. Luke, on the contrary, has yellow hair, arranged in slight curls. The border in these two miniatures is about an inch broad, the sides in both being composed of interlaced dragons, and the top and bottom broken, in both, in the middle to make room for the symbolic animal above and for the feet of the saint below, and composed of interlaced ribbons and the Chinese-like Z-pattern modified.

St. Mark, copied in my Plate 26, and St. John, are apparently by another hand, with the heads disproportionately large. They are represented as standing without any chair, the hair arranged in long flowing curls, the nimbus red or purple (in St. Mark dotted with yellow). Each holds his Gospel: the feet are naked. St. Mark has long moustaches and beard, of which St. John is destitute; and the latter has a rudely-drawn eagle above his nimbus, whereas St. Mark has no special symbol, but, on the contrary, the four symbols occupy the four angles of the drawing (as seen in my plate). This circumstance induces me to consider it possible that the border of this miniature was originally intended to have contained a figure of the Saviour, to have been placed at the beginning of the volume; but that St. Mark, with a dotted nimbus, was added; or else that the drawing is really intended for the Saviour, although the nimbus is not cruciferous, and that the drawing of St. Mark is wanting. (This cruciferous nimbus of the Saviour is, however, shown in the two miniatures in the volume in which it is represented as white, with red dots. In both the latter drawings, however, the Saviour is represented as beardless.) The curious treatment of the symbolical figures in this drawing will be noticed, especially the long hind toe of one of the feet of the Eagle, the scroll in the hand of the Angel, and the long straight topknot of the Lion and Calf. The arrangement of these symbols thus—

| St. John, | St. Matthew, |
| St. Mark, | St. Luke, |

will also be noticed for its departure from the ordinary treatment. The frames in which these two figures of St. Mark and St. John are enclosed are unlike those of the other two Evangelists. Here the sides are two inches wide, the middle in the former miniature being lozenge-shaped, and in the latter circular, filled in with the spiral pattern: the remainder of the side borders being formed of small compartments, with the spiral pattern, interlaced ribbons, and monstrous animals, together with the Chinese Z and step-patterns, enclosed in bars, which are ornamented with rows of red dots.

The "Liber generationis ih" and the "Xpi autem generatio" of St. Matthew, copied in my 26th Plate; the "Initium Evangelii" of St. Mark; the "Quoniam qui[dem]"

2 L

of St Luke; and the "In pr[incipio]," &c., of St John, are by one hand, each occupying entire pages, the right-hand sides of each being margined with an ornamental border about an inch wide, formed of the ordinary patterns, and extended in some of the drawings (as in my Plate 26) along the upper and lower margins, terminating above in the head of an animal or bird, and at the other end in St. John's Gospel in a fish's tail. There is great diversity in the patterns in the different small compartments of which these gigantic letters are composed, especially in that of St. John, which is the most elaborate, although far less delicate in finish than in the Gospels of Kells or Lindisfarne. The spiral pattern is introduced to a considerable extent in all these title-pages; but the marginal rows of red dots, which afford so striking a feature in some of the other contemporary Books of the Gospels, are here entirely wanting, except round the great initials. The remaining letters in these pages are large angulated capitals, as in the Gospels of St. Chad and Mac Regol, &c.

The only ornamental cruciform page remaining in the volume is copied in the left-hand division of my 27th Plate, the most striking feature being the four groups of interlaced animals, resembling those of which some of the similar pages in the Books of Lindisfarne and St. Chad are entirely composed.

The two most remarkable drawings in the volume represent the Crucifixion and Glorification of the Saviour, copied in my 27th and 28th Plates. More barbarous designs could scarcely be conceived. In the scene of the Crucifixion the dotted (not cruciferous) nimbus, purple arms, blue legs, unwieldy garments covering the whole body, but twisted round in a most impossible manner, the wavy stream of blood extending from the point of the spear (not from the side of the Saviour) to the eye of Longinus and the long moustaches of the sponge-bearer, will all attract attention.

The other miniature, in my Plate 27, has been described as representing Christ teaching in the Temple; but I do not hesitate to regard it as intended rather for the Glorification of the Saviour. The cross resting on the right shoulder of Jesus Christ, the two Angels blowing trumpets at the sides, and the twelve Apostles in the lower part of the drawing holding books, must surely be regarded as representing the heavenly state of the Redeemer. One of the most remarkable sculptured stones published in Mr. Stuart's elaborate work is a fragment of a pillar now supporting the font at Rothbury, in Northumberland; on one side of which the same subject is represented almost in the same manner, the chief difference being that the Saviour is seated at full length on a cloud; and there are only eleven instead of twelve Apostles. Another fragment of the same stone, now in the Museum at Newcastle-on-Tyne, represents the Saviour in the act of benediction and holding the Gospels, young and beardless, exactly as delineated in the oldest Christian ivory carvings. (Stuart's "Sculptured Stones," ii. Pl. 85, 86.)

The St. Gall MS. No. 60 contains only the Gospel of St. John (divided into 232 paragraphs), having prefixed a portrait of the Evangelist with his Eagle, executed in a most barbarous style. The head is entirely surrounded with a yellow nimbus, and the garment is composed of yellow and dirty red longitudinal stripes. An attempt has been made to represent the arms holding an open book on the breast, on which is inscribed the name IOHANNIS. The figure is supposed to be standing within a large frame or chair.

the sides of which extend higher than the head of the Saint, each being terminated by a rude bird's head. The framework is equally rude, composed of knotted yellow ribbons on a black ground, and small squares, each with a sort of circle crossed by diagonal lines. The open spaces are filled in with rows of red dots. The initial page of the Gospel, containing the words "INPrincipio erat Verbum" is in the usual style, but very rudely executed in red, yellow, and purple colours. The cover of the manuscript is composed of an elegant ivory carving, 10 inches by 3½ wide, the design of which consists of a charming flowery arabesque formed of branches and foliage, forming twelve circles in pairs, the first, third, and fifth pair of circles filled in with a large vine-leaf; the others with wild animals (bears, lions, tigers, &c.), attacking oxen, designed with wonderful skill and freedom.

The Book of Fragments, No. 1,395, contains three illuminated leaves, two of which probably belonged to a Book of the Gospels, and the third to a Penitentiale.

One of the former contains a rudely-drawn figure of St. Matthew seated, writing his Gospel, upon a chair, seen sideways, the back of which only reaches up to his elbow, having a small conical cup on its top, in which he is dipping a style ("ohne allen Zweifel eine Feder"—Keller);[*] his left hand (with one of the fingers strangely distorted) holding a knife, and the square book resting on his knees. The head, with curling hair, is surrounded by a *cruciferous* yellow nimbus; the beard is long, straight, and divided into four points; the upper garment or mantle is purple, with yellow bands and border, and the lower garment or tunic, seen at the wrists and from the knees downwards, dark green, edged with yellow; he wears a pair of black shoes, with broad red borders, higher behind than in front. Below the seat of the chair appear outline figures of three objects, two of which may be open rolls, and the third a bundle of rolls, tied together across the middle. In front of the figure is represented the symbolical Angel, with curious outspread wings, holding a book in its hand in front of its face, from which the Saint appears to be copying his text. The framework of this picture is composed of the narrow Z-like pattern rudely drawn, with small rosettes and diagonal patterns at the angles.

On the reverse of this miniature are twenty-three lines of Irish text, of which a copy is given in the Record Commission plates, and a reading, with a translation by Dr. Todd, in Dr. Keller's memoir.

The second of these illuminated leaves is intended for one of the cruciform pages introduced into the Books of the Gospels, the design being 8 inches high by 6 wide. In the centre is a space about 1½ inch square, formed of red and yellow interlaced ribbons. Above and below this are two squares, each filled in with two distorted human figures, with long interlacing tails and legs; and at each of the sides is another square with birds similarly treated. These four squares are connected with the central one by narrow bars, formed of narrow white interlaced ribbons, leaving the four angles of the design plain (possibly from the illumination not having been completed). The square frame enclosing the whole is narrow, and composed of rudely-drawn interlaced ribbons and the Z ornament.

---

* Keller refers to the Codex No. 60. in the "Ministerialbibliothek" of Schaffhausen, for a figure of Venerable Bede seated writing. I regret not to have seen the drawing.

The third illuminated page is the initial of a Penitentiale, copied in the right-hand portion of my 28th Plate, which is to be read

reoea

vim

es dne peccav

imus parce n*

(The last letters of the fourth line were evidently written wrong, and an unsatisfactory attempt has been made to correct them.) The text is continued on the verso of the leaf in a very clear and beautiful rounded Irish hand: "parce peccatis nostris et salva nos qui gubernasti noe super undas dilu(vi)i exauli nos," &c., with the commencement of a litany— "See maria ora p . See petre ora p . See paule ora p," &c.

It will be perceived from my plate that the execution of the ornamental details of this page, although not devoid of elegance in the design, is large and coarse, as compared with some of the above-described illuminations in other manuscripts.

The St. Gall Library also contains a fine MS. of Priscianus "de Grammatica," written in a fine Irish hand, with many curious Irish marginal explanations; the initial letters of the various divisions formed in the genuine Irish style of outline animals, men, or birds, with various interlaced knots, in a style nearly resembling that of the Book of Armagh. Dr. Keller has given a number of these initials and other peculiarities of the manuscript in his memoir on the Irish MSS. in Swiss libraries, above referred to. The most remarkable of these initials is the letter P, of which the round open part is filled in with the distorted kneeling figure of a man, one of whose feet is grasped in the mouth of a monstrous head, forming the end of the whorl of the P; two gigantic birds with long interlaced topknots, at the sides of the man, peck the top of his head, whilst the bottom of the straight stroke of the letter is extended downwards, the end being curved upwards into the neck of another monstrous head, with a prettily curved topknot.

THE GOSPELS OF MÆIEL BRITH MAC DURNAN

Plate XXII.

THIS small volume of the Gospels, from which three of the most interesting pages are here reproduced, is certainly one of the most beautiful of all the Irish manuscripts which have come down to our times. Unlike all the volumes described in the preceding articles, this is of small size, being only 6⅜ by 4⅜ inches in size, and is written in minuscule characters, with many of the words contracted. It is preserved in the

---

* The same appears in the Stow Missal, published in fac-simile by O'Conor. The text, together with some of the Irish Liturgical texts contained in the same manu-

script, is published in detail by Bishop Forbes, in the "Liber Ecclesie de Arbuthnot," p. xlviii

Archiepiscopal Library of Lambeth; but its pages bear red-pencil references and notes in the handwriting of Archbishop Matthew Parker, whose collection of manuscripts is preserved at Corpus Christi College, Cambridge; but it is to be observed that the volume is neither inserted in the Catalogue of that library nor in that of the Archiepiscopal MSS. at Lambeth published in 1812.

The volume comprises the four Gospels entire, without the Epistle of St. Jerome to Pope Damasus, or the Prefaces to the Gospels, Capitula, &c. The 1st leaf is blank on both sides. The recto of the 2nd leaf bears the following laudatory verses, in a comparatively modern hand:—

DE EVANGELISTIS

Hoc Matthæus agens hominem generaliter implet
Marcus ut alta fremit vox per deserta Leonis
Jura sacerdotii Lucas tenet ore juventi (ni)
More volant aquilæ verbo petit astra Joh(annes)
Matthæus instituit virtutum tramite mores
Et bene vivendi justo dedit ordine legem
Marcus amat terras inter cælumq; volans
Atq; volans Aquila stricto secat em(olja) lapsu
Lucas uberius describit prælia Christi
Jure sacer vitulus qui munia fetur avita

These lines are evidently copied from the inscription on the leaf over which that on which they are now written has been pasted, but which had probably become partially illegible, as the two lines applicable to St. John at the end are omitted, the page itself having probably before the last binding of the volume formed the outside of the book. These lines refer to the drawing on the verso of the same 2nd leaf, on which are represented, of a small size, the four symbolical symbols, arranged in small oblong compartments in a frame, the centre of which is occupied by a small circle, ornamented with spiral lines forming a kind of rosette, from which extend the four arms of a cross, ornamented with small squares, filled in with diagonal patterns and uniting with the marginal border, the angles of which are ornamented with red, yellow, and green lozenges. Except in the heads and feet, these four symbols are similarly treated, each covered with parti-coloured patches like a harlequin, and having four wings, one pair extending to the upper and one pair to the lower angles of the drawing. That of St. Mark's Lion is represented in the open space of the middle compartment in my 22nd Plate; that of St. Matthew is given in my " Palæographia," together with the heads of the Eagle and Bull. The heads of the Lion and Bull are surmounted with a curious yellow topknot, which may possibly be intended for a nimbus.

Each Gospel is preceded by a page filled with a figure of its writer, in an elegant border, in which the ornamental designs, from the small size of the framework, are very delicately drawn, the patterns being formed of interlaced ribbons and monstrous birds and beasts, and with the Z-pattern modified in various ingenious manners. The spiral pattern is, however, wanting throughout the illuminations of this volume.* SS. Matthew and Luke are represented in the first and third compartments of my 22nd Plate, and St. John is given in my " Palæographia." All the four Evangelists hold a book with the naked right hand against the breast. In St. Mark the book appears to be enclosed in its case, which buttons over at the side. All are also destitute of a beard. All except St. Mark

* In the third compartment of my plate I have introduced the border from the commencement of St. John's Gospel, that surrounding the miniature of Saint Luke in the original being plainer and only formed of wide interlaced ribbon patterns.

have a curious cap or head-covering or nimbus, with curled ends over the shoulders;
and all except St. Luke, whose feet are naked, wear ornamental shoes, extending in the
middle in front up the instep, and (as shown in the figure of St. John copied in my
"Palæographia," who stands with his toes most uncomfortably bent outwards) with the
back part of the shoes also extending upwards as high as the front part.   There is no
appearance of tonsure in any of these figures; all of which, moreover, are represented as
standing, except St. Mark, who may be supposed to be seated, as the sides of the
drawing are occupied by two very slender animals, standing erect on their two hind legs,
and with a curved fore leg, and the head occupying each upper angle of the design, with
long red tongues, and which may be considered as representing the carved sides of the
chair, as in the Gospels of St. Chad.   The same Saint also is distinguished by having his
symbolical Lion very tamely represented at the top of the drawing, the deflexed wings
partially concealed by, and interlaced with, the lines of the frame of the drawing.

St. Matthew holds in his right hand a very long pastoral staff, with a plain head
and a sharp point at the bottom; whilst St. Luke holds in his right hand the short staff
or camhatta, rounded at top but truncated at the bottom.*   These are the only representations hitherto discovered in any of these manuscripts of the pastoral staves or cambattæ
of the early Irish bishops; indeed, with the exception of the figure of St. Matthew, habited
as a bishop, with a long pastoral staff like that of our St. Matthew, in that singular
manuscript, the "Sacramentarium of Gelloni" (figured by Silvestre and also by Count
Bastard, "Bull. Com. Hist. France," iv. 485 and 857), I know no other early figures
in which the Evangelists are treated as ecclesiastics, nor do I believe that any earlier
representations of the pastoral staff exist than those here figured.†

In all these four figures, the inner garment, like a gown, extends from the neck to
the feet, and is of a green colour, dotted with white or streaked with red; whilst the outer
garment is of very ample size, with many folds, and hanging down in curved folds over the
arms and at the sides, arranged without the slightest regard to nature, and totally destitute of
shading.   The flesh is coloured with opaque white paint, whilst the features are expressed by
fine black lines, drawn in the most inartistic manner.   St. Matthew is, moreover, interesting
from holding in his right hand a quill pen or pencil, which he is dipping into a small
conical pot of red paint, fixed at the end of a long thin stem.   The quill is considerably

---

* The pastoral staves of the Irish Bishops form the
subject of a separate chapter in the Appendix to the present
volume.

† The memoir of Count Bastard above referred to, and
"Le Bâton Pastoral" of Messrs. Barrault and Martin, may
be advantageously referred to on this subject.   An examination and sketch made by myself of the ivory head of a
pastoral staff preserved with the utmost veneration, as that
of St. Gregory the Great, in the sacristy of the church of
San Gregorio, on the Cælian Hill at Rome, enable me to
state that it is a production of a much more recent date,
being a whorl terminating in a dragon's head, with wide
gaping mouth, the open space occupied by a ram (with
curved horns) holding a cross, thus resembling the Bude
specimen, recently in the collection of Prince Soltykoff
(figured twice by Messrs. Barrault and Martin, and twice by
Count Bastard), and that of the Ashmolean Museum in
Oxford, except that the cross is surmounted by a dove (the
symbol of St. Gregory), of which one of the wings is broken
off, thus differing from all the other pastoral staves of this
type hitherto figured.   Count Bastard has published a miniature
of St. Gregory (Bull. Com. Hist. France, pp. 499 and 530),

wearing a low mitre, and bearing a long pastoral staff, terminating in a plain whorl, with a dragon's head alone, from the
MS. of the letters of St. Gregory (Bibl. Imp. Anc. f. lat.
2288).   The same church of San Gregorio does, however,
possess two contemporary relics of St. Gregory, which, from
his connection with the English Apostle St. Augustine and
the Early English Church, are of considerable interest.
These are, his white marble chair or Episcopal throne,
bearing on the seat an inscription commencing with a ✠
of which only a letter or two are now decipherable; the
arms terminating in finely-carved lions' heads; and the white
marble table, resting on elegantly-carved feet of the chair-
cal period, on which we are told, by an inscription in verse,
that St. Gregory fed every morning twelve poor pilgrims,
when an angel appeared as the thirteenth.   This is the subject
of the ceremony of the visit of the "Apostles," as they are
now called, which is one of the most striking scenes of the
"Holy week" at the Vatican.   Another marble chair of
St. Gregory is preserved in the Church of San Stefano
Rotundo, near San Gregorio; it is without back or arms,
but has the lower sides elegantly carved with the classical
honeysuckle pattern.

curved; but the upper part distinctly shows the barb of the feather. In his left hand he holds a knife or style, formed of a thin stem, with a knob at the top, and with the other end pointed.

The borders of these four miniatures are far more carefully executed than in any of the other small copies of the Gospels executed in Ireland.

The genealogical portion of the first chapter of St. Matthew's Gospel is regarded as a prologue, without any ornamental border, and with only the LI(ber) of an enlarged size, and but slightly ornamented. The "XPI AUTEM GENERATIO SIC ERAT" is, on the contrary, treated in the most elaborate manner, being in fact a miniature reproduction in the style of the same page in the most elaborately executed large copies of the Gospels, the five words occupying the whole of the centre of the page, and being written in angulated capital letters upon green bars, with yellow edgings, the ground itself being purple, with white dots, whilst the great initial X, formed of interlacing black bands, with the open parts green and purple, is placed upon a white ground, decorated with rows of red dots. The entire page, with its borders formed of compartments filled in with interlaced dragons and with delicate diagonal Z-pattern tracery, is a perfect palæographical gem. I attempted to reproduce it in my "Palæographia," but the result was far too coarse, and has evidently misled Mr. Noel Humphreys, who has copied it incorrectly, and without acknowledgment (and of an enlarged size), in his "Art of Illumination."[*]

The three other Gospels have the first page of each enclosed within an elegant border in the same style as the former; that of St. Mark, however, copied in the middle compartment of my plate, being the most elaborate and by far the most elegant. The border itself, formed of interlaced lacertine animals and ribbons, intertwined in a most unusual manner, is to be regarded as the body of a monstrous animal extending along the two sides and bottom of the page, and terminated at the top on the right side in a large lion's head and mane, with long red tongue, and with a kind of yellow topknot, which is curled into an elegant star-shaped rosette,[†] whilst the top of the left side of the pattern terminates in two hind legs and a curved yellow tail. The right side of the border and three of the angles are ornamented with interlaced animals, that of the border being unusually elegant in its design. The initial word Initium will be seen to occupy only portion of the enclosed space, the remainder being filled with the continuation of the text, written in a small minuscule hand. The initial letters themselves exactly resemble the same letters in the Book of Armagh.

The "Qm quidem" of St. Luke and the "In principio erat verbum" of St. John in like manner only occupy portion of the enclosed space within the ornamental border with which each initial page is surrounded. The former has the long tail of the Q angulated, and extending down the left margin of the frame, somewhat as in the Gospels of St. Chad, but terminating in the recurved head of an animal with a pointed topknot, like several initials in the Book of Armagh. That of St. John is copied in my "Palæographia," omitting the ornament within the open space of the initial, which consists of three squares similar to that in the centre of the bottom margin of the beginning of St. Mark's Gospel, copied in my Plate 22, and also omitting the patches of green paint in all the open parts of the letters of these four first words, and the straw-coloured ground on which they are written. The border of St. John's initial (as above stated) is

---

* Mr. Humphreys' note of the conjunction of the X and P, and the unnecessary repetition of the latter letter, is erroneous, the great initial being entirely formed of the X, as in the St. Gall MS. represented in my 26th Plate.

† This most unusual ornament occurs also at the tail of the first stroke of the X in the initial page of St. Matthew's Gospel, given in my "Palæographia," and again as the terminal scroll of the upper left-hand stroke of the X in the same situation in the Book of Armagh.

represented in my plate surrounding the figure of St. Luke. The step-like pattern in the two small square compartments in the middle of the two side borders is very unusual, and would form a very striking mosaic pattern if drawn mathematically correct.

Four twelfth-century illuminations of French origin, with burnished gold backgrounds, representing the Betrayal, Scourging, Crucifixion, and Entombment of the Saviour, have been inserted at the beginning of the different Gospels. Several charters of King Canute, containing grants to the cathedral church of Canterbury, have been copied upon blank pages of the manuscript; one of which (fol. 4 verso) bears a much earlier inscription, written in large capital letters angulated in the Anglo-Saxon style, as follows :—

> ✠ MÆIEL BRIDUS MAC
> DURNANI ISTU TEXTU
> PER TRIQADRU DO
> 925 DIGNE DOGMATIZAT
> ✠ AST · AETHELSTANUS ·
> ANGLOSAXANA · REX · ET
> RECTOR · DORVVERNENSI ·
> METROPOLI · DAT · P · ÆVV ·

The date 925 is, of course, a comparatively modern addition. The translation of the first four lines is difficult : but Mæiel Brith, the son of Mac Durnan, or Tornan, has been satisfactorily shown by Dr. Todd to have been Abbot of Derry in the ninth century, and afterwards Archbishop of Armagh, to which see he was promoted in A.D. 885, and died A.D. 927. Athelstan ascended the Anglo-Saxon throne in 925, and died in 941; so that it is possible that the Archbishop may have sent the volume as a gift on the occasion of the accession of the king. The inscription certainly does not indicate the Archbishop to have been the writer of the volume, and, from its palaeographical peculiarities, I have no doubt that it was written by the same hand as the Gospels in the Book of Armagh, which is now ascertained to have been written (not by Aidus in A.D. 698, as stated by Sir W. Betham, but) by a scribe named Ferdomnach, in 807, which may probably be regarded as near the date of the Gospels of Mæiel Brith Mac Durnan. (See article by Dean Graves, in " Proc. R. Irish Acad.," iii. 316.)

There are several short Irish notes written in the margins of some of the pages : and at the end of St. Matthew's Gospel the scribe has written, " Amen : Do gtas ago ; " at the end of St. Mark, " Finit, Amen, finit ; " and at the end of St. Luke, " Do gtas ago,"—according to the custom of Irish scribes in the eighth and ninth centuries.

THE GOSPELS OF THE CATHEDRAL OF TREVES.

Plates XIX. and XX.

AMONGST the many valuable MSS. in the library of the Cathedral of Treves (for an opportunity of examining which I am indebted to the learned Canon Wilmovski, under whose superintendence such great light has been thrown on the Roman portions of that most interesting building—see Didron's " Annales Archæologiques"), is a quarto copy of the Latin Gospels of very great interest, from the singular combination which it contains of Celtic and Teutonic or Franco-Byzantine art and caligraphy, of which my two plates afford abundant evidence.

The text is written partially in a fine Hiberno-Saxon hand, resembling, but rather larger than, that of the Gospels of Lindisfarne, and partly in Merovingian uncials as large as, but closer and neater than, the writing in the first division of the 44th plate in the "Nouveau Traité de Diplomatique," the two hands occurring sometimes on the same page, and even in the same line; so that the writing of both must have been simultaneous.

On the first leaf of the manuscript is inscribed, within a square compartment surrounded with red dots, and written in the Hiberno-Saxon hand of portion of the text,—" Scribtori vita eterna. Legenti pax perpetua. Videnti felicitas perennis. Habenti possessio cū salute. Amen. Do gracias. Ora pro me. Ds tecum."

The verso of this page is occupied with representations of the four Evangelical symbols, each in an oblong compartment separated by bars, forming a cruciform design, having a central circle an inch and a quarter in diameter, within which is a bust of the Saviour, young and beardless, holding a book, and with a plain yellow nimbus with a red edge, the open parts of the circle dark blue, with white dots arranged in triangles. The "Vitulus" of St. Luke and the "Aquila" of St. John are almost identical with those of the Paris Gospels. The "Leo" of St. Mark is better drawn than in most of the Hiberno-Saxon Gospels; and St. Matthew's representative is a fair figure of a man, 3½ inches high, holding a roll in his right hand, with sandals on his feet, and destitute of nimbus. The ornaments in the framework of this miniature resemble those of the border of St. Matthew in the Paris Gospels, represented in Plate 21.

The second and two following leaves are occupied with the Prefaces, "Plures fuisse," &c., with the several headings written in Merovingian capitals, rudely coloured.

The extraordinary drawing represented in my 20th Plate occupies the verso of the fifth leaf, and is intended for a conjoined figure of all the four Evangelical symbols, as appears from the inscription of the names of the four Evangelists themselves,—" Mattheus euang(elista)," &c., written in Hiberno-Saxon letters of large size, resembling in form those used in our finest manuscripts.

The principal figure in this design consists of the upper half of the "Homo," the feet of which appear at the bottom of the drawing. Below the central cross-line will be perceived the wings and claws of the Eagle; below these are two of the legs of the Lion; whilst below, resting on the blue dress of the Man, are two of the legs of the Calf.

The Man, with a short grey pointed beard, wears a blue under-garment, on which are seen over the right shoulder and above the feet the two yellow vittæ, which occur in the dresses of the earliest Christians in the catacombs and mosaics, and which we see again in the dress of the two Angels in Plate 19. These, as will be clearly seen, are not a detached portion of the dress, but simply two ornamental bands fastened on the lower garment; and it will also be seen that they are continued as a border between the feet of the principal figure. The upper garment on the left shoulder of the figure, and on either side below the wings of the Eagle, is dirty orange, relieved with dark brown and opaque yellow stripes to indicate the folds. But the most curious part of this design consists of the two objects which are held by the Man, and which are evidently instruments of ecclesiastical use; but whether the star-like object held in the right hand be identical with the object held in the hands of the Angels in the miniature of the Virgin and Child in the Book of Kells, and with that held by St. Luke in the Gospels of St.

2 F

Chad; or whether it be intended for a "flabellum" or for an "aspergillum" is difficult to decide; but I think no doubt will be entertained that the object in the left hand is intended for an ornamented knife. (See articles in the Appendix on the "holy spear" and flabellum.)

The bold character of the ornament, and especially of the whorls terminating in dogs' heads at the angles of the frame, will be noticed, as well as the inscription at the bottom, "Thomas scribsit," in red Hiberno-Saxon characters, identical with portion of the text of the volume.

The Epistle of St. Jerome to Pope Damasus commences on the recto of the sixth leaf, the "Novum opus" being written in large Hiberno-Saxon characters, with the initial N in the style of the Gospels of Lindisfarne; but the two lines of the heading, "Beato papæ Damaso Hieronimus," are in Merovingian capitals.

After this Epistle occurs a page which contains the fine drawing copied in the lower part of my 19th Plate, representing the two Archangels, Michael and Gabriel (whose names are inscribed over their heads in large elegant Hiberno-Saxon characters), holding a purple panel (resting on a central pedestal, the capital of which rests on a boss formed of an interlaced line), inscribed in angulated Hiberno-Saxon capitals, INCIPIT EUANGELIUM SE✠CYNDUM MATTEUM, surmounted by a scroll of classical design, above which is a Celtic ribbon-knot. These Angels (of which I know no other equally early MS. example) are of a very Byzantine character, and are a satisfactory proof that art of a superior kind had not quite died out in the eighth or ninth century, although instances of its occurrence in MSS. of that date are of the greatest rarity. The band across the head, the long wand, the two narrow yellow bands down the lower garment, and the square patch of gold on the outer, are indications of Angelic or noble rank.

To this page succeed the Euschian Canons, occupying several pages, enclosed in ornamental columns with rounded arches, the writing being entirely in Hiberno-Saxon; the upper portion of the first Canon ("Canon primus in quo iiii."), in which the same facts are mentioned by all the four Evangelists, is copied in Plate 19. It will be at once perceived that the style of Art is entirely unlike that of any Celtic work, the birds (here cocks in connection with the head of St. Peter), including an excellent pair of parrots, occupying the upper angles of the Canons, being entirely in the style of the Caroline MSS. With one exception, the columns, capitals, and arches are ornamented in the classical or Byzantine style; but in the fourth Canon, the base of the columns is filled with the usual Celtic spiral pattern. Each of the tables has the arch surmounted by a bust (as in the drawing before us), evidently representing an Evangelist or Apostle, each figure holding a book or scroll, and in the act of giving the benediction in the Latin manner, with the third and fourth fingers closed, except in the fourth Canon, where the first, second, and fourth fingers are extended; and also the first, which represents St. Peter, excellently designed, holding, apparently, two keys in his right hand, his left hand elevated, and with only the first finger extended; the crown of the head is tonsured. The second of the Canons, where three of the Evangelists narrate the same facts, has the name THOMAS inscribed at the sides of the medallion in the same hand as the text.

Then follow three leaves, with interpretations of Hebrew names:—

> " Abraham, pater videns
> " populum
> " Aminadab, po-
> " pulus meus voluntarius
> " Asia, pater dñi." &c

These five lines being written in fine Hiberno-Saxon characters, whilst the remainder of the page and the two following are in the Merovingian hand. It thus appears that the Anglo-Saxon scribe wrote the most important parts of the manuscript, either from that style of caligraphy being the most esteemed, or (more probably) from the fact of the scribe himself being a more important personage in the monastery when the book was written.

The verso of the succeeding page has a portrait of St. Matthew ("Imago Sci Mathei Euang." written in the Hiberno-Saxon capitals), the page arranged exactly as in that of St. Matthew in the Paris Gospels represented in my Plate 21, although the figure of St. Matthew is very different. Then commences, on the recto of the next page, St. Matthew's Gospel, "LIBER GENERATIONIS," which words occupy the top of the first column, just in the style of the Paris Gospels, as copied by Silvestre. I perceive in a fac-simile I made of one of the lines of this genealogy, that the scribe has written ", Asa autem genuit iosahath," the word *autem* being written in the conventional contracted manner, like a h' with a reversed comma attached to the top of the curve. The whole of the genealogy, occupying two pages, and the next page, being the commencement of the historical part, are in the Hiberno-Saxon hand; but the verso of the latter and the greater part of the text are in the Merovingian writing, as are also the Argumentum, Breves Causæ, and Capitula of St. Mark, except the heading of the Argumentum.

On the verso of the following page is represented St. Mark, very rudely drawn, surrounded by an ornamental frame, by the same hand as the conjoined symbolical figure copied in my 20th Plate. The figure is standing in front of a tall chair, with his left hand pointing downwards towards an open book, which seems fixed in an impossible manner to the outside of the chair, and with a strange bird-like animal, intended for a winged lion, at the side. At the foot of the drawing is written "Incipit textus sci euangelii secundum marcum feliciter," with a flourish of the pen forming the outline of an exaggerated kind of oak-leaf. The whole of the text of St. Mark, with the Prefaces of St. Luke, are written in the Merovingian hand, except the initial I of the Gospel, which is long and narrow, and the word "Lucas" at the beginning of the Argumentum of St. Luke's Gospel, which are executed by the Hiberno-Saxon artist in the ornamental character.

These are followed by the portrait of St. Luke, copied in outline in my Plate 52, fig. 3 (being precisely in the same style as St. Mark), surrounded by a narrow interlaced border. This figure has the head (not tonsured) surrounded by a yellow nimbus and a blue border ornamented with white dots. In his left hand he holds what I consider to be an open book resting upon its satchel or cover,* the tags or fastenings of which hang down, terminating in knobs. In the original the two open leaves of the book are yellow; the bar which crosses them is also yellow, with the dilated ends orange; the cover is blue with white dots, with an angulated orange line forming the top of the lower border. The ends of the four fingers support the book, the thumb being directed downwards. At the back of the Saint is his chair, the supports of which terminate below in spiral and interlaced patterns. At the side of the figure opposite the book is the representation of an object (the four divisions of which are coloured red, purple, blue, and yellow) of which I have never met with another representation, and the nature of which, although quite problematical, I can only suggest to be intended for an ornamental lectern, but without any support. Above this object is a large bird occupying the upper half of the right side of the design, having a calf's head and a lion's fore legs, and supporting a book, whilst the lower half of this side bears the inscription, in Hiberno-Saxon characters, "Incipit euangelium secundum Lucam."

* See Appendix for article on the ornamental book-covers of the Irish.

The whole is enclosed in a narrow border, with broad and slightly interlaced ribbons, the angles and sides ornamented with rudely interlaced knot-work. Below the frame is again written, in small red Hiberno-Saxon letters, "thomas scribsit," the second word being in a much more cursive character than the name. Below this again, enclosed in an oblong space ornamented with red dots, is the numeration of the quaternion, qxx t, in large black letters, with red patches, the whole page forming a very striking composition.

To this succeed five leaves (the last with the numeration [q t t t t], proving it to have been misplaced in binding), containing the Argumentum and Breves Causæ of St. Matthew's Gospel, the whole written in the fine Hiberno-Saxon hand, except the title of the Argumentum, written in large Merovingian capitals, with patches of different colours and red dots.

The Prefaces, &c., and the whole of St. John's Gospel are written in the Merovingian hand, except the two initials I and I, which are elongated and ornamented in the Hiberno-Saxon style. The miniature of St. John is wanting. I had not time to collate the text, but found the curious passage indicating the divinity of the Holy Ghost, John iii. 6, 7, thus written:—"Quod natum est de carne caro est Et quod natum est de sps sps est qia ds sps est et ex do natus est noli mari [sic] quia dixi tibi, oportet vos nasci de novo;" the words here printed in italics being written on erased lines. This passage, which was supposed to be unique in the Vercelli Codex, I found in the Book of Kells, and here in a volume partly emanating from the Hiberno-Saxon school, I found it again in the Treves Gospels.

From the preceding description, there can, I apprehend, be no doubt that this MS. is one of the most remarkable productions of the eighth or early part of the ninth century. We have also seen that many of its illuminations and the most curious portions of the text are written in fine Hiberno-Saxon characters by a scribe, evidently a person of importance sufficient to warrant his name appearing in the most remarkable places in the book. We have also seen that in many particulars the illuminations bear great resemblance to the Paris Gospels, which are traditionally affirmed to have emanated from Epternach, and to have belonged to St. Willibrord. We may therefore reasonably infer that the Treves MS. originated from some Irish establishment at no great distance from Epternach. We learn from Kugler (Kleine Schriften z. Kunstgeschichte, ii. p. 341) that this was one of nine manuscripts of the Gospels bequeathed to the Cathedral library of Treves by Count Christoph v. Kesselstadt, "Dom dechanten" of Paderborn, and the Treves Libraries contain various manuscripts from the great monasteries founded by the Irish on islands in the Rhine, or its vicinity. Now, amongst these was the monastery of Honau, called in Latin records Honaugia and Hohenaugia,—"constructa in insula quæ publice ab omnibus Hohenaugia* nominatur, super fluvium Rhenum in honore S. Michaelis archangeli [whose portrait we have seen is contained in the volume before us] ceterorumque sanctorum," as it is described by the Abbot Benignus in his charter, dated at Maguntia (Mayence), in the tenth year of the reign of Charlemagne.

The island lies a short distance north-east of Strasburg, on the east side of the Rhine, occupying a bend of the river, and insulated by a narrow channel. The monastery itself was founded a little before A.D. 720 by an Irish bishop called Tubanus, who took the title of Abbot Benedict, to whom the site of the abbey was granted by Adalbert, Duke of Alsace. Thirty years afterwards, a Bishop Dubanus is recorded in several charters as then Abbot, "ubi Dubanus episcopus nunc temporis præesse videtur."

---

* This name Hohenaugia has been translated Hohenau, "High-meadow;" but I apprehend that it was rather employed in reference to the other Irish monastery on the Rhine, named Augia.

In 770, Carloman, son of King Pippin, at the prayer of the Abbot Stephanus, exempted the monastery from all judicial interference, and in 783 and 786 grants were made by Charlemagne to the Abbot Beatus, whose charter is signed by himself as Abbot,—"qui hanc chartam fieri rogavit," followed by no fewer than seven Irish names with the accompanying title "Episcopus," and one Irish "Presbyter." These bishops, it appears, were the ministers of so many churches tributary to Hohenaugia, including one which Beatus had built in Mayence, the others being in the Palatinate of the Rhine, near Mayence. It appears, however, from a list of the Abbots given by Dagobert, that between Dulianus and Stephanus the monastery was presided over by an abbot named Thomas, whose abbacy consequently must have occurred between A.D. 750 and 770. I have no doubt that we have here the writer and illuminator of the volume before us, probably executed, indeed, before he was made abbot, which would bring its execution within the first half of the eighth century.*

COMMENTARY ON THE PSALMS BY CASSIODORUS.

Plates XVII. and XVIII.

THE noble manuscript of the eighth or early part of the ninth century which has furnished the drawings for these two Plates is preserved in the Library of the Cathedral of Durham (No. B, 2, 30), and is traditionally affirmed to have been written by Venerable Bede,—"de manu Bedæ," the text being written in double columns, in a hand nearly resembling (but somewhat smaller and more evenly written than) the Harleian MS. 2965. (Astle, tab. XV. iv., and the Royal MS. 2 A. 20, Astle,t ab. XVIII. i.: both of which are also referred to the eighth century.)

It is of a folio size, and contains a commentary on the Psalter, which, after a preface, commences on the verso of the fifth leaf, the B of the "Beatus vir" being of the rounded minuscule form, in black ink, surrounded with red dots.

The figure of David seated, playing on a harp of antique form, copied in my Plate 18, forms the frontispiece of the volume (p. 81 verso). The drawing of the Psalmist has probably been copied from some earlier type, but modified according to the taste of the Anglo-Saxon artist. The Psalmist is represented beardless, with curling hair, green eyes, the head surrounded by a green circular nimbus, having a broad white border edged on each side with red, and marked, *cross-like*, with three red bars. The under-garment is left white, having only a narrow red border round the neck and wrists. The outer garment is lilac, with narrow red bars, and with the lower edges hanging over the knees, edged with a narrow white border and a fringe. Some slight attempt has been made to express the folds of the drapery by black lines slightly shaded. The hands and feet are not drawn in so exaggerated a style as in some of the MSS. of this period. The harp

---

* A memoir on this monastery, with a notice of the fourteen charters connected with it (first published by M.dillon, "Ann. Ord. S. Benedicti," ii. App. pp. 603—700), was read before the Royal Irish Academy by the Rev. Dr. Reeves, on the 10th Jan. 1857. *Proc.* vi. 152.

precisely resembles that in the hands of David in the so-called Psalter of St. Augustine, copied in my Plate 3, except that there are only five instead of six strings. The framework immediately surrounding the figure, ornamented with knotted ribbons of different colours, terminating at the top on each side in dogs' heads, with long interlaced ribbon-like tongues, is evidently intended for a seat, on which the Psalmist is supposed to be seated. We have already seen several such chairs represented in the earlier plates of this work. The concentric rings of red and black dots surrounding the figure, and which also form two circular panels enclosing the name "DAVID"—"REX" (written in fine Anglo-Saxon minuscule letters), are a very distinctive feature of this manuscript.

From the importance of the Psalter it is not surprising that portraits of its inspired author should be of common occurrence in Biblical and religious manuscripts, which it is interesting to compare together in order to trace the variations in the styles of art in different periods. The picture before us may therefore be compared with the figure of David and his attendants, above referred to, copied in my Plate 3; also with the strange figure of David, seated and playing on the harp, in the Psalter Vitellius, F. XI., in the British Museum, of which I have given a tracing in Plate 51, fig. 6; also with that in the great Anglo-Saxon Psalter of Boulogne (see Plate 37), with that in the Psalter in the Public Library, Cambridge (Palæogr. sacra,—Anglo-Saxon Psalters, plate 1), and with the remarkable drawing in the Cottonian Psalter Tiberius, C. 6, representing David playing on a harp, surrounded by his four attendants, three of whom are playing on different musical instruments, whilst the fourth, Ethan, is engaged in throwing up and catching knives and balls; which was copied and engraved by Strutt, in his "Horda Angel-Cynan" (plate 19, and has been repeatedly copied).

The framework of the miniature before us is extremely elaborate in its details, and at the same time equally effective in the arrangement of its few and simple colours. The curious and ingenious manner in which the narrow white borders of the black ribbon (upon a red ground) are interlaced, in six of the compartments, will be noticed, as well as the wonderful variation in the numerous knots in the four compartments occupying the angles of the frame.

The other miniature of David, as a warrior, represented in my 17th Plate, occurs on page 173 of the MS. It is a bold, although rudely-drawn figure, far superior to many of the contemporary figures of Evangelists. Here the King is also represented as beardless, but with the hair arranged in spiral curls, the eyes yellow, and the head surrounded with a yellow circular nimbus, with a lilac border destitute of the cross-like bars seen in the other drawing; the lower garment, extending like a gown from the neck to the knees, is of a buff colour, with a narrow red border and stripes; whilst the upper garment, which hangs in natural folds over the left arm, is lilac, the folds indicated by black lines. The right hand holds what is doubtless intended for a small circular shield (inscribed with the name "Dauil"), such as we see in the small figure in the Psalter of St. Augustine (Plate 3, upper division of the right side of the plate), and in the warrior in the Book of Kells (Plate 8).

The long spear which the Psalmist holds in his left hand is identical with those in the hands of the two warriors in one of the initials of the Psalter of St. Augustine (also copied in my Plate 3). The remarkable black and white tessellated patterns at the angles of the framework, and the various arrangements of the knots in the other six compartments, will especially be noticed, as well as the two-headed bar on which the Psalmist is standing, which may possibly have a symbolical meaning.

BEDE'S ECCLESIASTICA HISTORIA GENTIS ANGLORUM
BIBL. COTT., TIBERIUS. C. 2.

Plate LII. figs. 7 and 9.

I HAVE selected this MS. of the famous work of the father of English history for illustration in this volume, not on account of its being the earliest copy (being apparently somewhat more recent than that of the Public Library of Cambridge, written in A.D. 737), but on account of the illuminated capitals which it contains at the head of the divisions of the history.

The "Brittania oceani insula cui quondam Albion nomen fuit," at the beginning of the first book, occupies the whole of the first column, the first letter being a very finely proportioned b, of the rounded form, 5½ inches high, whilst the remainder are arranged on three transverse yellow and red bars, enclosed in differently coloured plain borders, the letters being about three-quarters of an inch high. The great B is composed of a main stroke about three-quarters of an inch wide, formed of a number of compartments, in which monstrous animals intervene with interlaced ribbons and the Z-pattern, the oval open portion of the letter being divided into four parts by a narrow cross foliated at the ends of the limbs, having a monster in each of the open spaces, which are coloured red and dark and light green. The top of the main stroke of the B terminates in a handsome design like the top of the h in my Plate 52, fig. 9 (the open spaces being filled in with red, yellow, and green of two shades, which are the only colours used), the whole letter being surrounded with double rows of red dots. The animals are of a very unusual character, those in the middle of the B resembling the one in the lower part of the S in my fig. 7, with the tails tied into a knot; but in three of the compartments of the body of the B the animals are of much more elegant character, with the tails formed into a series of circular whorls, of an arabesque character, each whorl terminating in a leaf or dog's head. A somewhat similar, but far less elegant, treatment will be observed in several of the compartments of the arch in my Plate 14, whilst the remainder of the letters resemble those of the second division of the Prayer-Book of Bishop Æthelwold, given in the right-hand division of my Plate 24, many being similarly elongated, and terminating in grotesque heads of men and animals. The page is altogether a very striking and unusual specimen of early Anglo-Saxon caligraphy.

The initial H (is temporibus) of the second book is copied in my Plate 52, fig. 9. The open part of the letter is coloured red, with a yellow margin, the bird being pale green. The foliage of the branch on which it is standing is treated quite in a conventional manner. The initial S of the fifth book is copied in my fig. 7, the open upper part being yellow and the lower red; the bird is coloured green, red, and white; the large leaf green and yellow, and the monster pale green.

I have introduced these outlines as specimens of very rare occurrence, where an attempt has evidently been made to represent natural foliage and birds, of which indeed I have met with no other instance, except as above mentioned, in any of the elaborately ornamented MSS. which have been already described.

There are, however, several carved stones of a very early date still existing in Northumberland, in which the same treatment is adopted, and which, from its great similarity to work of the Norman period, might be considered several centuries more recent than the real date of their execution. Illustrations of these stones have been recently published by Mr. J. Stuart, in his "Sculptured Stones of Scotland;" namely, at Rothbury, pl. 85; Hexham, pls. 88, 93, 94; Jarrow, pls. 82, 116; Jedburgh, pl. 118; and in the Museum of Newcastle-on-Tyne, pl. 115.

THE BOOK OF ARMAGH.

Plate LIII. fig. 10.

THIS volume is one of the most valuable of the early manuscripts of Ireland, not only on account of the great number and nature of the documents which it contains, but from the beauty of its writing and curious drawings. It long belonged to the Church of Armagh,[*] and was held in such veneration that the family of Mac Moyre held lands from the see of Armagh by the tenure of the safe-keeping of this MS.; it was indeed long regarded as the autograph of St. Patrick himself, from the statement on one of the pages, "Hucusque volumen quod Patricius manu conscripsit sua;" but the entry proceeds, "septima decima Martii die translatus est Patricius ad Cœlos." The volume must, therefore, be considered as a transcript from an earlier volume, possibly the autograph of St. Patrick, containing not only his Confession or Epistle to the Irish, but other memoirs of the life of the Irish Saint. The volume is preserved in a strong black leather case, with raised ornaments of animals arranged within circles and raised interlacing ribbons. Besides the top, bottom, and closed ends, it is furnished with a flap similarly ornamented, which shuts over the upper side, and is fastened by a very ancient brass lock and eight brass staples, or half-rings, which being fixed on the upper side, in a row, passed through as many holes of the flap, a bolt or pin being probably arranged to pass through the rings and fasten with the lock. I possess a careful drawing of this cover.[†] Towards the close of the seventeenth century the volume passed into the hands of Arthur Brownlow, Esq., and in 1846 it was deposited in the Museum of the Royal Irish Academy by the Rev. Francis Brownlow.

A very long account of the volume was published by Sir W. Betham in the second part of his "Irish Antiquarian Researches," with several plates of fac-similes of its writing

---

[*] Whether, notwithstanding the later character of its writing, this be the identical volume described as the Gospels of St. Patrick, which was preserved in the Church of Armagh in the eleventh century, as stated in St. Bernard's life of St. Malachy may be doubtful. In 1836 Mr. Petrie exhibited at the Royal Irish Academy, a MS. of the four Gospels, said to have been given by St. Patrick to the first Bishop of Clogher, enclosed in a brass case of curious workmanship, called the DOMNACH AIRGID, on which the circumstances of the gift are represented in highly raised

figures. He had previously read a paper on it, published in the 18th volume of the Transactions of the Academy. The writing agrees with that of the Book of Kells in character, and Dr. Todd refers it to the fifth century.

[†] Specimens of such leather satchels are of the greatest rarity. Mr. Petrie possessed one, figured in his work on the Round Towers. I found another amongst the laid manuscripts in the convent of St. Isidore at Rome; and a very curious one, with its straps, is preserved in the library of Corpus Christi college, Oxford, containing an Irish Missal

and drawings. It is of the small quarto size, 8 inches high by 6 wide, and contains 221 leaves of vellum, the first twenty-four of which are occupied with various early Latin lives of St. Patrick, by Tirechan,* Aidus, and other writers, including the "Sancti Patricii Confessio sive Epistola ad Hibernos," commencing, "Ego Patricius peccator rusticissimus et minimus omnium fidelium et contemptibilis," and terminating, "Et hæc est confessio mea antequam moriar."

On the 25th leaf commences the Epistle of St. Jerome to Pope Damasus, usually preceding the Vulgate Gospels; followed by the ten Eusebian Canons, explanations of Hebrew names used in the Gospels, various Prefaces and Arguments; followed by the four Gospels and the remaining books of the New Testament, not placed in the usual order, terminating with the Acts of the Apostles, preceded by the Apocalypse, almost all the Epistles having an Argument by Pelagius at the commencement.

The last thirty leaves of the volume are occupied with the life of St. Martin of Tours, by Sulpicius, with two short Epistles by Sulpicius and Severus, terminating with a very singular prayer.

At the commencement of St. Matthew's Gospel is a page (of which a fac-simile is given by Sir W. Betham) divided into four squares, containing representations of the symbols of the Evangelists,—" Homo," " Leo," " Vitulus," and " Aquila," each with four wings, rudely designed, but neatly executed in outline, in the style of the 10th figure in my 53rd Plate. The Homo wears an under-garment, reaching from the neck to the feet, and an outer cloak hanging from the shoulders almost as low, but thrown in a round fold over each arm. He bears a book, whilst the Eagle carries a fish in its talons.† Each Gospel commences with a fine ornamental letter, very similar to those in the Gospels of Mac Durnan, except that they are simply in ink outlines; and the Xpi of St. Matthew i. 18, only occupies the upper part of the left-hand column of a page, the book being written in double columns. The ornamented initials of the "Liber generationis," "Xpi autem generatio," "Initium Evangelii," and "Apocalipsis Ihu Xpi," are represented in fac-simile by Sir W. Betham.

The initial Q of the "Quoniam quidem" occupies nearly half the first column of the page on which St. Luke's Gospel commences, the open part of the letter filled in with the spiral pattern, neatly executed, and the tail of the Q terminating in a recurved dog's neck and head, with a very long interlaced topknot. Over the letters XPI and QM we find a fish used as a mark of contraction. At the end of St. Luke's Gospel is given another remarkable figure of the "Vitulus," with four wings, three of which bear in the centre small circular medallions, in which are represented the heads of the three other symbols,—namely, the Man, Lion, and Eagle; whilst at the beginning of St. John's Gospel is the representation of his symbol, copied in my Plate 53, fig. 10 (from a tracing made for me by Mr. H. O'Neill), in which the body and two of the wings bear similar circles with the heads of the Man, Lion, and Calf. I know no other instance of such a remarkable combination of these symbols.

The text of the volume, which appears to have been entirely (with the exception of a few short marginal notes) written by one hand, is extremely neat, but full

---

* In one of these lives, St. Patrick is stated to have set up stone crosses in various places, and at one place "recidit Patricii dens et dedit dentem Brono suo in reliquias." The FIACAIL PHADRUG, or St. Patrick's tooth, long preserved in a silver and brass case, at Cong, in the County Mayo, was deposited, in 1845, in the Museum of the Royal Irish Academy.

† Miss Twining (Christian Symbols, pl. 52) has copied this Eagle, and describes the fish as the Symbol of Baptism; but the fish occurs commonly in the Book of Kells, and indeed in the Book of Armagh itself, as a mark of contraction, simply used as an ornamental bar. In the former book even a fish is represented as being devoured by a cat.

of contractions and curious orthographical errors, exactly such as are found in the Gospels of Mac Durnan, which I cannot but think was written by the same hand, the ornamental details being in several curious respects (mentioned in my article on that volume) identical.

From a short passage at the end of one of the lives of St. Patrick,—" Hæc pauca Sancti Patricii peritia et virtutibus Muirchu Maccu Machtheni dictante Aiduo Sleptiensis civitatis episcopo conscripsit,"—Sir W. Betham arrived at the incorrect conclusion that the volume was written by Aidus, bishop of Slepten or Sletty, in Queen's County, about A.D. 698 : but the Rev. C. Graves, in two communications to the Royal Irish Academy in 1846 and 1847, has satisfactorily shown that in no fewer than eight instances, Ferdomnach, the real scribe, had written his name in different parts of the volume, but that it had been nearly effaced in each instance. Two scribes of this name are recorded in the Irish Annals ; but from some additional passages connected with one of the signatures, Mr. Graves has been able satisfactorily to determine that this volume was written by Ferdomnach, " dictante Torbach herede Patricii " (the latter being the title of the Irish primate), which would give the year 807 as the date of the volume, Torbach having been Archbishop of Armagh only during one year.

THE PSALTER OF ST. COLUMBA, OR ST. COLUMBANUS.

THE ancient family of O'Donell in Ireland has long been the hereditary keepers of a remarkable brass box, or Cumhdach, known under the name of " THE CAAH," the upper side of which is a silver plate, ornamented with large precious stones and adorned with chasings (probably of the sixteenth century), representing in the centre a juvenile sitting figure, with long flowing hair, in the act of benediction (which has been considered to represent St. Columba), but which I regard as intended for the Saviour, with two Angels swinging censers at the sides of the head. To the left is a bishop, in a low triangular mitre, with a long pastoral staff, standing, in the act of benediction ; and to the right a figure of the Crucifixion, with the Virgin and St. John (not the two Marys as described). At the top and bottom are rows of monstrous animals, and at the sides foliage. Affixed to the left side of the box is a small globular silver cross suspended by a short chain.

On one of the additional covers of the case it is styled "hereditarii Sancti Columbani pignoris ;" but the box has ordinarily been regarded as a relic of St. Columba, and not of St. Columbanus.

Notwithstanding the superstitious tradition that evils innumerable would fall on the family of O'Donell whenever its contents should be developed, the box was allowed to be opened by Sir W. Betham, when it was found to contain a considerable portion of the Psalter, written in a small rounded hand of early character, of which a facsimile was published by Sir W. Betham from the beginning of the 103rd Psalm. I also published another fac-simile from the commencement of the 91st Psalm in my "Palæographia." Each Psalm commences with a large initial letter, the two or three following gradually diminishing in size. These initials are rudely executed and ornamented, with none of the elegance which we see in other early Irish manuscripts. The size of the MS. was originally about 9 inches long by 6 wide. This valuable MS., with its cover, is now, by the kind permission of Sir R. O'Donell, placed in the Museum of the Royal Irish Academy.

THE BOOK OF DIMMA MAC NATHI.

THIS is a small copy of the Latin Gospels formerly in the possession of Sir W. Betham, described by him in his "Irish Antiquarian Researches," where fac-similes are given of the drawings of three of the Evangelists,* the fourth being represented by his symbolical Eagle, drawn with four wings, seen in front, and holding a book in its claws. Nothing can be ruder than these figures, which are clothed in garments composed of patches of yellow, red, and green colours, the outer portion of which is thrown over each arm, forming a large shield-like patch standing out obliquely from the dress. The first and fourth of these figures are enclosed in a framework border, composed of rudely-drawn interlacing ribbons and diagonal patterns. A description of the text and its peculiarities, with fac-similes, will be found in my "Palæographia sacra." Sir W. Betham has also given a page of fac-similes of the more rudely-written portion of the volume, including a Service for the Sick, or "Missa pro infirmis," the text of which was published by Sir W. Betham, under the title of "Visitatio Infirmorum;" but much more correctly by Bishop Forbes (from the reading of Dr. Reeves) in the "Liber Ecclesie de Arbuthnott," 1864.

This MS. is preserved in a brass box, richly plated with silver. It has been frequently repaired; but the bottom face is figured by Sir W. Betham. It is engraved with interlaced circles and square compartments of an early character, on which is affixed a metal chasing of the Crucifixion, with the Virgin and St. John (not the two Marys, as stated by Sir W. Betham) on each side of the cross.

The book and its cover were purchased by the Royal Irish Academy some years ago from Sir W. Betham, at the price of £200.

The name of the scribe, Dimma, and Dimma Mac Nathi, is repeated several times in the volume; and, according to Colgan, there were many Irish saints of the name of Dimma; one with the addition of Mac Nathi is repeatedly mentioned in the life of St. Patrick in the Book of Armagh. Another was celebrated for his skill in penmanship, and is recorded to have been requested by St. Cronan, who died in 621, and whose grandfather was also named Mac Nathi, to write for him a copy of the Gospels, which occupied forty days' and forty nights' incessant labour, the writer "nec desiderio cibi vel potus sive somni gravatus est." The MS. is remarkable for its readings, including the

* These three figures wear shoes of the genuine early Irish pattern.

singular "lance: passage following St. Matthew xxvii. 48. An account of these readings is given by Mr. Henry Monck Mason in the "Transactions of the Royal Irish Academy." The manuscript was preserved until the dissolution of monasteries, in the Abbey of Roscrea, of which St. Cronan was the founder.

The MEESHAC or Miosach, another remarkable Cumhdach, or metal covering of a sacred volume, also formerly in the possession of Sir W. Betham, and described and figured in the first part of his "Irish Antiquarian Researches," afterwards came into the possession of the Duke of Sussex, at whose decease it was sold with his library and effects, and was ultimately presented by Lord Adare to the College of St. Columba at Rathfarnham.

The groups of Ecclesiastics repeated four times on the cover, as well as the four representations of the seated and crowned Virgin Mary, with the crowned Child on her knees, have apparently been cast in moulds. The date of the inscription, in *Gothic text*, which Sir W. Betham read "ao dõni ccccciii." (A.D. 503), is clearly to be read "aº. do. m. ccccciii." (A.D. 1503).—See Dr. Todd's article in "Proc. Roy. Irish Academy," v. p. 461.

THE PSALTER OF ST. JOHN'S COLLEGE, CAMBRIDGE.

Plate XXX.

THE manuscript from which the three illuminations given in this plate are taken, is one of the most remarkable hitherto described. It contains the Psalter and Canticles, written in a moderate-sized Hiberno-Saxon hand, with illuminated capitals, and with three most singular miniatures, two representing scenes of the Victories of David, and the third the Crucifixion, of which I published a fac-simile in my "Palæographia sacra," which Mr. Ruskin has republished as the rudest specimen of pictorial art which he had ever seen.

The volume is a large octavo, the lines written entirely across the page, with many contractions, in a semi-uncial or rounded minuscule hand, apparently by an Irish scribe (there being some few Irish and many Latin glosses covering the blank spaces of the pages). It stands in the catalogue of the MSS. of St. John's College, under the number C. 9, and is merely described as a "Psalter written about the year 800, very much glossed about the year 1200." It is very difficult to fix the date of the small handwriting of the glosses found in Irish manuscripts, but I should be inclined to regard the volume as written after the middle, rather than in the early part, of the ninth century, if, indeed, it be not referrible to the tenth century, as the later style of the initial letters seems to indicate.

The 1st Psalm, "Beatus vir," as well as the 51st Psalm, "Quid gloriaris," and totst. "Dne exaudi orationem meam," have larger initials than the other Psalms, and are enclosed in ornamental borders: the first and third of these are copied in the middle compartment of my Plate 30, the large initials being formed of strangely convoluted animals, with their limbs and tails wonderfully interlaced. The ornaments in the compartments of the borders throughout the volume are rather coarsely designed and executed. The curious spiral ornament is wanting. The initial Q of the Psalm "Quid gloriaris" is large, and exactly like the same letter in the Psalter of Ricemarchus, published in my "Palaeographia." In this manner the Psalter is divided into three nearly equal portions: in which respect also the last-named Psalter agrees with the one before us. Here, contrary to the usual plan of writing the Canticles at the end of the Psalms, they are interpolated at the end of each of the three divisions, and several short prayers are also added to the text.

The three miniatures are placed at the head of the three divisions of the Psalter, the Crucifixion facing the 51st Psalm. This miniature is reproduced and fully described in my "Palaeographia sacra." It is evidently by the same hand, and in the same rude style, as the two other miniatures represented in my 30th Plate; the three being very similar in style (although clearly by a different hand) to the two miniatures of David contained in the Cottonian MS. Vitellius, F. XI. In one of these two miniatures David is represented as having just discharged the stone from his sling against Goliah, who holds up his hand to protect his face; but in the miniature now before us, occupying the left-hand division of my plate, Goliah is overcome, head downwards, the artist not being able to express, nor the space allowing, the giant to be represented as fallen to the ground. The staff which David holds in his hand is much longer than in the Vitellius miniature; the circular shield of Goliah is intended to be represented as lying on the ground, the hand being raised to the head when the fatal wound was received.

The other miniature, occupying the right-hand division of my plate, is evidently intended as an attempt to delineate David's exploit with the Lion (1 Samuel xvii. 34, 35, and 36); but there is no authority in the sacred text for the introduction of the quaint little figure laying hold of the tail of the sheep or ram, rather than a lamb. It would, I think, be impossible, in the whole range of Christian art, to meet with more extraordinary examples of rude conventionalism and design than are afforded by the two drawings before us.

THE COTTONIAN PSALTER, VITELLIUS, F. XI.

Plate LI. figs. 5 and 6.

THIS copy of the Latin Psalter was unfortunately greatly injured in the Cottonian fire, but has been carefully repaired and mounted. It is of the octavo form, written in Hiberno-Saxon semiuncial characters, with slightly illuminated initials (the large initial of the 1st Psalm being greatly injured), its most remarkable feature consisting of two miniatures of David, precisely in the style of the drawings in the St. John's College

Psalter, described in the preceding notice, although probably by a different hand. Unfortunately the fragments are so singed and blackened that it has been with the utmost difficulty, and only with the aid of a magnifying-glass and by holding the pages in different lights, that I have been able to make out the lines of the figures; whereas the beautiful patterns of the ornamental borders (omitted in my Plate 51, but in the same style of ribbon and Z-like patterns, but wider and more carefully executed than those in the Cambridge Psalter, copied in my 30th Plate) are more easily determined by the colours, which have better withstood the action of the fire.

The first of these drawings (fig. 5) represents the combat between David and Goliah, the former of whom holds in his left hand his short shepherd's crook, terminated appropriately in a dog's head, whilst in his right hand, suspended from the little finger, he holds one end of his sling, from which he has just discharged a circular stone, which is seen about to strike the head of Goliah. (The late Mr. Eugene Curry informed me that a discussion had been carried on in the pages of *Saunders' News Letter* respecting the nature of the Irish sling. Mr. Clibborn, considering it to have been nothing else than a stick cleft at the end. The drawing before us will set the question at rest. The Anglo-Saxon Cottonian MS. Claudius, B. IV., of the tenth century, also contains the figure of a man using a sling of nearly similar form, copied by Strutt in his "Horda," plate xvii. fig. 4, and "Sports and Pastimes.") The drawing of the giant, although very rude, is expressive. By figuring him kneeling upon one knee, the artist has contrived to introduce him as of larger size into the picture; whilst this attitude, combined with his closed eye and his hand held up to protect the face, indicate his fear of the coming stone. He wears a conical helmet; his beard is long and plaited, and he carries a small circular shield, ornamented with concentric rings, variously coloured. Across the middle of his body is apparently a representation of plate-armour, indicated by rows of round rivet-heads. As a representation of a Celtic warrior of the ninth or tenth century, the drawing is very valuable, from the great rarity of such illustrations in early Irish art.

The other drawing (fig. 6) represents David playing on the harp, and will be equally interesting to the Irish antiquary, as one of the earliest pictorial representations of that favourite instrument, the form of which is very curious, being of an oblong form, resting apparently on a narrow stand, with one of the upper angles rounded off, the other terminating in a dog's head biting the tail of another dog, which forms the outer portion of the instrument. It is furnished with twelve strings, although there are only seven pegs represented, round which they are fastened at the top. The long plaited and curled hair, the long moustaches and the pointed beard,* the stiff arm and hand, the strangely attenuated body and diminutive feet of the Psalmist will be noticed, as well as the curious seat, seen sideways, formed of an animal with a long neck (of which other instances have already been given in this book).

In Plate 51, fig. 9, I have reproduced a small group of Ecclesiastics, carved in metal-work, on the Cumhdach or cover of the small Stow Missal. One of these figures holds the short pastoral staff or cambutta; another a small sacred hand-bell, whilst between them is an attendant harper, surmounted by the winged bust of an Angel. I presume this to be a work of the seventh or eighth century.

---

* By way of comparison, I have placed the miniature of the Betrayal of Christ, in the Book of Kells, in postposition with this drawing. (See Plate 51, fig. 1.)   It will be seen that the two Jews in the former have similar moustaches and beards.

THE PSALTER OF ST. OUEN, ROUEN.

THIS very remarkable MS. now in the Public Library of Rouen, contains the Latin Psalter of the Gallican version and that made by St. Jerome from the Hebrew, written in parallel columns, with a multitude of glosses written in very minute Irish characters.

The initial letter of each Psalm is about an inch and a half high, elegantly formed of black interlaced and knotted strokes, and terminating in dogs' heads. Of these beautiful letters, an extensive series is given by the Benedictines in the second volume of the " N. Tr. de Diplomatique," as also by Messrs. Silvestre and Champollion in their " Palæographie universelle." Specimens of the text are also given in these works, as well as in my " Palæographia." By the French authors above named the volume was referred to the seventh or eighth century. From its close similarity to the Psalter of Ricemarchus and some other nearly contemporary MSS. executed in this country, I infer that it is probably not earlier than the tenth century.

THE PSALTER OF RICEMARCHUS.

IN the Library of Trinity College, Dublin, is contained a small copy of the Latin Psalter (not written in the Gallican version commonly employed in England in the tenth and eleventh centuries) executed, as appears by some autograph verses at the end, by Ricemarchus, Bishop of St. David's, in the latter half of the eleventh century, facsimiles of which are given in my " Palæographia sacra," as well as in an article which I published, containing a more detailed description of the MS., in the first volume of the " Archæologia Cambrensis."

It is written in Hiberno-Saxon minuscule letters, each Psalm commencing with an ornamental capital letter about two inches high, formed of black strokes, elegantly interlaced, terminating in dogs' heads, and surrounded entirely with red dots. The initials of the 1st, 51st (Quid gloriaris), and 101st Psalms (Dñe exaudi) are of a considerably larger size, the whole of the first verse of each of these Psalms occupying an entire page, surrounded with borders formed of rudely interlacing lacertine animals, the borders themselves terminating above in the large head of an animal, and the lower end of the border ending in the hind legs and tail of the creature. Red, yellow, and green are the only colours used, the lines of capital letters in which the page is written being inscribed on yellow bars, the spaces between the lines being coloured green. The volume is destitute of miniatures.

THE PSALTER OF KING ORWIN.

AMONGST the Cottonian MSS. almost destroyed in the deplorable fire of 1731, was a small copy of the Psalter (Galba, A. 5) described by Casley, 130 years ago, as written in the Irish hand, 900 years old, which is recorded in the early catalogues of the Cottonian Library as having belonged to a King Orwin. It is written in very small characters, with a vast number of contractions, the initial letters of each verse daubed with red and yellow, and with the initials of each Psalm about an inch high, in the style of those of the Psalter of Ricemarchus, but much less elaborate. I have given a fac-simile of it in my "Palæographia," Irish Biblical MSS., plate 1, fig. 3; and regard it as a production of the eleventh or twelfth century.

THE PSALTER OF THE MONASTERY OF ST. ISIDORE.

THE Irish Monastery of St. Isidore at Rome possesses a certain number of MSS. of Irish origin, amongst which I found the fragments of a Psalter which, in its original state, must have been one of the finest of the later works of the Irish scribes. It is of a folio size, and the text is written throughout in letters a quarter of an inch high. It is much glossed throughout with notes in minuscule characters, and the initials of each Psalm are of an enlarged size, corresponding with the text, and in the style of those of the Psalter of Ricemarchus, with the open spaces filled in with patches of red, yellow, green, and purple colours. I presume it may be referred to the eleventh or twelfth century.

THE STOW MISSAL.

IN the "Bibliotheca Stowensis," and "Scriptores Rerum Hibernicarum Veteres," Mr. O'Conor described and illustrated another small Irish manuscript, containing a copy of the Latin Gospel of St. John, and a Missal according to the service of the early Irish Church, now with the rest of the Stow collection in the Library of Lord Ashburnham, which, from the style of its writing and illuminations, appears nearly contemporary with the Gospels of Mac Durnan. It measures only 5 inches by 4, and contains a full-length figure of St. John, entirely like the drawings in the last-mentioned volume, with the head and wings of the Eagle occupying the space above the head of the Evangelist, who holds a book in both naked hands against his breast : his feet are naked. The figure is enclosed in a frame ornamented with interlaced ribbons and the diagonal Z-pattern, as is also the first page of the Gospel, with the " I N P(rincipio)" occupying the whole length of the page, and ornamented at top and bottom with knots terminating in the rudely-drawn heads of dogs.

The Missal commences with the "Peccavimus dñe peccavimus, parce peccatis nostris," &c., as in one of the St. Gall MSS. described above, the P, of a square form, with the tail extending the whole length of the left side of the page, whilst the other sides are enclosed in a border filled in with interlaced dragon-patterns, and terminating at the top in the head, and at the bottom in the hind legs and tail, of an animal ; the initial P is ornamented with lozenge-shaped yellow and red compartments, and the open centre is filled in with a diagonal pattern.

THE BOOK OF DEIR, CO. ABERDEEN.

Plate LI. figs. 2 and 3.

ATTENTION has only recently been directed to this curious little volume (preserved in the University Library of Cambridge, numbered I. i. vi. 32), by Mr. Bradshaw, the present lynx-eyed librarian. It is of a small but rather wide 8vo. form, and contains the Gospel of St. John, with portions only of the three other Gospels, in Latin, together with a short Office for the Visitation of the Sick, in an Irish hand, and several grants, written in blank spaces of the volume, to the monastery of Deir, founded by Columba and Drostan, who came thither from Iona, towards the end of the sixth century, and concerning both of whom there is a legend in the volume, in connection with the Abbey of Deir. These grants are not earlier than the middle of the twelfth century, but the Gospels are written in a fine Hiberno-Saxon minuscule character, which may be ascribed to the ninth century, and not very unlike the Bodleian Cædmon (Astle, tab. xix. fig. viii.).

The initial letter of each Gospel is alone enlarged and ornamented with patches of different colours, being about two inches high, the ends of the principal strokes of the letters terminating in dogs' heads, somewhat in the style of the letters in the Psalter of St. Ouen, and especially like the initials given in my 1st Plate of Irish Biblical MSS., No. 4, from the Harleian Gospels 1802, and in my 2nd Plate, No. 5 of the "Palæographia sacra." These pages, as well as the miniatures in the volume, are surrounded by ornamental borders, chiefly formed of rudely-interlaced ribbons, and with some modifications of the Z-patterns, both in the lozenge and rectangular forms. Mr. Stuart, amongst the illustrations to the second volume of his "Sculptured Stones of Scotland," has given fac-similes of not fewer than eight of the ornamental pages of this volume. One of these, from the last leaf of the volume, with four quaint little figures, is copied in my Plate, 51. fig. 3 ; and another miniature, not published by Mr. Stuart, representing St. Mark, is copied in my fig. 2. These comprise the whole of the drawings in the volume.

The figure of St. Matthew (Stuart, ii. plate 5) is a standing figure, in the style of those of the Gospels of Mac Durnan, &c., with the beard of moderate length, divided into four points, the feet naked, and the right hand holding a sword of very unusual form, turned downwards, the point of the scabbard resting between the feet. The handle of the sword is guarded not only in front of the hand (as in Hewitt's "Ancient Armour," p. 33, figs. 9, 10, and 11), but also behind the hand, the guards being curved, but reversed; the scabbard itself appears at first sight, owing to the curved border of the dress, to be shod at the end like Hewitt's fig. 2, p. 32. The Sword is a rare symbol of St. Matthew, but it is given as such in Eusenbeth's lists of the Emblems of the Saints. On either side of the head of the Saint is a small figure, possibly intended for an angel. St. Mark is represented in my 2nd figure. St. Matthew, in the Gospels of St. Boniface, represented in my 4th figure of the same Plate 51, is really well drawn as compared with this St. Mark, of which the most noticeable feature is the object held to the breast like a casket, which may represent a book in an ornamental binding suspended from the neck, with the Cumhdach or case in which it is preserved (of which the Missal of Corpus Christi College, Oxford, is an example). I need scarcely add that the Book is a very constant adjunct to the figure of the Evangelist in these early drawings, as seen in many of my plates.

Mr. Paley, on the contrary, describes this ornament as "a rather large square apparel, or rationale, suspended from the neck by three strings." I presume the two curved bars extending from the cheeks to the middle of this ornament are intended for the arms of the Saint, the hands being covered; whilst the two large oval parts of the dress marked with a cross may represent the looped-up sides of a garment, possibly a chasuble. St. Luke, however (fol. 29, v.), is represented like St. Mark, but has in addition a pair of arms thrown upwards from the upper angles of the book or rationale, and then extending outwards, so as to pass through and beyond the side borders of the frame. St. John is also represented in the same manner as St. Mark, with the addition of a small cross between his feet, and with three quaint little figures on each side (like those in the upper part of my Plate 51, fig. 3), and with a marginal little sketch of a dog, and a quaint little outline flourish, forming a series of leaves.

My fig. 3 represents the recto of the last folio, 86, and is probably intended to represent two of the Evangelists, with two Angels (being analogous to the tessellated pages of the Books of Lindisfarne, &c.), whilst a similar composition, the centre formed of a six-leaved rosette, occupies the verso of the first folio. At the end of St. John (folio 84, verso) is also a group of two of these Evangelists (?), and on the verso of the following folio (85 v.) is a group of four of these figures (without books), two with uplifted and one with outstretched arms, the fourth without arms. Quaint little flourishes resembling fern-leaves, and small animals and birds, occupy many of the open spaces and margins of the pages.

The following observations by Mr. Paley on the dress of these curious representations of the Evangelists will be read with interest, although it may be doubted whether the portion referring to the supposed apparel or rationale is not unfounded:—"Assuming that the dress of all these figures is meant to represent the chasuble, considerable interest must attach to a representation, however rude, of the vestments worn by a Gaelic priest in the ninth century. If, as is probable, the chasuble was derived from the toga,—which is indicated by the original circular form of both, the appearance of the rounded ends over the knees would be accounted for. The collar, or rather the neck-folds, seem to be most ample, and quite unlike any fashion that we are acquainted with in the Middle Ages. The square apparel on the breast is the most characteristic and well-marked feature of these portraits. It is described by Dr. Rock in his 'Hierurgia,' [and also in the 'Church of our Fathers,' i. 369, where several figures are given of it from 13th and 14th century illustrations;] and is evidently the origin, combined with the broad strip or orphrey down the middle of the peaked chasuble, of the large cross now worn on the back, but formerly on the front of the officiating priest. In some early incised slabs, especially those existing in the Churches of Rome, this combination is very clearly seen. The broad strip itself was the laticlave of the Romans: this was a purple border extending down the breast of the tunica, and worn as a badge of distinction by senators and certain priests. In allusion to its position, Juvenal says "latum demisit pectore clavum." From the symbolical and cross-like form produced by the combination of orphrey and rationale, it was found convenient and appropriate to exhibit it on the side more conspicuous to the people, i.e. the back of the celebrant priest. This latter device is, however, comparatively modern, and there seems to be no precedent for it in any representations of ancient art."—*Paley*, p. 486.

The first seventeen verses of St. Matthew's Gospel are treated as a prologue, followed by the inscription " Finit prologus. Item incipit nunc Euangelium secundum Matheum."

At the end of St. Mark's Gospel is the fragment of a Mass of the Gallican family, as published by Mabillon, commencing " Item or. alia an(te) dominicam orationem. Corpus cum sanguine dñi nri ihu xpi sanitas sit tibi i vitam perpetuam et salutem," &c. This Missa infirmorum has been published by Mr. Paley (*Home and For. Rev.*, i. 482), and by Bishop Forbes in his " Liber Ecclesie de Arbuthnott."

At the end of St. John's Gospel is also inscribed the "Credo" entire, occupying sixteen lines, followed by three lines of Gaelic, being a short prayer, of which the following is a translation:—" Be it on the conscience of every man to whom shall be any advantage from this book, to pray for a blessing upon the soul of the wretch who wrote it."

The whole of the pages containing Gaelic inscriptions in the volume, several of them with drawings, including the legend of Columbkille and Drostan, and the Latin Charter of King David (A.D. 1120—1156), have just been published in fac-simile by the photo-lithographic process of Sir W. James, at the head of the national work on the Historical Documents of Scotland. They were also printed, with translations, by Mr. Stokes, in the *Saturday Review* for 8th December, 1860, the language of the former being considered as identical with the oldest Irish Glosses in Zeuss's " Grammatica Celtica."

Martyrii Campo ubi S. Bonifacius archiepiscopus cum sociis gloriose occubuit, manus fidelium recollegerunt ac in Sacrarium Fuldense deportarunt."

These three MSS. are in three different characters. One is of Italian origin, containing portion of the New Testament, written in narrow uncials, and corrected by Victor, Bishop of Capua, in the year A.D. 546, as appears by an autograph note.—(See fac-similes in " N. Tr. de Diplom.," iii. plates 34, 45, and 57.) It is without illuminations.

The second is of Lombardic origin, and is written in cursive Lombard characters, containing a treatise of St. Isidore of Seville (N. Tr. de Diplom., plate 59, iv. 2), with ornamented initials, in which fishes are introduced in the genuine Lombardic style. This book is pierced, cut, and stained with the blood of the Apostle of North Germany.

The third is a small 8vo. volume, containing the four Gospels in a true Irish, very small minuscule, character, like that of the Gospels of St. Mulling (Pal. sacr.). The vellum is coarse, and each Gospel is preceded by a rude figure of the Evangelist : that of St. Matthew (with a style and book, copied in my Plate 51. fig. 4) resembling the figures of the Evangelists in the smaller Irish copies of the Gospels.

The curious verses on the Evangelists quoted above, from the Gospels of Mac Regol, are contained, with some verbal variations, in this volume, as quoted by Schannat.

At the end of the book is the following entry, in golden letters :—" Hoc Euangelium Sanctus Bonifacius martyr Domino gloriosus ut nobis seniorum relatione compertum est, propriis conscripsit manibus, quod etiam venerabilis Abba Huoggi obnixis precibus a rege piissimo Arnulfo impetravit et sancte Fuldensi Ædclesiæ honorabiliter restituit cui Salvator Jesu Christe premia sempiterna pro devotione sua in caelestibus elementer redde cumque nobis feliciter dominari tempora longa concede." It happens, however, unfortunately for this tradition, that the real scribe of the volume, Vidrug, has inscribed his name, in the ordinary Irish fashion, at the end of St. John's Gospel,—" Finit. Amen. Deo gratias ago. Vidrug scribsit." Moreover, it appears from one of the Epistles (the 3rd) of St. Boniface, that he could not read (scarcely less write) the " minutas et connexas" letters of the minuscule writing, and requested Daniel, Bishop of Winchester, to send him books " claris discretis et absolutis litteris scriptos." A fac-simile of the first page of St. Matthew is given by Schannat (Vindem. Liter.), and partly copied in " N. Tr. de Diplom.," iii. plate 59. VI. vi. p. 446.

[The celebrated GOSPELS OF ST. KILIAN, who was martyred in A.D. 687, stained with spots of blood, were found on opening his tomb in 743. They are now preserved with great veneration at the Cathedral of Wurtzburg, and are exposed on the high altar on the anniversary of the Saint's death, having an ivory carving and precious stones on the cover. The text is entirely written in narrow semi-uncial letters of true Italian character, without any ornament.—(See the first fac-simile in the " Chronicon Gotwicense," partly copied in the 3rd vol. of the " N. Tr. de Diplom.") It has been necessary to give this detail to prevent confusion with the blood-stained book of St. Boniface, and because Mr. Petrie, by some accident, has stated that the volume is adorned with designs similar to those of our Irish manuscripts (Cromlech on Howth, p. 18).]

A SMALL copy of the Latin Gospels, written in a small Irish minuscule character, was for many ages preserved with religious veneration in its metal covering, or Cumhdach, described in Vallancey's "Collectanea," under the name of the LEATH MEASICITH and LEATH FIAL, or the Stone of Destiny, by the family of Kavanagh, by one of whom it was presented to Trinity College, Dublin. The covering is ornamented with very large crystals, but without any chased figures. On one of the blank pages at the end of St. Matthew's Gospel the scribe has written a small Office for the Visitation of the Sick, of which a careful reading has been published by Bishop Forbes (in the "Liber Ecclesie de Arbuthnott").

The volume being described in my "Palæographia sacra," I need here only state that the initial letters of each Gospel are neatly executed, about two or three inches high, in the style of those of the Book of Armagh, without colours, and surrounded by double rows of red dots. There are three figures of the Evangelists, drawn nearly in the style of the Gospels of Mac Durnan, each holding a book with the left hand against the breast; two also supporting the book with the right hand; whilst the third dips a pen into an inkstand by his right side. Each figure has a circular nimbus, and one with long flowing hair, hanging in outstretched curls over the shoulders, as in the Gospels of Mac Durnan. In two the feet are naked; but the third wears shoes, extending upwards over the instep and heel. There is no Evangelical symbol; so that it is impossible to appropriate these figures to the respective Gospels.

In two of the figures the outer garment hangs in tolerably well-arranged folds over the left arm. Each is about five inches high, and is surrounded by the usual interlaced ribbon and dragon-like borders rudely executed.

At the end of St. John's Gospel the scribe has written a precatory note, terminating "Nomen autem Scriptoris Mulling dicitur : finiunt quatuor euangelia."

St. Moling, who was Bishop of Ferns at the beginning of the seventh century, has been supposed to be identified with the scribe who thus writes his name Mulling.

The Cumhdach also contained portion of another copy of the Gospel of St. Mark, with the Epistle of St. Jerome to Pope Damasus, the Eusebian Canons, Prefaces to the Gospels, &c.

THE HARLEIAN GOSPELS, Nos. 1802 AND 1023.

THESE are two small Irish copies of the Latin Gospels, which have been the subjects of much discussion, the former having by some writers been referred to the ninth or tenth century, but which is now clearly proved by a number of historical facts recorded in notes on the blank pages of the book by the original scribe, to have been written in the year 1138. A detailed account of the peculiarities of these two MSS. is given in my "Palæographia sacra," so that it will not be necessary here to allude further than to their artistic elements. They are certainly of great interest, as proving how late the genuine Irish style of writing and ornamentation was retained in Ireland; since, were it not for the historical evidence contained in the former volume, it would, from the style of its execution, be assigned to the ninth or tenth century; there is in fact great similarity between the text and that of the Gospels of Mac Durnan. The initials are like those of the pages found in the Cumhdach of St. Mulling's Gospels, the open spaces of the initials being daubed with plain patches of red, yellow, green, and purple colours, slightly separated from each other by curved or straight lines. The Evangelists are replaced by their symbols, the Lion (of a very conventional character) in the MS. 1802 being copied in my "Palæographia," in which work a fac-simile is given of the commencement of St. Mark's Gospel, with its initial letter; whilst the beginning of St. John's Gospel, and the entry at the end, are carefully given in fac-simile by Mr. Purton Cooper, in Appendix A to his Report.

The figures of the symbols of St. Matthew and St. John are wanting in the MS. 1802, and only the Lion and the Eagle are represented, very rudely, in No. 1023, in which the initials are very poor.

A careful description of the former MS. has been published by the Rev. Dr. Reeves, in the "Proceedings of the Royal Irish Academy," vol. v., January, 1851. This volume was formerly in the National Library of Paris, whence it was stolen by the villain Aymon, and sold to the Earl of Oxford.

THE RED BOOK OF THE PEAK.

THIS curious volume is preserved in the Library of Corpus Christi College, Cambridge, and is of a thick 8vo. size, in which is inserted the following note, in a comparatively modern hand:—

     "The rede boke of Badge in the Peake in Darbyshire.—This booke was sometime had in such reverence in Darbieshire, that it was commonly beleved that whosoever should sweare untruche upon this booke should run madd.*"

It contains a fragment of the Anglo-Saxon Dialogues between Solomon and Saturn, written in a very ancient hand, in Anglo-Saxon verses, many of which are marked with certain characters which have been described as Runic letters, together with a number of early musical notes, or neumes.

It also contains a more recent Latin Pontificale, or, rather, "Missa," written, as would appear from the prefixed Paschal Table, in the year 1081, together with a Calendar and several curious illuminations.

* Sir Davies, "Iron. Ideall," p 189.

THE IRISH GOSPELS OF CORPUS CHRISTI COLLEGE, OXFORD.

THIS beautifully-written MS. measures 8½ inches by 6, and bears the number 122. It contains not only the four Latin Vulgate Gospels entire, but also the Preface of St. Jerome, "Novum opus," &c., together with the Eusebian Canons, inscribed on eight pages at the beginning of the volume, within plain rounded arches. The writing is evidently that of an Irish scribe of the eleventh or twelfth century, and abounds in contractions; together with a scheme, or table, inscribed, ".Mea Evangelii, quam Dubinsi Episcopus Bennchorensis detulit a rege Anglorum, id est a domu Adalstani, regis Anglorum, depicta a quodam Francone et a Romano sapiente, id est, irit."

Each Gospel commences with a large illuminated initial letter, occupying portion of the upper part of the page (that of St. John having been abstracted). The L, IN, and Q, initials of the three other Gospels, are formed of elongated animals, the bodies of which are coloured in patches of blue and lilac, with tails and topknots coloured yellow, forming a succession of interlaced knots all round the letter, upon a red ground. This interlacement is by no means so regular and delicate as in the earlier Codices, and somewhat resembles that of the initials of the Psalter of Ricemarchus. The remaining letters of the first line in each Gospel are about a quarter of an inch long, with patches of red, blue, and yellow. The manuscript is curious for having the initial letter of the 17th verse of the 1st chapter of St. Matthew, "Omnes ergo generationes," ornamented, being transformed into the head of an Angel with great staring eyes, and a large pair of wings extending below the letter. The "Xpi autem generatio sic" is also more elegantly ornamented, the X being 2½ inches high, with the interlaced and spiral patterns, having a human face quaintly introduced into one of the whorls; the remainder of the line elegantly written in large Hiberno-Saxon minuscule letters, with the open spaces coloured with patches of red, yellow, blue, and purple. The initial of the Preface of St. John's Gospel (fol. 103, v.) is of the minuscule shape, and formed into a purple dog, with a wonderfully elongated and knotted yellow tail, on a red ground.

Mr. George Waring, who carefully compared the readings of this manuscript with those of the Gospels of Mac Regol, thus speaks of the former, which he considers to have been written circa 1100:—"From the later copy of the Gospels the more barbarous forms of spelling and grammar have disappeared; omissions have been supplied and interpolations weeded out: the text had evidently undergone considerable recension since the days of Mac Regol, yet without entire sacrifice of the national characteristics of this distinct and remarkable class of MSS."—Proleg., iv. lxii.

THE IRISH MISSAL OF CORPUS CHRISTI COLLEGE, OXFORD.

THIS curious volume measures 6½ inches by 5, and is of great bulk, owing to the size of the writing, of which there are only eighteen lines on a page. It is of Irish origin, and may possibly be assigned to the twelfth or thirteenth century, having many characteristics in common with the Gospels in the same library last described. It bears the number 282, and contains the office of the Mass, the first page being occupied by a gigantic "Per omnia," contracted and formed into a mass of rude interlaced work, now so obscured and blackened by use as to be with difficulty followed. The "Vere dignum" occupies part of the verso of the first leaf, and the "Te igitur" the recto of the second; the initial letters, formed, as they are throughout the volume, of monstrous animals, generally coloured in purple patches, with elongated yellow tongues, tails, and topknots, forming a great variety of knot-work upon a red ground, of which the outline generally follows the curve of the initials, without any edge-line or other circumscribing margin. These initials are very coarse, both in their design and execution; every prayer commencing with a moderately enlarged and coloured initial.

On the reverse of fol. 7 commences a "Missa de S. Trinitate," on fol. 12 a "Missa de S. Maria," with Prayers for the Dead, &c.; and on the 43rd folio the "Officium Missae," with Prayers, Lessons, &c., for the whole course of the year.

The outer leaves of the MS. are blackened by use; portions of its original wooden covers remain, polished by long wear; and the volume is preserved in its original black leather satchel, of which the front was ornamented with diagonally impressed lines and circles, now nearly obliterated by constant use. At the upper angles are affixed the strong leather straps, fastened with leather ties to a broader central strap, which passed over the shoulders, so that the volume thus suspended offered no trouble to the priest in his long peregrinations, of which its worn state affords most abundant evidence.

came into the possession of the latter from his connexion with the Emperor Otho. The character of the writing of the portion of the volume containing the Psalter supports such an opinion, being written in elegant Caroline minuscule characters. The Calendar, however, at the beginning of the volume, with the Rules for finding Easter, Lunar Tables, &c., is written in small early Anglo-Saxon characters, one of the rules for finding "quotus sit annus incarnationis Dni" being calculated for the year 703. At the end of the volume is also a series of short Prayers (one for each Psalm), written in similar characters. A series of fac-similes of the different handwritings employed in this little Psalter, including the beautiful initial of the first Psalm, is given in my "Palæographia sacra," in which the other peculiarities of the volume are detailed.

On the second leaf of the volume has been affixed a beautiful fifteenth-century miniature of a king kneeling to the Creator, who appears in the clouds. This miniature is probably intended for King David, and there is reason to suppose that it was placed in its present position by Sir R. Cotton, by whose orders the inscription, "Psalterium Regis Athelstani," was written in gold capitals on a blue ground. It is also probable that, like the miniature introduced from the Psalter of King Henry VI. into Athelstan's Coronation Oath Book (as suggested in my "Palæographia," and subsequently proved to have been the fact), this miniature of King David was also derived from the Henry VI. Psalter.

The verso of this second leaf is occupied with the miniature of Christ seated in Glory, holding a book in his left hand, with the right hand extended downwards and open. To the back of the chair, or throne, on which is a cushion in the Byzantine style, are attached the Cross, Spear, and Sponge, as implements of the Passion, the latter represented like a bunch of large grapes. A choir of Angels, with the bodies bent in the attitude of veneration, occupies the upper angles of the miniature; one of the Angels holding a blue vase, from which apparently four blue flames are emitted, possibly intended for a censer. The Saviour is young and beardless, and has a plain (not cruciferous) nimbus, as have also the Angels. Below are two rows of busts, the two principal figures offering a lamb and what appears to be intended for a cornucopia, being the first-fruits of the earth and of the flock. These represent the "Chorus Prophetarum;" whilst below are grouped the full-length figures of the twelve Apostles, nimbed, the head of the Virgin Mary occupying the centre of the group; whilst St. Paul, aged, and St. Peter, tonsured, and his garment marked apparently with the letters E (reversed) and R (being the monogrammic manner in which the wards of the two keys of St. Peter were occasionally represented, to form the letters PETR), occupy the centre of the group; the angles of the drawing are ornamented with lions' heads. The outlines of this little drawing are rude, and formed by thick strokes of a pen; and the colours, except the blue, dull, heavy, and opaque.

The other drawing of the Saviour seated in glory, within an oval pointed "Vesica piscis," occupies the 21st leaf. Here our Lord holds the Cross in his left hand, with naked feet, and with his dress opened to show the wound in his side. He has a cruciferous nimbus and long flowing grey hair, but without any beard. His right hand is open and extended upwards: on either side are the letters A and ω. The Saviour is surrounded by a great number of heads, representing the choruses of Martyrs and Confessors: many of the former are tonsured; and two groups of female busts, representing the "Chorus Virginum." The angles are filled in with four Angels; whilst the upper angles of the frame terminate in heads, and the lower in conventional foliage.

The 120th leaf is occupied by the drawing of the Ascension (Ascensio DNI), copied in the upper right-hand portion of my plate. Here the Saviour—very young in appearance, with long flowing hair and naked feet, the head surrounded by a cruciferous nimbus—is seated on a cushion within an oval space, supported by two Angels; the middle of the picture is occupied by two other Angels, half-hidden by clouds, who direct the attention of the "VIRI *galilei*" and "Maria" to the rising Saviour. The Virgin here occupies the centre of the group, separated from her companions by neatly-drawn plants.

In the upper left-hand part of my plate I have given a fac-simile of another drawing of the "NATivitas Xri," pasted as a single leaf into the MS., "Rawlinson, B. 484," in the Bodleian Library (being a collection of Irish paper documents), to which my attention was obligingly directed by the Rev. W. Macray, one of the Librarians, and which I immediately recognized as a companion to the "Ascensio Dni" in the Athelstan Psalter. The Virgin is reclining on a couch. The "Præsepe Dni" has rather the appearance of a temple than a manger, the heads of the ox and ass alone giving it that character; whilst "Joseph" is seated on the left side, regarding the Virgin. Although the Child is seen "wrapped in swaddling-clothes" in the upper part of the picture, he is again represented in the lower part as being washed in a large vase, into which one of the females pours water. Besides the same style of drawing and identical size of the frames of the two pictures, the minute and beautifully-formed capitals, inscribed in different parts of both, will be seen to be unquestionably by the same hand.

It will, I think, be evident that the two miniatures in the upper part of my plate are by a different hand to the two lower ones, even if the latter are not also by two different artists, which appears to me most probable. The designs in the upper drawings are entirely Byzantine in their treatment; but the small descriptive capitals, especially the angulated S, are apparently of Anglo-Saxon origin: the long-tailed A is, however, very rarely seen in Anglo-Saxon writing.

The twelve Zodiacal signs represented in my plate, occur at the heading of the respective months in the Calendar at the beginning of the volume, and were unquestionably executed by Anglo-Saxon artists. At the foot of the different pages of the Calendar are also introduced small figures, probably of personages introduced into the Calendar, one of whom, representing an ecclesiastic, is given in my "Palæographia sacra."

It will at once be perceived that the drawings before us exhibit a character of art quite unlike that of any of the specimens described in the preceding pages of this work. In the middle of the ninth century, in fact, the influence of the artists of the schools of Charlemagne became evident in the productions of England; for although many of those schools were presided over by Alcuin and other Anglo-Saxon learned men, yet the more frequent communication with Rome necessarily led to a higher appreciation of classical art, and to the decline of those rude notions of design, of which the most striking examples have already been laid before the student in this work and in my "Palæographia sacra;" and, at the same time, to the adoption of a more realistic treatment of the human figure, as well as to a more general adoption of foliage as an element of ornamental design; indeed, after the ninth or first half of the tenth century, I have been unable to find any Anglo-Saxon MS. executed in the Lindisfarne or Irish style: although, as we have seen in some of the preceding descriptions, it remained for several centuries longer in use in Ireland, considerably modified however in its ornamental details, which exhibit but little of the extreme delicacy of the earlier productions.

THE MISSAL OF BISHOP LEOFRIC.

Plate XXXIII.

THIS interesting volume, now preserved in the Bodleian Library, No. 579, was presented to the Cathedral Church of Exeter by Leofric, the first Bishop, in the first half of the eleventh century. It is of a quarto size, and is described by Wanley in Hickes's Thesaurus as a " Missale vetus or Sacramentarium Gregorianum, with additions." The greater part of the volume, consisting of an older copy of the Sacramentarium, is written in a pure Caroline minuscule hand, with plain capitals about an inch high, and with four pages of the Canon of the Mass, beautifully ornamented in the Franco-Saxon style of the time of Charles the Bald, or the middle of the ninth or first half of the tenth century; the "Vere dignum" and the "Te igitur" occupying entire pages, each followed by a page with purple bars, on which the Mass is continued in golden minuscule writing.

The Calendar, Paschal Tables, &c., are more recent, and are fixed by the dates of the calculations to the year 960. This part is written in an elegant Anglo-Saxon hand; but there are many subsequent pages written in several distinct and very strongly-marked Anglo-Saxon characters. In this part of the manuscript are contained the four pages represented in my plate, which afford an excellent specimen of a style of art which was usual in Anglo-Saxon miniatures in the tenth and eleventh centuries, the figures consisting entirely of outlines in different colours, drawn with a pen with wonderful neatness and precision, and in which an elaborate folding of the drapery, which is represented as fluttering in a most unnatural manner, is perceived.

These four drawings have reference to Paschal calculations, as well as to computations of life and death. The left-hand drawing contains the figure of a large hand with outstretched fingers, inscribed "Dextera nam Dñi fulget cum floribus Paschæ," with two figures ingeniously introduced into the lower angles of the square, which is surrounded by a framework with foliated patterns, common in the later Anglo-Saxon drawings. The opposite page in my plate contains other Paschal calculations within two ornamental circles, one of which contains the bust of a priest, with the head tonsured, inscribed "DIONISIVS."

The two central figures allegorically represent Life and Death, the latter being inscribed MORS. The former of these, crowned and holding a cross as a sceptre, has entirely the conventional appearance of the Saviour, with the drapery folded and fluttering in the late Anglo-Saxon style, and is surmounted by six verses on the chances of life and death.[*]

> Collige per numerum quicquid cupis eou profundum
> Junge simul nonus feriam lunæmque diei
> Collectamque una summam per jura trigenos
> Quodque super fuerit rotulos discernet utrique
> Quos retinet vitæ res mea et mortis imago
> Si super fuerit vivet mortuus et infra

---

* Careful descriptions of the miniatures in this MS. are given by Dr Waagen, " Treasures of Art in England," vol. iii. pp. 49. 62.

The lower figure is a singular representation of Death, quite unlike the conventional treatment. The head is surmounted by a pair of horns, and the shoulders with a pair of wings, the ears flapping like leaves, whilst the hair of the head seems to be developed into six dragons; the elbows, knees, heels, fingers, and toes, are armed with spurs, and the breast and body clothed with shaggy hair. A precisely similar pair of drawings exist in the Cottonian Psalter Tiberius C. VI.*

INITIAL LETTERS FROM THE CODEX PSALTERII VOSSIANUS.

Plate XXXIV.

THIS beautifully written MS., preserved in the Bodleian Library, Oxford, numbered Junius 27, formerly belonged to the famous Anglo-Saxon scholar, Francis Junius, who procured it from Isaac Voss; whence it has obtained the name of the Codex Vossianus. It contains the Latin Psalter, preceded by the Calendar, and is written in an elegant Anglo-Saxon hand, with an Anglo-Saxon interlineary translation, apparently by the original scribe. By Wanley the volume is assigned to the time of King Athelstan. A fac-simile of the text is given in the first plate of Anglo-Saxon Psalters in my "Palæographia sacra," and I have in the accompanying plate collected a series of the most striking of the initial letters at the beginning of each of the Psalms, the volume containing no other miniatures or ornamental borders. The peculiar style of these initial letters, in which birds and monstrous animals or dragons are represented as biting each others' tails or bodies, and in which foliage is introduced in a very conventional manner, appears to have been a favourite one with the Anglo-Saxon artists of the tenth and eleventh centuries, as they occur in many manuscripts; such as the Lambeth Aldhelm, the Bodleian Cædmon, the Psalter of Salisbury Cathedral, and a fine MS. in the Library of Trinity College, Cambridge, &c.; but nowhere are they so elegantly drawn and coloured as in the manuscript before us. It is rarely that figures are introduced; but in one of those now before us, being the letter D, David's conflict with the lion is represented with considerable spirit; in another (d), the head of a monk, showing the tonsure, is introduced; whilst a squirrel and a bird, fairly drawn, are seen in other letters, b and d. It may be well to add that the initials represented in the two divisions of my plate are intended for

A A A		d I b
b B		d d
b D b		M g M
d d		I N K

* M. Denis, in his splendid edition of the "Imitation de Jésus Christ," published by Curmer, has given a very fine initial S of the tenth or eleventh century, from a Psalter formerly belonging to the Cathedral of Exeter, &c. "Notice," p. 32. No further reference is unfortunately given to the locality of this MS.

THE PSALTER OF SALISBURY CATHEDRAL.

Plate XXXV.

THE earliest manuscript in the Library of the Cathedral of Salisbury is a Psalter with the Gregorian Liturgy, having an Anglo-Saxon version evidently anterior to the time of Osmund, the first bishop, in the latter half of the eleventh century, from which Mrs Elstob transcribed some of the hymns, and from which the accompanying figures are copied. They are entirely drawn with a pen, and represent the signs of the Zodiac, executed with a certain amount of freedom, together with an entire page containing the commencement of the 119th Psalm, "Ad Dominum cum tribularer clamavi et exaudivit me." The fine initial A has the body of the strokes formed of dragon-like animals, and is surmounted by a figure of the Saviour, with hands open and directed downwards in the attitude of compassionate attention, as indicated by the words, "Clamavi et exaudisti me." The columns, arch, and capitals enclosing the design are ornamented with conventional foliage of bold design, the columns resting on bases in which dragons are conjoined, and which also rest on the feet of animals.

The initials of the Calendar and of the Psalms are formed of birds and dragons, exactly in the style of those of the "Codex Psalterii Vossianus," although only in outline. The "Te decet hymnus" (Ps. lxiv. 1) commences with a dog standing on its hind legs, holding two dragons in its mouth, which form the top bar of the initial. The figure of the Bishop holding a cross and a book, copied in my plate, forms the initial of the 65th Psalm, "Iubilate Deo omnis terra;" the Anglo-Saxon gloss of the first three verses of which is as follows, the Saxon letters being here printed in ordinary type :—

1. Heriath God ealle eorthan Saln cwothath naman his; gifath wuldor lofe his.
2. Cwethath gode ba egeslice synd wuorc thine on manifaildnesse mæies thines leogath the fynd thine.
3. Ealle eorthan wyrthiath and singath the ——.

THE GREAT GOSPELS OF BOULOGNE.

Plate XXXVI.

AMONGST the many invaluable MSS. contained in the Public Library of Boulogne is a very large and fine copy of the Latin Gospels, with drawings executed by an Anglo-Saxon artist of a very unusual character, although in the style of the Benedictionals of St. Ethelwold and of Rouen, with which I consider it to be coeval.

J F

The text is written in a minuscule character of the Caroline type, in which the peculiar early Anglo-Saxon forms are lost, and which was much in use among the later Anglo-Saxon scribes. In the drawings gold-leaf has been employed to a considerable extent, which has in many places become tarnished.

The Eusebian Canons, written in columns, with arches boldly ornamented with various curious designs, precede the text. In one of these pages, containing the Canons of the four Evangelists, the text is enclosed in four rounded arches resting upon foliated capitals of a depressed form, above which arise four other arches springing from short columns and enclosing the four evangelical symbols, each with six wings, drawn in an extremely spirited manner. In another of the Canons the two rounded and two conical arches are surmounted by a large single arch, beneath which are drawn two archers, one discharging an arrow at a lion and the other at a stag, which is already wounded. The action of the hands of the archers is exactly portrayed, and the animals are drawn with great energy. In a third of the Canons two musicians are engaged playing on the harp and lyre.

The genealogy of Christ at the beginning of St. Matthew's Gospel is treated in a very remarkable manner; the various persons recorded in the genealogy up to Jacob are represented in rows, six in each row, under rounded arches, the head and upper part of the body of each being given. The features of these curious figures, as in the other drawings in this MS., are chiefly formed by fine red pen lines. The lower part of the same page is occupied with a fine drawing of the Annunciation of the Archangel Gabriel to the Virgin,— "Angelus intactæ cecinit properata Mariæ." Here the Virgin is seated, in front of a wide rounded arch, from which curtains are suspended; her head is surrounded by a golden nimbus; the attitude of attention is well expressed by the leaning forward of the body and the uplifted hands. The Angel stands to the left, facing the Virgin, holding a golden rod in his left hand, and with the right hand stretched out as in the act of benediction, whilst to the right is an open book, resting on a thin column. The figures are considerably larger, and the treatment far more natural, than in the same more carefully treated subject in the Benedictional of St. Ethelwold (Archaeologia, xxiv. plate 10). To the right of the picture, in a small compartment, is represented the Salutation of the Virgin and St. Elizabeth, both drawn in the curious humpbacked position of the Angels in my Plate 36.

The Gospels of SS. Luke and John are preceded by their full-length figures engaged in writing their Gospels, each enclosed in a framework, having ornamental rosettes in the angles, in the style of the Rouen Benedictionals, &c. These figures are boldly drawn and coloured, with the lights chiefly formed by the employment of white body-colour. St. Luke, seven inches in height, is seated on an architecturally-ornamented stool with a cushion; his right hand holds a quill pen with the web on both sides which he is dipping into an inkpot fixed at the side of the seat: he has a plain golden nimbus. The open spaces of the drawing are filled in with architectural accessories. My copy of this drawing especially attracted the attention of Dr. Waagen.

The curious drawing represented in my 36th Plate is intended for the commencement of the Gospel of St. John, the centre figure, with its ornamental top and bottom, being intended for the initial I. The Saviour is here represented seated within the "Vesica piscis," upon a rainbow, the upper part of the groundwork being inscribed with the Alpha and Omega, and studded with stars to represent Heaven, whilst the green lower part is probably intended for the earth. Here, as in the figures of the two attendant Angels, the many-folded and fluttering drapery is exactly treated as in the

Leofric Missal, &c. The ornamentation of the column with red foliage, and the bold interlacement of the top and bottom of the I, are especially to be noticed, as well as the elegant manner in which the lower fold is extended at the sides into dogs' heads with long tongues, and above into graceful foliage, serving as a base to the column. The Angels have the upper part of their bodies bent, almost as if humpbacked.

The inscription in fine golden capital letters of various sizes is to be read:—" PRINCIPIUM FINISQ. PATRIS VERBUM D(EU)S. HIC EST INITIUM SCI EVANGELII secundu(m) Iohanne(m) IN PRINCIPIO erat verbum et verbum erat;" the continuation of the Gospel being written on the reverse of the leaf, in fine uncial letters, with red patches, as represented in the lower part of my plate, the bottom line of small writing being the ordinary text of the volume. It will be seen that this passage, of the "Word made flesh," is throughout marked with peculiar characters, which are early musical notes or neumes, showing that the passage was sung in the service of the Church, and not read.

THE LAMBETH ALDHELM.

Plate XXXI.

THIS is a beautifully-written copy of a famous work in praise of virginity, by Aldhelm, the Anglo-Saxon Bishop of Sherburn, a prince of the royal family of Wessex, and the best poet of his age (A.D. 705), contained in the Archiepiscopal Library of Lambeth, No. 200, which was referred by Strutt to about the year 680, but which he must, I apprehend, have antedated by two or three centuries. It is of the quarto size, measuring 11 inches by 8, and is written in a fine Caroline minuscule hand, with very little trace of the Anglo-Saxon form of the letters ; the most peculiar letter being the r, which has the first stroke prolonged below the line, but the second forms only a small curve at the top of the line. The capital letters, however, in the inscriptions, exhibit several of the angular letters in use ; whilst the initials throughout the work are of great elegance, in the style of those of the Vossian Codex of the Psalms (Plate 34). Those contained in the lower portion of the right-hand division of my plate represent the letters A, Q, C, T, H, S, and M. The two lines of text are to be read, "IGITUR SI SCA VIRGINITATIS GLORIA ANGELICA beatitudinis germana erolitur et pulchra supernorum civium sodalitas," &c.

The first page of the manuscript, copied in the right-hand division of my plate, is exceedingly interesting, from the mixture of ornaments introduced into the borders and initial letter J. The central compartments are filled in with the oblique Chinese Z-like pattern of the older MSS., somewhat modified, and by no means so carefully drawn, as may be noticed in the upper compartment. The remainder of the border is an elegant arabesque, with birds and animals introduced into the whorls of the interlacing branches and foliage, in a very unusual manner in Anglo-Saxon MSS.; but of which a beautiful example occurs in the Great Psalter of Boulogne (Plate 38). The great initial J is divided into compartments, in which we perceive a strong similarity to the ornaments in the second border, copied in Plate 49, from the Arundel Psalter, No. 60.

The alternation of rows of red and green capitals in this title-page is also a comparatively late style of ornamentation.

The miniature at the head of my plate faces the first page of the text in the MS., and represents the Bishop seated on a curule chair, with dogs' heads and a cushion, presenting the volume to a company of nuns, several of whom, in the decorated hanging sleeves and the jewelled head-dresses, exhibit a love of finery which the bishop's treatise especially condemns. The figures are, although only in outline, spiritedly drawn, in the later Anglo-Saxon style, in which the fluttering drapery (especially shown in the right-hand figure) is to be observed, as well as the awkward, almost humpbacked, drawing of some of the females, as noticed in the Angels described in the last page.

Unfortunately the drawings in this MS. are only in outline, of which the ink has faded to a brown colour; and the one before us is the only miniature in the volume, which may, I apprehend, be safely referred to the latter part of the tenth century.

THE GREAT PSALTER OF BOULOGNE.

Plates XXXVII. XXXVIII. and XXXIX.

THE manuscript which has furnished the materials for these three plates is one of the noblest copies of the Latin Psalter ever written, and is now preserved in the Public Library of Boulogne. It was written in the Abbey of St. Bertin, between the years 989 and 1008, during which period Odbert presided over the abbey; but it possesses so many Anglo-Saxon peculiarities, and is in several respects so precise a duplicate of portions of the Cottonian Psalter Tiberius, C. VI., that it can only be supposed to have been executed by or under the influence of Anglo-Saxon artists. From a special charter of this celebrated convent, it is known that various fine manuscripts were executed there about the year 1003, by Odbert and his monks, and we find the fact recorded in the volume before us, in the following curious acrostic, written on the verso of the first leaf of the volume, the first letters of the lines forming the words HERIVEUS SCRIPSIT ME SCO BERTINO; whilst we further learn that Odbertus himself decorated the volume, and Dodolinus supplied the gloss.

H une Petre Davitirum librum conscripsit habendum
E cce sacer tibi cui claves concessit Olympi
R ex Christus simul ac terræ, supplex Heriveus
I n Patris egregii Psalteri fuas amore
V nica opes mundi nam Christus in hoc titulatus
E cclesiæ sibimet sponsam sancivit in ævum
U nus et hic rerum pater est qui cuncta guberna
S pū et sanctos summo descriptus honore
S ic pater Odbertus Christi solamine faltus
C oenobii qui Sithiensis sic coenctio sancta
R ite deo psallit, quorum penetralibus altus
I stud opus exeptum, domino patrante peregi
P ax sit multa patri precor Odberto super album
S it que salus cunctis Sithiu degentibus omnis
I n Christo valeat mihi quisque juvamen adamsis
T artara possideant nec quisquam foraverit ex hinc

M e compuit Herivala et Odberta decoravit
E accrpsit Dotoresvs et hos Deus aptet Olympo
S ancta cohors latare monachorum Sithicnsis
C cenobii modulans domino gratissima David
O rgana quæ cecinit sancto spiramine plenus
B artistes tibi namque manum fert congemiscis
E ximia Felgebar Silvino que patronis
R egna beatipoli retinere que sorte perentii
T empla nitent tibi tampana redimita canoris
I naumeris libris superas vicinia septa
N ec quisque superare valet quot pignora compta
O ptineas merito sanctorum relliquiarum

The first page of the volume comprises a remarkable symbolical description of the Christian Church, commencing, "Fundamentum ipsius cameræ est fides, Altitudo ejus est spes, Latitudo ejus est caritas," &c.; and ending, "Cathedra Christi est serenitas mentis: Sponsa Christi est sancta anima; Cameraria Christi, spiritales virtutes sunt, Prima sancta caritas dicta est, illa regit cameram Christi; secunda est sancta humilitas, illa est thesauraria in camera Christi; tertia est sancta patientia, illa facit luminariam cameræ Christi; quarta sancta puritas, illa scopat cameram Christi." This description evidently faced a drawing of the mystical temple, now wanting in the volume.

The second leaf is occupied with the miniature of the Psalmist, with musical instruments, copied in my 37th Plate. The King is seated at the door of a temple, between columns, of which the bases and capitals are elaborately ornamented with sculpture representing conventional foliage, supporting a conical arch surmounted by a foliated pinnacle, and inscribed, "✚ Hic est David filius Iesse tenens Psalterium in manib; suis. Hec est forma Psalterii." The Psalterium is square in form, with one of the upper angles produced and rounded: it is provided with ten strings. At the side of the drawing and on the following page are represented a series of musical instruments, of which a similar series occurs in the Cottonian MS. Tiberius, C. vi., copied in Strutt's "Horda," plates xx. and xxi. Our plate contains the Bunibulum, fistula ærea, tabula, and chorus; whilst the following page represents the semicircular nablum (Strutt, pl. xx. f. 1,—a triangular variety, like the letter delta, being described); the cithara (Strutt, xx. f. 4); the tintinnabulum (Strutt, xx. f. 5); the two tubi, or calami (Strutt, xx. fig. 7), with three pipes at the end; the Psalterium (Strutt, xx. f. 2); the tympanum, strangely formed in two parts, terminating in three dogs' heads (Strutt, xx. f. 3); the sabuca, not in the Cottonian MS.; the fistula (Strutt, xxi. f. 1); the pennula, like a kite; and the chorus (pellis simplex, —Strutt, xxi. f. 2, but with the middle part circular).*

The first page of the Psalter is a beautiful specimen of illumination, and is represented in my 38th Plate. The framework of this elegant composition is arranged as an arch springing from two side-columns, with capitals formed as quatrefoils, and bases as truncated quatrefoils, both forms of great rarity at the period of the execution of this volume. The transverse base, columns, and arch are ornamented with flowing convoluted branches of gold, edged with fine red lines, each convolution enclosing a fanciful bird or beast, in silver,—an ornamental treatment of the greatest rarity (of which we have another instance in the Lambeth Aldhelm, Plate 31). The four spaces within the quatrefoils contain representations of the exploits of David; namely, his contest with the bear and his fight with Goliah, whose head he cuts off, and presents to Saul, in the lower compartments. The quaint manner in which the limbs of these figures are arranged, so as to occupy

---

* From a series of articles on Musical Instruments contained in the first and second volumes of the "Annales Archæologiques" of M. Didron, it would appear that there are drawings of similar instruments in MSS. in the Libraries of St. Emeran, St. Blaise, and Angers. See also the elaborate separate work of M. Coussemaker on the subject of early musical instruments.

the irregular spaces of the design, deserves attention, as well as the sling of David, the helmet and other accoutrements of Goliath, who is evidently habited in scale armour, and the chair, crown, and sceptre of Saul.

The beautiful initial B encloses in the upper part a figure of the Saviour, young and beardless, with a cruciferous nimbus; and in the lower part the Descent of the Holy Ghost on the *twelve* Apostles, the Virgin Mary being absent. The entire ground of this miniature, with its borders, is of a beautiful purple colour.[*]

The division of the Psalter into three portions, of which several instances have been noticed in the previous pages of this work, is kept up in the volume before us by the enlarged size of the initials of the 51st and 101st Psalm, both copied in my 39th Plate, the Q of the former, "Quid gloriaris in malitia," containing in its centre the scenes of the Birth of Christ, whilst the D of the latter, "Dñe exaudi orationem meam," is occupied with the Death of the Saviour and his Descent to Hades. The manger of Bethlehem is here a beautiful temple, the Virgin reposing on a large ornamented cushion or bed, whilst to the left an Angel descends from the heavenly choir through a slit in the clouds, to announce the glad tidings to the shepherds, one of whom in a cloak holds his staff, and another his cow's horn, used as a trumpet or probably as a drinking-vessel. This miniature is executed entirely by fine pen-lines in red ink, whilst in the Q the drawing is done in fine black lines. Here the Saviour is nailed to the cross with his feet apart, and clothed only round the middle of the body; the head is surrounded with a golden cruciferous nimbus, and over his head is inscribed the names IHC XPC (Jesus Christ, written contractedly in Greek capitals). On either side are two busts, evidently intended for Sol and Luna, nearly defaced. Longinus with the sponge and a bucket, and his companion piercing the side of the Saviour, together with St. John and the Virgin, stand at the sides of the Saviour. The long attenuated form of all the figures will be noticed. Below, the three Marys visit the sepulchre with golden vessels in their hands, and with fluttering drapery entirely in the late Anglo-Saxon manner: the Angel is seated upon the flat cover of the tomb, partially removed, with the napkin lying near his feet. Below are four guards, whose alarm is quaintly expressed, owing to the confined space in which they are drawn.

On the left hand, within the main stroke of the D, the Saviour is represented with a twisted rope in his hand, drawing up the spirits of the dead, who are represented as rising from their tombs. I have nowhere else seen this curious treatment of this mysterious subject.

The noble proportions and the elegant ornamentation of these two letters will merit careful attention. They are quite unique, so far as my knowledge of illuminated manuscripts extends.

The initials of five other of the Psalms are executed in the same style as the two large ones; but they are only three or four inches high. The 41st Psalm commences with a Q, in which Zachariah and the Angel are figured; Ps. 72, Q. with the Murder of the Innocents,—a single soldier alone has cut off the heads of a number of children; Ps. 97, C, with the miracle of the Water turned into Wine; Ps. 106, C, with the Deposition from the Cross; and Ps. 109, D, with the Ascension of the Saviour in the Vesica piscis, borne by four Angels.

Another series of initials, of still rather smaller size, contains the following miniatures:—Ps. 43, the Fall of Adam and Eve; Ps. 48, the Murder of Abel; Ps. 58, Samson pulling down the palace; Ps. 81, the Saviour standing alone, holding a book and a cup;

---

[*] In the printing of the plates the purple tint has incorrectly been extended beyond the borders of the design.

Ps. 90, 91, 92, and 93, four scenes of the Temptation; 96, the Miraculous Draught of Fishes; 108, the Ascension of Christ with his Disciples.

The whole of the remainder of the Psalms have the initials drawn with the greatest skill, and ornamented in the most elegant manner. I only regret that want of space prevents me from publishing the extensive series of fac-similes which I made from them, as well as from many of the small sketches with which all the blank spaces in the MS. have been filled, forming an invaluable series of archæological subjects.

THE POEMS OF PRUDENTIUS.

Plate XLIV.

THE writings of Prudentius, and especially the "Psychomachia, liber de Pugna Vitiorum et Virtutum," an allegorical poem, in which the Virtues and Vices are clothed in human attributes, were especial favourites with our Anglo-Saxon forefathers. Several fine MSS. exist of them, illustrated very extensively with outline drawings, of which the finest is the one until recently preserved in Archbishop Tenison's Library in St. Martin's-in-the-Fields, which was sold by auction, on 1st July, 1861, when it was acquired by the British Museum, being knocked down at the price of 260 guineas. It contains as many as 80 drawings, in the style of those represented in my 44th Plate. Not only from the character of the writing, but also from the fluttering style of the drapery, and from the conventional manner in which foliage is treated, as in the Winchester books (*see* especially the lower left-hand drawing in my plate), it is evident that it must be referred to the end of the tenth century. The drawings are of great value as containing a series of representations of the habits and customs, dresses, arms, &c., of the later Anglo-Saxons. With the exception of a single figure copied by Mr. Hewitt (Ancient Armour, p. 65), no other portion of these drawings has hitherto been published. In my 1st compartment Pride is represented as starting in his car, drawn by two prancing horses, and in the second he is overturned, the horses as well as the chariot being represented in the air; whence we may infer that the artist had the fate of Phaeton in his mind. In the former drawing, the form of the chariot and the harness of the horses (omitted in the latter drawing) will be noticed. In the third drawing, the musical instruments, the banners, and long fluttering robes of the dancing female, merit attention; whilst in the fourth, the large circular Anglo-Saxon cloak floating in the breeze, or folded over the arm in a knot, is especially interesting; I recollect no other instance in which it is so precisely represented. Amongst the many other drawings of which I had made copies, but of which want of space will not allow the publication, I may especially direct attention to a chariot-race, a dinner scene, a combat between two females, with beautiful conventional shrubs and flowers; a priest holding the chalice and wafer (marked with four dots forming a cross), in his covered hand before an altar; Abraham receiving the three Angels at the door of his tent; a female, with a group of warriors on foot, and another group of warriors on

I 1

horseback, driving an ox and a pig before them. Amongst the minor details are to be noticed a cat-o'-nine-tails used by a horseman; also swords, bow and a quiver of arrows, cymbals (two circular discs fixed on long handles), holy-water bucket, a warrior sheathing his sword, and another with a large trumpet, &c.

An extremely fine copy of the " PSYCHOMACHIA," with 89 miniatures, in the same outline style as the above, is also preserved in the Library of Corpus Christi College, Cambridge. It formerly belonged to the church of Malmesbury, as appears by the following inscription in the volume, written in large Anglo-Saxon characters :—

> Hunc quicunque librum Aedhelmi depresserit almo
> Damnatus semper maneas cum sorte malorum
> Sit pietate Dei sine qui vel portet ab isto
> Cenobio librum Aedhelmi hunc vel vendere temptet
> Qui legis inscripti a verbis regitare memento
> Christum ac in torpie semper die vivat Athelward
> Qui dedit hunc librum Aedhelmo pro quo sibi Christus
> Moneta larga fent largitor crimina laxans

Another very beautifully-written copy, of small size, is contained amongst the COTTONIAN MSS. (CLEOPATRA, C. 8). It contains 83 drawings, about 3½ by 2½ inches in size, delicately but very spiritedly drawn with a pen with red and black ink. The style of the drapery is fluttery, as in the later Anglo-Saxon drawings. Strutt used this MS. very extensively in his " Horda Angel-cynan," and other works, copying them, however, coarsely; and from his copies they have been introduced into more recent works illustrating the manners and customs of the Anglo-Saxons; such as the " Pictorial History of England," by C. Knight; " Old England," &c.

Mr. Shaw has copied three of the miniatures very carefully in his " Dresses and Decorations," vol. i., representing groups of warriors, females, a fenced city, &c. Three others—1. Wisdom seated on her throne, a charming little female figure, very insufficiently copied by Mr. Fairholt (Wright's " Domestic Manners," p. 60); 2. Abraham's offering of Isaac, with the ram caught in a thicket; and 3. a Priest standing before an Altar, with the chalice in his right hand and the wafer in his left (the latter covered by the chasuble), with an aged man offering a lamb as a sacrifice (Strutt's " Horda," pl. xv. f. 3)—are especially clever and interesting, and were copied for this work. Want of space, however, renders their omission necessary.

The COTTONIAN MS. TITUS, D. XVI., a small 12mo. volume of the end of the eleventh century, also contains a copy of the " Psychomachia," with 46 drawings in the later Anglo-Saxon style, slightly tinted with colours and the drapery fluttering. Amongst them, as interesting illustrations of costume, &c., are to be noticed armed figures on horseback, warriors both in chain and scale armour, armed with nasals, kite-shaped shields, swords, spears, &c

THE ASTRONOMICAL TREATISE OF ARATUS.

Plate XLVIII.

THE astronomical poem of Aratus has attracted considerable attention in this country in consequence of the elaborate memoir of the late William Young Ottley on the various MSS. in which it is contained in the British Museum Library, one of which, namely the Harleian MS. 647, he was induced to consider, from the style and character of the drawings with which it is adorned (and which, in many instances, are partially filled in with lines of writing of different lengths, consisting of Roman rustic capitals), "that they are genuine remains of ancient Roman art, and that the manuscript which they decorate may vie in antiquity with the far-famed Virgils and Terence of the Vatican." The drawings are, however, accompanied with a series of verses of Cicero, written on the same pages beneath the former, " in bold, well-formed minuscule characters;" and Mr. Ottley's endeavour to prove that the latter characters were in use among the Romans, extended to not fewer than 98 pages of the "Archæologia," vol. xxvi. (pp. 47—144). Notwithstanding Mr. Ottley's arguments, the Harleian MS. is, however, clearly to be ascribed to the ninth century: such is the opinion of the best palæographers, and it cannot be doubted that the drawings were copied from ancient ones.

Of this practice of copying ancient drawings in manuscripts of a more recent period, Mr. Ottley's memoir itself afforded very ample evidence, as it comprised an account, with figures, from two MSS. of the tenth century (MS. Harl. 2506, and MS. Cotton., Tiberius, B. 5), both of which contain copies of the poem of Aratus; whilst in the latter the drawings of the Harleian MS. 647 itself have been copied by an Anglo-Saxon artist, with the usual modifications. Orion, the dog Sirius, the Hare, the ship Argo, the Dragon (Coetus), Eridanus, the Fish (Piscis), the Altar (Ara), the Centaur, the Hydra, the dog Anticanis, the Pleiades (seven female heads), and the group of five heads, Jupiter, Saturn, Mars, Venus, and Mercury, appear in both MSS., and are contrasted by Mr. Ottley, the Harleian one being regarded as a classical work, "full of vivacity, replete with classic feeling, and in every detail of the costume corresponding with the productions of classic times. But in order duly to appreciate the merits of the original artist, his performances should be confronted with those of the Saxon copyist in the Cottonian MS." Several of the figures of the constellations in the Harleian MS. are, unfortunately, not copied in the Anglo-Saxon one; whilst, on the other hand, the figures of Sol (in a quadriga) and Luna (in a biga, drawn by two oxen), contained in the Anglo-Saxon MS. copied in my 48th Plate, are wanting in the Harleian volume; so that we are unable to contrast them, as we cannot but suppose that the figures in my plate were copied from an earlier drawing in the Harleian volume which has now disappeared: they, however, appear in the later Bodleian No. 614. We have here, therefore, various details, evidently modified to suit the taste of the Anglo-Saxon artist and the costume of his own day; thus the banded legs of Sol were probably sandals in the original, as they are in the original figure of Orion, whilst the fluttering drapery and the large circular cloak of Luna will be recognized as Anglo-Saxon by comparison with my copies from the Tenison Prudentius, described in p. 107.

L K

Mr. Ottley incidentally mentions (pp. 149, 171) the Leyden volume, which was used by Grotius ("Syntagma Arcteorum"); and it is curious that, as he considered that there was "every reason to believe that it was written and decorated in ancient Roman times," he did not more particularly allude to, or describe, the drawings or writing of the MS. I have myself examined it very carefully, and made many fac-similes of the drawings. It is written throughout in very fine Roman rustic capitals of large size, nearly a quarter of an inch high, with only the first line—

"AB IOUE PRINCIPIU MAGNO DEDUX, ARATUS."

being written in red letters rather larger than the text, without any illumination or ornament, and terminated by the line—

"VALE FIDENS IN DNŌ, XPI VESTITUS AMORE."

written in smaller rustic capitals, and somewhat more negligent than the text.

The miniatures are fine classical figures, about six inches high, drawn with much greater freedom than those of the Harleian volume, and coloured in a broad classical style, in the manner of the wall-paintings of Pompeii; so that both writings and drawings would lead to the idea that the manuscript was not more recent than the fifth century. The figures of the constellations differ in their attitudes from those in both the Harleian volumes, although Perseus bears a closer resemblance to that in the MS. 2506. He has, however, a long robe flying behind, fastened on his left shoulder, and holds the Gorgon's head in his right hand. The heads of the five planets are much more individualized, Mercury having a pair of small wings attached to his head, and the caduceus on his shoulder; Venus with a peacock's feather, &c. Unfortunately, however, for the antiquity of the volume, I found inscribed on the margin of the planisphere (resembling that of the Harleian 647,—Ottley, pl. 22), the words, "altissima in Virgine, humillima in piscibus esse videtur," written in a beautiful minute Caroline hand of the ninth century.

Lastly, I may add that the Cottonian MS. Tiberius, C. 1 (about A.D. 1100), contains a series of outline figures of the constellations similar to those of the Aratus, and that the little Bodleian MS. (No. 614), executed in this country about 1100, has some of the figures of the constellations clearly copied from the Harleian 647, or the Anglo-Saxon Tiberius; e. g., Perseus, Sol and Luna, or Apollo and Diana, much less spiritedly designed than in my plate. The group of the planets is increased to seven by the figure of the Sun, crowned, and bearing a torch in each hand, and placed in a larger central circle; and Luna, with a crescent and a single torch below, between Venus and Mercury, the latter of whom is represented as an aged man. Some of the figures in this little MS. are beautifully drawn, and many of them are evidently copied from Tiberius, B. 5. The drawings in the Basle MS. of Aratus are quite of a different character to those in any of the MSS. above described.

THE METRICAL PARAPHRASE OF BIBLE HISTORY BY THE PSEUDO CÆDMON.

THE remarkable MS. formerly belonging to Junius, and now one of the chief ornaments of the Bodleian Library (Jun. No. 11), contains not only a poetical paraphrase of the Bible account of the Creation of the World and the history of our first parents and their immediate successors, but also an introductory account of the fall of the rebel Angels, the pride, rebellion, debates, and punishment of Satan and his companions, "with a resemblance to Milton so remarkable, that much of this portion might be almost literally translated by a cento of verses from that great poet" (Conybeare's Synopsis, in "Ill. of Ang.-Sax. Poetry"). In fact, after taking into consideration the circumstances which have been recorded relative to the production of "Paradise Lost," I conceive there can be no doubt that the three first books of that poem were an afterthought, induced by the publication by Junius, in 1655, of the Anglo-Saxon poem contained in the Bodleian MS.; Milton's Tragedy, as it was intended to be called, having originally commenced with what now stands as the 32nd line of the 4th book. After the account of the overthrow of Pharaoh's host in the Red Sea, the poem takes up the first five chapters of the prophet Daniel, followed by another poem, the subject of which is the triumphal entry of Christ into Hades, the return of the Saviour to the earth, his appearance to his disciples, and his ascension to heaven. The leaves of the volume measure 12¼ inches by 8; the text is written in a fine round Anglo-Saxon hand, with capitals in the same style as those of the Lambeth Aldhelm and Vossian Psalter. The text is (up to the 109th page) illustrated by an extensive series of drawings, full of imagination, and often very quaint; but rudely executed in outlines, either entirely drawn in a brownish ink, or having different parts of each subject drawn with either red, green, or black outlines. The figures are greatly attenuated, the drapery fluttering, and the foliage is treated quite conventionally.

There are clearly two hands traceable in these drawings; the one which executed those in the latter part, relating to Noah and Abraham, is far neater than the earlier ones. Only a single figure (the Deity beholding the excellence of his productions, represented without a nimbus, but with a fillet round the head; the right hand elevated in the act of Latin benediction, the left holding a book) is finished in thick opaque colours. At the foot of one of the pages is a small side portrait of an ecclesiastic (as seems to be the case from his dress, although not tonsured), drawn within a circle, inscribed "Ælfwine;" and it is to be observed that the little Prayer-Book, Titus. D. 27, of the Cottonian Library, was written for an abbot of New Minster of that name. One of the pages contains a very rudely-designed group of two men talking earnestly together, one seated. They are of large size, and seem to form no part of the illustrations of the text. At page 225 is the commencement of a tessellated design, in outline, of considerable elegance, formed of a series of quatrefoils within diamonds, containing foliated rosettes, and with a curious border of a branching design.

As the whole of these outline drawings are most carefully engraved in the 24th volume of the "Archæologia," I have not thought it necessary to reproduce any of them in this work.

THE COTTONIAN BOOK OF PRAYERS, TITUS, D. 26.

THIS small volume of Prayers, of the latter half of the tenth century, contains an interesting little drawing of St. Peter (with the head disproportionably small), seated on a throne beneath a triple rounded arch, and holding two keys in his right hand, whilst an open book rests on his knees. At his feet is represented the small figure of a monk in his cowl, standing and holding a book in his hand. The drawing is very neatly executed in bistre outlines, slightly tinted with green, whilst the central rounded arch is coloured red and blue. The style so strongly resembles that of the miniatures in the MS. Titus, D. 27, that I am inclined to regard both as having the same origin, and even probably as the work of the same artist.

THE COTTONIAN MS. CALIGULA, A. XV.

THIS book of Anglo-Saxon Homilies and Prayers, Paschal computations, &c., in Latin, and also in Anglo-Saxon, by different writers, contains only two small drawings near the end of the volume, at the tops of two pages of a calendar. One on fol. 122 v. represents four monks kneeling or extended in front of a small church with rounded arches, above which hovers an Angel with outstretched wings, with the right hand pointing upwards, whilst the left holds a long scroll inscribed " NAT. VIII Kl Ap Idus Ap." This scroll is received by the first prostrate figure, over whose head is inscribed " Pachom' abb' " and whose left hand is elevated, with all the fingers stretched out, as are also the hands of the other monks. The drawing is very carefully executed in outline, and slightly tinted with red and green, very much in the style of those of the MSS. Titus, D. 26 and 27.

On the opposite page is a similar-sized drawing by the same hand, in the centre of which Christ is seated within a red-edged vesica piscis, holding a book in his left hand, and with the right hand elevated in the act of benediction. On either side an Angel stands, holding a long triple-tongued banner, and at each end of the drawing is a six-winged Cherubim standing on clouds. These figures are drawn with great skill and boldness, having somewhat the character of those of the Harleian Psalter, No. 603.

THE COTTONIAN CALENDAR, JULIUS, A. 6.

THIS little Book of Prayers is especially interesting for the series of illustrations which it contains of the employments of our ancestors throughout the year, one being appropriated to and placed across the foot of the page containing the calendar of each month. The figures are about an inch high, drawn with very great spirit and delicacy. In January, the operations consist of ploughing with oxen and sowing seed; in February, pruning trees, which are treated in a completely conventional manner; in March, digging, sowing, and raking the ground; in April, a drinking-party celebrate the Easter festival; in May, shepherds tending their grazing flocks; in June, felling and carting timber; in July, mowing grass and making hay; in August, reaping and loading the harvest cart; in September, driving the swine to the forests; in October, hawking (a respectably-drawn ostrich is well delineated among the birds); in November, a bonfire, one of the men bringing logs from a stack of firewood; in December, thrashing and winnowing corn. The whole of these charming little groups have been engraved with his usual care by Mr. H. Shaw in his "Dresses and Decorations," vol. i. On fol. 71 v. is an elegant initial D.

THE COTTONIAN MANUSCRIPT TIBERIUS, B. V.

THIS large MS. consists of various treatises, including the Abbot Joachim's treatise on the Prophets, now bound up separately as Part II., whilst Part I. contains not only the Anglo-Saxon copy of the astronomical poem of Aratus, with its 27 illustrations described above (see Plate 48), but also a variety of chronological and other matters, such as lists of kings, and archbishops of Canterbury; bishops of Rochester (by which we learn that the volume was executed in the latter half of the tenth century); a calendar, with a series of illustrations of the occupations of the month (quite similar to those in the MS. Julius, A. 6, but drawn much larger and coarser), the whole of which are copied by Strutt ("Horda," plates x. xi. and xii.). This is followed by a "Descriptio topographica Orientis," full of wonders and monsters of various kinds, all of which are rudely represented in 37 coarsely-coloured drawings, two of the best drawn of which were engraved by Dibdin in his "Bibliographical Decameron," Strutt having, also published one of them in his "Horda," pl. xiii. f. 1. These monsters, which appear to have served as the prototypes of the grotesque figures introduced into the borders of illuminated manuscripts of a later period, are described at great length, with wonderful properties attributed to them.

3 M

[The COTTONIAN MS. VITELLIUS. A. XV., of the 4to. size, and written in Anglo-Saxon characters, in the tenth century, contains a variety of treatises, &c. (including the poem of Beowulf), amongst which is a copy of the "Descriptio topographica Orientis," with a series of figures similar to those in the preceding MS., but excessively rude both in their drawing and colouring.]

THE COTTONIAN MS. HERBARIUM, VITELLIUS, C. 3.

THIS folio MS. of the tenth century contains the "Herbarium Apulei Platonici" in Anglo-Saxon, and is illustrated throughout by rudely drawn and coloured figures of the various plants and animals described in the text, preceded by two large ill-drawn miniatures, each occupying an entire page, surrounded by borders of foliage, somewhat in the Canute style, but very rudely executed and much injured: of these, fol. 11 v. contains the figures of a priest fully robed vanquishing a lion; a monk presenting a book, and a warrior, much defaced, complete the design. The other drawing (fol. 19 r.) represents three figures, Æsculapius, Plato, and Centaurus, with animals, enclosed in a border of the same style as the other miniature. Among the small drawings illustrating the text are several representing scorpions, well drawn, showing that the figures must have been copied from some classical original, executed where opportunities would occur for seeing these obnoxious animals alive and representing them correctly.

[The COTTONIAN MS. VITELLIUS. A. XIX., contains the Life of St. Cuthbert, by Venerable Bede, in fine Anglo-Saxon characters, the verso of the 8th leaf of which has the centre stained purple, upon which has been scratched, with a hard point, a figure of a priest standing erect, with the right hand in the act of benediction, and the left holding a maniple (evidently intended subsequently to have been finished in colours). On the opposite page is a finely-drawn initial P, in the style of the Lambeth Aldhelm.]

THE ROYAL. MS. 13. A. 1. (BRITISH MUSEUM).

THIS small manuscript of the early part of the eleventh century contains a work on the exploits of Alexander the Great, King of Macedon, together with his Epistle to Aristotle, and a treatise on Philosophy. It is beautifully written, and contains an interesting frontispiece, in which are two carefully drawn figures, representing the king

THE PSALTER OF THOMAS à BECKET.

THIS Latin Psalter and Hymns is contained in the Library of Corpus Christi College, Cambridge, No. 411, and has been described as of the quarto size, and as written in the ninth century. It was formerly covered with silver gilt plates and gems, and ultimately became the property of the famous Thomas à Becket, as appears in a very old inscription in the volume. It appears to me rather to be of the latter half of the tenth century, and is plainly written in large characters, but is further interesting as containing a contemporary portrait of Eadrig.

THE HARLEIAN PSALTER, No. 2904.

Plate XLIII.

THIS magnificently-written Psalter so entirely corresponds with the Winchester Books of St. Æthelwold, &c., that we may satisfactorily place its date at the close of the tenth century. It contains only, as illuminations, the drawing of the Crucifixion (the finest of its kind), and the initial B (the noblest with which I am acquainted), both represented in my Plate 43. The miniature is executed with the pen with the greatest freedom, and very carefully shaded with pinkish bistre. The Saviour is represented as already dead, having "bowed his head and given up the ghost." Here we see the hands, side, and feet pierced, and still bleeding; the head surrounded with the cruciferous nimbus; the beard short and forked; the body girt round the middle. Save in the too slender form of the body, the figure is finely proportioned. The words of the titulus over the head are unusually arranged—"Hic est Nazaren. HIC Rex judeor." As usual, in order to give more effect and dignity to the principal figure, the attendants are drawn of a smaller size; and, in order to fill up the space, they are mounted on small rocks. The Virgin, weeping, to the left, with covered hands, holds up her outer garment to her face, and is drawn in the peculiar humpbacked manner adopted by the later Anglo-Saxon artists, whilst the lower part of the body and legs are greatly attenuated.

3 N.

The beloved disciple, indicated by a scroll, on which is written, "Hic est discipulus qui testimonium perhibet," bends eagerly forward to catch the last word or sigh of his Master, with a quill pen in his hand.

The grand initial B, followed by noble golden capitals, the largest and finest of all executed at this period which I have hitherto met with, is ornamented entirely in the style of the Hyde Abbey books, with conventional foliage and branches of varied colours springing from a noble lion's head at the juncture of the two curves of the second part of the letter, whilst the top and bottom of the main stroke are ornamented with knot-work terminating in dogs' heads. The black line of text at the bottom of the page is from the following leaf, and exhibits the ordinary writing of the volume.

THE LATIN PSALTER OF THE ARUNDEL LIBRARY.

(BRITISH MUSEUM, No. 155.)

THIS manuscript was supposed by Wanley to be of the time of King Canute. It contains in the Calendar the names of St. Edward the Martyr, St. Gregory, and St. Cuthbert. In the character of the writing and the ornamental details it closely resembles the New Minster volumes below described, and ought probably to be assigned to about the year 1000.

The 1st, 51st, and 101st Psalms, as usual, have the first words splendidly illuminated, with the initial letter of each of large size, each enclosed within a broad rectangular frame, with large rosettes at the angles filled with conventional foliage.

The commencement of the 1st Psalm is given by Mr. Humphreys, in his "Illuminated Books of the Middle Ages," where it is erroneously referred to the Arundel MS. 83. The "Quid gloriaris" is similarly treated; and the D of the 101st Psalm has a figure of David, occupied in cutting off the head of Goliah, in the open space of the letter, very rudely executed. There is, moreover, a large, rude coloured and gilt illumination of St. Benedict and his monks, in their hoods, with a monk kneeling below kissing his feet. Another drawing of the Abbot Pachomius, and an Angel under an arch, is very spiritedly designed in outlines (fol. 9 v.); and on the opposite page (fol. 10 r.) is a group of three monks, seated, in outlines. At the end of the volume are a series of prayers, with a Saxon gloss.

[Amongst the fine MSS. preserved at Holkham is also a copy of the Gospels illuminated in the Winchester or Canute style. I am only acquainted with this through a fac-simile contained in a series of copies from the Holkham MSS. shown me by the late Mr. Dawson Turner, from which it appeared to be less elaborately ornamented than usual in this class of MSS.]

THE GOSPELS OF THE ROYAL LIBRARY, COPENHAGEN.

Plate XLI.

THE volume which has furnished the accompanying plate of St. Matthew possesses great interest to the student of Anglo-Saxon art. It is a noble folio copy of the Gospels, written with all the luxury of the finest MSS. of the end of the tenth century, and is preserved in the Royal Library of Copenhagen. Having completed my drawing of St. Matthew from the Gospels of Lindisfarne (copied in Plate 13) only a few days previous to starting, in 1850, for Denmark, the reader will easily judge of the pleasure with which I found, in the fine MS. now under notice, a miniature of the same Evangelist in which the same extraordinary and hitherto unique treatment was retained; and on carefully comparing the Copenhagen drawing with my copy of the Lindisfarne one, which I had taken in my portfolio with me, it was quite evident that the artist of the later volume had copied his figure, in all its details, from the Lindisfarne one, modifying only various parts according to the fashion of the period: thus the whole of the garments exhibit the multitudinous fluttering folds so common with the tenth century Anglo-Saxon artists.

The practice of copying miniatures in mediæval MSS. from earlier volumes was doubtless not of uncommon practice; but, from the destruction of so many of the early libraries, it is now of the greatest rarity to meet with examples where this can be shown to have been the case. Here, however, we have one of the highest interest, where a remarkable feature—namely the introduction of a nimbed head at the side of a curtain—is found in both drawings, and, so far as I have observed, in no other of the hundreds of early figures of the Evangelists so universally introduced into the copies of the Gospels.

Other instances of this practice are afforded in the present volume by the Utrecht Psalter, p. 14, copied into the Harleian Psalter No. 603, and thence into the Eadwine Psalter of Trinity College, Cambridge, and again partially into the Psalter No. 1194, of the Paris Library; and by the "Aratus," as illustrated in the 24th volume of the "Archæologia," and in my 48th Plate, and afterwards in a little volume in the Bodleian MS. No. 614, of the twelfth century, of which I have made an extensive series of copies, but of which no account has hitherto been published.

The border in the drawing before us is formed of bars of gold and other colours, as in the Æthelwold style, but less elaborately finished; although the foliage introduced into the semicircles of the frame partakes entirely of the treatment of the borders of the contemporary MSS.

I apprehend that this fine volume was carried to Denmark by King Canute himself, whose character has earned for him amongst his countrymen the title of a Saint, and whom we shall, in a subsequent page, see, with his wife, in connexion both with New Minster, in the Hyde Abbey Book, and with another Book of the Gospels described below.

THE COTTONIAN PSALTER TIBERIUS, C. VI.

Plate XLVI.

THIS MS. is doubly interesting to the Anglo-Saxon student, not only on account of the Anglo-Saxon interlineary translation of the Psalms which it contains (unfortunately all after Ps. 114 is wanting), but for the fine series of drawings with which it is illustrated. In my plate I have introduced as the date, the end of the tenth century; but the character of the handwriting is somewhat more recent than that of the Winchester volumes of that date; so that possibly it may be half a century more recent. In this volume we observe the fashion already commenced of inserting a series of pictures both of Old and New Testament subjects at the head of the Psalter.

The volume commences with paschal and lunar computations enclosed within rounded arches, supported by plain columns with foliated bases and capitals; at the head of one of these is represented a party seated at a feast, with servants offering meat on long spits, from which it is cut by the guests (copied in Strutt's "Horda," pl. xvi. f. 1, and "Pict. Hist. Engl.," i. 336). On fol. 6 v. is a singular representation of Life and Death contrasted, the former as Christ with a cruciferous nimbus, and standing on the wings of the latter, very similar to the drawings in the Leofric Missal (*see* Plate 33). On fol. 7 v. commences the series of drawings of which the two given in my Plate 46 are specimens. They are—

1. The Spirit of God as a dove sitting upon the face of the water, the Creator holding a pair of scales and compasses supporting the spheres (*see* Mrs. Jameson's "Hist. of our Lord," i. 72, with a wrong reference to the MS.), being an attempt to embody the grand poetry of the 11th chapter of Isaiah, especially verses 12, 13, and 22, and the description of the Wisdom of the Almighty in the creation of the world, Proverbs viii. 22—31. There is a similar drawing in a large folio MS. Bible in the British Museum, of the Norman period.

2. David killing the Lion.   3. David killing Goliah.   4 and 5. David and Saul.

6. David playing on the harp, inspired by the Holy Ghost as a dove (more like an eagle) standing on the top of the sceptre. (Miss Twining, "Symbols of Christian Art," plate 31, f. 1, has given the upper part of the drawing.)

7. The contest between Christ and Satan in the wilderness.

8. The entry of Christ into Jerusalem, copied in my "Palæographia sacra."

9. Christ washing the Disciples' feet; an Angel from above holds a large napkin over the head of the Saviour.

10. The Betrayal of Christ.   11. Christ bound and brought before Pilate.   12. The Crucifixion.

13. The three Marys at the Sepulchre, copied in my plate. Here the foremost of the females bears a censer, as well as a box of precious ointment. The Angel, a grand figure, holds a sceptre and open book. The architecture of the tomb is remarkable, and quite unlike that of any of the other early representations of the tomb which I have seen.

14. The "Harrowing of Hell,"—Christ represented as treading upon the devils, and drawing the souls out of the infernal regions.

15. The Incredulity of Thomas.—Except in the figure of Christ being rather too tall, this is perhaps the most pleasing of the series; the figure of the Apostle is very natural, and that of the Saviour very spirited, being seven inches high.

16. The Ascension.—The upper part of the figure of the Saviour hidden by the clouds.

17. The Descent of the Holy Ghost as a dove, with flames of fire issuing from its mouth, the tail held by a hand in the clouds.

18. The Contest between St. Michael and the Dragon, copied in my plate. Drawn, like the rest, with a pen, with wonderful freedom, in different coloured inks, and destitute of any shading, these designs teach us the ideas of composition entertained by the later Anglo-Saxon artists. They may very advantageously be contrasted with the drawings of the Benedictional of St. Æthelwold and the Missal of Rouen.

To these succeed several pages of illustrations of musical instruments (copied in Strutt's "Horda," similar to those in the Boulogne Psalter), including a figure of David playing on the Psalterium (of which a reduced copy is given in "Pict. Hist. of England," i. 321).

These are followed by a figure of Christ seated within the Vesica piscis, with an Angel sounding a trumpet on either side, and with the Virgin and two priests standing below. This is enclosed in an ornamental frame, and is highly finished in thick glazed body-colours, as are the illuminated initials of the principal Psalms.

Fol. 19 r. is surrounded with an illuminated border, somewhat in the style of the Canute Gospels and Rouen Books, enclosing the commencement of the treatise on the Origin of the Psalms, with a fine large ornamented "D(avid) filius Jesse cum esset in regno suo"), &c. The miniature of David, with his four attendants, three of whom play on different instruments, whilst the fourth acts the part of a gleeman, or juggler, throwing up and catching three knives and three balls, occurs on fol. 30. (Another illustration of this gleeman is to be found in the Cottonian MS. Claudius, B. 4, fol. 33 r.) The drawing in the MS. before us has been copied, without the ornamental border, by Strutt, "Horda," pl. xix.; and "Pict. Hist. Eng.," i. 322.

The commencement of the 1st, 51st, and 101st Psalms, having the initial letter of large size, are enclosed within beautiful foliated borders. Preceding the 51st Psalm is a drawing of the Saviour, triumphantly standing upon the Lion and Dragon; and before the 101st is a priest, richly robed: each of these figures is represented standing beneath a rounded arch, and is executed in the same way as the drawings at the beginning of the volume.

On fol. 125 v. is a very remarkable drawing of the Trinity, within a plain quatrefoil surrounded by a circle; the Father is represented as an aged bearded man, the left hand holding a book and the right hand raised in the act of benediction; the Son is represented as the Agnus Dei, holding a book, and with a cross erect on its back; and the Holy Ghost as a dove; each of the three figures having a cruciferous nimbus.

THE ANGLO-SAXON PSALTER OF THE PUBLIC LIBRARY, CAMBRIDGE. No. F. f. 1. 23.

THIS fine MS. of the Psalter, remarkable for having the interlineary Anglo-Saxon version written of equal size with the Latin text, and in red ink, was bequeathed by Archbishop Matthew Parker to Sir Nicholas Bacon, by whom it was presented to the University of Cambridge.

The 1st, 51st, and 101st Psalms, as usual, have the initials of large size; the "B(eatus)" of the 1st being six inches high, ornamented in the ordinary later Anglo-Saxon style; and each is enclosed within an ornamental border of the Winchester style, but coarsely executed. Opposite each of these leaves is an illuminated page. That facing the 1st Psalm contains within a quadrangular frame, with rosettes at the angles, the figures of David playing on the harp, and his four attendants playing on the fiddle, sackbut, or lute, a horn with stops like a flute, and a small semicircular kettledrum with two sticks. This drawing is copied (without the border) in my " Palæographia," where, however, for convenience of space, Ethan and Idithun are placed at the sides of the Psalmist; in the original they occupy two compartments beneath the feet of the King, who is himself seated beneath a trefoil arch, above which are seen the tops of towers and other buildings. The form of the crown of the King, the harp of an elongated triangular form, and the Holy Ghost as a dove, flying towards the mouth of the Psalmist, who holds an object in his left hand, which may be intended for the roll of the Psalms rather than a plectrum, are to be noticed.

The Crucifixion (p. 167) is represented in coloured outlines. The cross is inscribed on the arms, "*Lignum vite*." In the place of the titulus is seen the outstretched hand of the Father. The upper part of the figure of the Redeemer is represented too short, probably from the attempt to delineate the bowing of the head, which is not higher than the cross-bars. The Virgin, on the contrary, is disproportionately tall and thin, being 7½ inches high. St. John is much superior, both in proportions and drawing; he is engaged in writing on a square tablet, "et ego vidi et testimonium" (Rev. xxii. 8; St. John xxi. 24). Above the arms of the cross are Sol and Luna weeping. Both St. John and the Saviour wear a fillet across the forehead, with a central gem. The Saviour has a green and red cruciferous nimbus, whilst the Virgin and St. John have the nimbus plainly coloured yellow.

The Ascension (p. 331) represents the Saviour holding a book with the left and blessing with the right hand, bearing in his arms a long scroll, inscribed, "Ego sum Ds qui reddo unicuiq: juxta sua opera." He is seated within a Vesica piscis, which is supported by two Angels above and two below, of a larger size than the Saviour. All the five have a plain green or red nimbus round the head, and all have the band across the forehead. The drapery is very fluttery.

Page 381 contains a very tall figure of the Saviour (more than eight inches high), standing upon the Lion and Dragon, inscribed: "Sup aspidem et basiliscu ambulabis." A tall wand, with an ornamental cross at the top, is borne in the right hand of the Saviour, the first and second fingers being extended as if engaged in the act of benediction.

The initials of most of the Psalms are drawn with considerable spirit, and show remarkable ingenuity of design. A letter M, formed of two acrobats tied together by the neck, and a Q, formed of the rotund face of a monk, are especially quaint.

THE ANGLO-SAXON PSALTER, ARUNDEL MS. No. 60.

Plate XLIX.

THIS is one of the most important MSS. of the Psalter of the later Anglo-Saxon period, both on account of its Anglo-Saxon interlineary gloss and for the drawings with which it is enriched, and the ornamental borders with which the latter, as well as the initials B, Q, and D of the three principal Psalms, are surrounded, and which, although in the style of the Winchester volumes, have the ornamental foliage of the frames splaying outwards, so as to leave the central part of the page open: they are also destitute of gold, although richly coloured. Opposite the 1st Psalm is a representation of the Crucifixion, which has been very carefully copied in outline by Mr. H. Shaw in the 4th plate of the Arundel Catalogue: it is drawn in blue, red, and green outlines. The Saviour is perfectly upright, with a cruciferous nimbus, a band round the head, and with a cloth round the middle of the body reaching to the knees; the hands and feet are attached by four nails to the cross, formed of the trunk of a tree with the branches lopped off. The hand of the Father descends from a cloud at the top of the cross. Sol and Luna, each with a flaming crown, look on unconcerned from two circles above the arms of the cross. The Virgin and St. John stand on either side, tall and meagre, with faces more like monkeys than human beings, each holding a book and each with the disengaged hand having the fingers stretched out widely.

On fol. 52 v. is the remarkable picture of the Crucifixion represented in my 49th Plate, which, although apparently of the twelfth century, agrees so entirely in its ornamental details with the rest of the volume, that we can only arrive at the conclusion that it is coeval therewith, and that the other Crucifixion opposite the 1st Psalm is an interpolation. We here see the body of the dead Saviour bent in a manner which at a later period was carried to extravagance by French miniaturists and sculptors. The two trees represented at the sides of the cross are, I think, an unique feature in this drawing. I must do Mr. Tymms, the artist who placed my fac-similes on the stone, the justice to say that he has excellently reproduced this remarkable picture, and the corresponding page with the commencement of the 101st Psalm, written in red, blue, and green capitals; the borders of the framework composed of foliage arranged in a very stiff and unusual manner, whilst the fine initial D has the foliage remarkably free in its movements.

THE ANGLO-SAXON PSALTER OF JEAN, DUC DE BERRI.

THIS curious Psalter, in which the Latin and Anglo-Saxon versions are written in opposite columns, is preserved in the Bibliothèque Impériale, Paris (MSS. Latin Suppl. No. 333). It formerly belonged to John, Duke of Berry, third son of King John of France, who was a great collector of curious books, and who, having inscribed his name on the last page, presented it in 1406 to the church of Bourges, and which, in a MS. catalogue of the middle of the last century, is described as " Les heures du duc Jean, reliées en long ; à côté du Latin, il y a une colonne d'une traduction qu'on croit d'ancien Anglo-Saxon *ou d'Hongrois*" ! It is a long and narrow folio, and in the margins are painted many scutcheons of the arms of France and Boulogne. A fac-simile page is given by Silvestre in his " Palæographie universelle ; " and Count Bastard, in his " Librairie du Jean, Duc de Berri," has given two plates, in which he has collected all the small marginal sketches made with a pen with great spirit on its various pages. Thus Psalm ii. 9 is illustrated by a small figure of the Saviour with a long rod breaking a vase ; Ps. iii. 3 has a small kneeling figure with the hand of God emerging from a cloud supporting his chin. Ps. iv. 5, a figure holding a chalice, and pushing forward a ram, approaches an altar. Ps. iv. 7, two figures, one with a large sack, and the other with a vase, press eagerly forward. Ps. v. 5 has the mouth of Hell open, with a number of the heads of the damned seen among the flames. Ps. v. 10, two warriors in deadly combat, engraved by Hewitt (Ancient Armour, i. p. 51), from a sketch which I communicated to him. Ps. vii. 2, a lion standing over a prostrate man. Ps. vii. 13, an angel discharging arrows on a guilty couple, &c.

Several fac-similes of this MS. are preserved in the British Museum library ; and two plates are given, with other specimens of the Anglo-Saxon text, in the Appendix B. to the Record Commission Report of Mr. Purton Cooper. The initials are quite plain, in gold or colours. The text has been edited by Thorpe (8vo., Oxon. 1835). The scribe of the volume thus records his name at the end of the book :—

"Hoc Psalterii carmen inclyti regis David Sacer Dei pulpitus (i cognōm to cada) manu sua conscripsit. Quicunq̃ legerit scriptu anima sua expetiat votum."

THE LATIN PSALTER OF MR. DOUCE, No. 296.

AMONGST the fine MSS. bequeathed by Mr. Douce to the Bodleian Library, is a Latin Psalter, executed about the year 1020, written in the same style as the Harleian Psalter, No. 2904, illustrated in my 43rd Plate, except that the initials are of a smaller size. The great B, however, of the 1st Psalm is five inches high, and very handsome, with a lion's head in the centre, and with the open parts of the letter coloured purple. The Q of the "Quid gloriaris" contains, in the open part of the letter, a warrior in ring armour, engaged in slaying a large dragon, which forms the tail of the letter. Instead of the Crucifixion, as in the Harleian Psalter, it has a figure of the Saviour, drawn in a very meagre style, treading triumphantly on the Lion and Dragon. Gold leaf is plentifully used in the initials.

THE BODLEIAN GOSPELS. No. 155.

THIS is a fine copy of the Latin Gospels, written in 4to. during the first half of the eleventh century, remarkable for having two of the usual figures of the Evangelists replaced by two Angels with six wings, drawn in black and red outlines, with very great freedom and correctness. One of these is a tall beautiful female figure, 8 inches high, holding a long scroll, on which is inscribed "Fuit in diebus Herodis regis judeæ sacerdos" (St. Luke i. 5); the other Angel is shorter in its proportions, and is looking upwards towards a hand stretched out from the clouds: it also bears a scroll inscribed "Credo videre bona dei in terra viventium."

The draperies of both the Angels are exceedingly fluttering, and the drawings are very characteristic of the art of the period. The ground on which they stand is raised into little rounded hillocks, common in the designs of this time.

THE GOSPELS OF WADHAM COLLEGE, OXFORD.

THIS copy of the Latin Gospels is of the 8vo. size and form, and was executed, according to Dr. Waagen (Treasures of Art in England, v. 3), between 1020 and 1030, having a drawing of the Visit of the three Marys to the Sepulchre, executed in outlines, in thick reddish purple ink, for a frontispiece. It agrees in general design with the same subject in my 46th Plate, except that the figures are reversed, the sepulchre being at the left side of the drawing. Below the feet of the Angel the three guards lie at full length asleep. The border, also in outlines, is in the style of the Winchester books, except that the foliage is directed outside the frame, which is semicircularly dilated in the middle of its four sides. St. Matthew is also delineated in red outlines, writing his Gospel, and is remarkable for holding a very good feather pen; the inkhorn being affixed to the desk. The border is in the same style as the other miniature. The Epistle to Pope Damasus commences with a large ornamental B(eato Papæ Damaso), coarsely drawn in red, blue, and green outlines; and the initial Q of St. Luke's Gospel contains St. Michael attacking a dragon, the tail of which forms the tail of the letter.

THE COTTONIAN BOOK OF PRAYERS, TITUS, D. 27.

THIS is a small nearly square volume, written at New Minster, containing Prayers, (some of which are in Anglo-Saxon), Hymns, the Office of the Holy Cross, &c. Prefixed is a Calendar, with tables of calculations; at the foot of which we have the following lines, showing the name of the Scribe, who was a monk of New Minster, and of the person for whom it was written, who was afterwards Abbot of that Monastery in 1035.

> Frater humillimus et monachus
> Ælfsinus me scripsit, sit illi longa salus   Amen
>
> Ælfwine, monachs. Decanc computum
> Istum possidet vel me possidet.   Amen.

It must have been written when Ælfwine was young, as the Paschal Table begins with A.D. 978, and the Calendar contains an entry, in the same handwriting, of the translation of the body of St. Æthelwold, which took place in 998; so that the volume must have been written between those two dates.

In the Calendar are recorded the deaths of two monkish artists:—XIII. Kal. (Maii), "Obitus Ætherici m° pict°;" and V. Non. (Jul.), "Obit° Wulfrici m° pictoris."

The volume contains two small but very excellently drawn miniatures in outline; one representing the Crucifixion, measuring 4 inches by 2¾, bearing at the top the inscription again recording the name of the monk for whom the book was executed.

> Hæc crux consignet Ælfsinum corpore, mente;
> In quâ suspendens trax(it)   D° omnia secum.

The Saviour, with a cruciferous nimbus, and having his garment fastened round the waist, extending nearly to the knees, and the feet separately nailed, bends the head down towards the Virgin, who stands with both hands open, looking towards her Son; whilst St. John looking up to the Saviour, writes the story in his opened page.   Over the head of the Saviour is the legend—"Hic e IHS Nazarenus rex judeor.," and the hand of the Father is stretched out from a cloud at the top of the cross in the act of bene-diction.   On either side above the arms of the cross, are Sol with a flaming crown, holding a globe in one hand and a flaming cornucopia in the other; and Luna, crowned with a crescent, holding a similar object in the left hand, and with the right hand out-stretched : both are three-quarter figures.   A copy of this miniature, from a drawing by myself, is published in E. Thomson's "Select Monuments of the Catholic Church."

The only other drawing is the singular little representation of the Trinity, of which an etching was published by Dr. Dibdin, in his "Bibliographical Decameron," vol. i.   Here the Father and Son are represented quite alike, and as aged men, each with a cruciferous nimbus, and each with a book; whilst the place of the Third Person is occupied by a figure of the Virgin Mary, holding an infant on her lap, and with the Holy Ghost as a dove resting upon her crowned head.   A demon bound in chains, beneath the feet of one of the two aged figures, is being thrust into the gaping jaws of Hades, whilst Arrius and Judas, both also chained, occupy the two lower angles of the design.   These two drawings are very superior in their style to the great majority of those which have survived, of this period.   They are very slightly but effectively tinted in green and red, which latter colour is employed for the outlines of the flesh and portions of the dress in the drawing of the Crucifixion.

THE BODLEIAN DUNSTAN MS.

THE Bodleian MS. N. E. D. 2, 19 (Bodl. 578), consists of various fragments collected together, and merits notice in this work on account of a drawing on the first page, which has attracted considerable attention, and which purports to have been executed by St. Dunstan himself (which has been published by Hickes in his "Thesaurus" and by Strutt in his "Horda," pl. 18), as appears by an inscription of a somewhat more recent date in partially Gothic characters, but still retaining the long-tailed r. : "Pictura et scriptura huius pagine subtus visa, est de propria manu Sci Dunstani." The drawing represents the Saviour standing erect : it is 8 inches high, but the feet and lower part of the drapery are cut off by a line. It is finely drawn in strong outlines, the body excellently posed, the head a little bent over the right shoulder, the hair long and flowing, the beard very small, the head surrounded by a red nimbus, marked with a white cross ; the right hand is held upwards towards the breast. A slender rod terminating at top as a trident formed of three lines of red dots, is grasped by the thumb and second, third, and fourth fingers of the right hand, of which the index is extended : over the rod is written :—" ✠ Virga recta est virga regni tui." The left hand holds a book inscribed " Venite filii audite me, timore dni docebo vos." The upper garment in well-arranged folds extends from the shoulders to the knees, and is fastened by a sash across the waist, the end fluttery, as in late Anglo-Saxon drawings. At the bottom of the right side of the drawing is a small side-faced figure of a monk kneeling, with the body bent to the ground, the face shaded with the right hand, the head tonsured, the cowl resting on the back of the neck ; the garment with a red edge above the feet, and with this inscription above the figure :—" Dunstanum memet clemens rogo xpe tuere. Tenarias me non sinas sorbsisse procellas." The writing over the rod and on the book is in narrow Anglo-Saxon letters, and the lines over Dunstan in rounded minuscule characters, the r having the first stroke produced below the line, as in the New Minster books of the end of the tenth century : the initials of the two lines are miniated in the same manner as the nimbus of the Saviour.

On the verso of the sheet containing the miniature is the commencement of a grammatical treatise (Eutex Grammaticus), written in a hand of the tenth century, and extending to a number of the leaves, followed by portion of an Anglo-Saxon treatise and a curious series of extracts from the Minor Prophets, &c., written in Greek and Latin parallel columns of an early date, of which I have given fac-similes in my "Palæographia."

These details are necessary because Dr. Waagen (Treasures of Art in England, iii.) has affirmed that the MS. is of the twelfth century (to which date indeed the superscription on the miniature can alone be referred), and consequently cannot represent the Archbishop Dunstan, of the tenth century.

Mr. Planché copied the figure of Dunstan in his "British Costumes," p. 39 ; but incorrectly referred it to the Royal MS. 10 A. 13, which led me, in my "Palæographia," to state that the latter MS. contained a copy of the Bodleian drawing. The Royal MS. drawing is alluded to beneath. Mrs. Jameson (Leg. Monast. Orders, p. 94) has given a not very faithful copy of this drawing, mixing it up in her comments with the portrait in Claudius. A. 3, which she subsequently describes.

3 S

THE COTTONIAN DUNSTAN MS. CLAUDIUS, A. 3.

Plate I.

T HIS manuscript consists of a variety of pieces, including a Pontificale and a series of Synodial Decrees for the reformation of the Church, probably drawn up by Archbishop Wulfstan, and afterwards confirmed by King Æthelred II.

The MS. contains the miniature, copied in my 50th Plate, representing an Archbishop, enthroned, *with a yellow nimbus* round the head, wearing the pallium and other gorgeous robes, seated beneath a highly-decorated arch. On his head is a small cap-like mitre, with the infulæ short; whilst the Holy Ghost, with a red cruciferous nimbus, flies towards his right ear.

Three ecclesiastics kneel at his feet, one wearing the black, another the white (slightly tinted with pale pink), Benedictine habit; and the third the dress of an Archbishop, with a pallium and a similar cap or mitre.* Two of these figures embrace the feet of the principal personage. Across the top of the drawing is inserted, in a somewhat later handwriting, " Dunstani Archiepiscopi ;" and hitherto the principal figure has been affirmed to represent St. Dunstan; whilst Mrs. Jameson (Legends Mon. Ord., p. 95), overlooking the close mitre and pallium, adds that the lower left-hand figure is intended for a priest or canon regular.

Dr. Rock, in the " Church of our Fathers," has twice repeated the principal figure as that of St. Dunstan, illustrating various interesting points of ecclesiastical costume, and relying more particularly on the presence of the dove as confirming one of the many legends of the saint. This miraculous story, which is given by the Bollandists in the " Acta Sanctorum Ord. St. Benedicti," t. iv. Maii, p. 364, and which does not speak very highly for the merciful character of Dunstan, is to the effect that three false coiners having been condemned to death, Dunstan, on his way to perform mass on the festival of the Holy Ghost (the day of Pentecost, or Whit-Sunday), inquired if the sentence had been executed. On learning that it had been delayed on account of the high church festival, the enraged Archbishop immediately gave orders for the execution. We may well agree with the historian when he adds that the " edictum nonnullis videbatur crudele." The order of Dunstan having, however, been performed, " lota facie, ad oratorium, *exhilarato vultu*, abiit." " Now," said he, " I trust that God will accept the sacrifice which I am about to offer ;" and, accordingly, at the moment when he lifted up his hands to pray that God would keep the universal Church in continual peace, " *nivea columba*, multis intuentibus, de cælo descendit et, donec sacrificium consummatum est, *super caput ejus* (Dunstani) expansis alis et quasi immotis, sub silentio mansit." After the Mass was ended, he retired alone, full of the manifestation which had been afforded of

---

* This is probably one of the earliest representations of a mitre in its simplest form. In earlier drawings, bishops are represented without any head-covering, and there is an mention of the mitre in the Benedictional of St. Æthelwold,   or the Pontificale of Æthelgar, where the episcopal consecration occurs. In the twelfth century it appears as a larger cap, depressed in the middle.—(Weiss, Kostumkunde, p. 677.)

the Divine grace, and having taken off his chasuble, as there was no attendant to hold it, it remained suspended in the air, for fear that, falling to the ground, it should disturb the holy thoughts of this servant of God.

Notwithstanding, however, the supposed confirmation which this story gives to the idea that the principal figure represents St. Dunstan and his white dove, I must observe, first, that the presence of the nimbus round his head indicates a sainted personage, which was not then the case with Dunstan; second, that the dove does not rest upon his head, but that it is flying towards his mouth,—a mode of representation of the act of inspiration by the Holy Ghost (to be followed by subsequent oral delivery of the inspired thoughts); and third, that this mode of representing the inspiration of the Holy Ghost has in all ages and countries been adopted.

Thus the dove, resting on his shoulders and whispering into his ear, has been a constant symbol of Pope Gregory the Great, of which numerous illustrations might be quoted. (See p. 70, n. 4.) St. Ephrem of Syria affirms that he saw a dove resting on the shoulders of St. Basil the Great, dictating his works. St. Jerome is so represented in a fine MS. of the Paris Library (Bibl. sacra, No. 6829); and in a grand Greek Psalter in the same library (MS. Grec, No. 139), a dove hovers over the head of David; and in the Cambridge Psalter (see ante, p. 120) one flies towards his mouth. In an early stained-glass window of the Cathedral of Sens, the protomartyr Stephen is also similarly represented. In Germany, St. Catherine is also figured with the Holy Ghost in one of the windows of the Cathedral of Freiburg, in Brisgau. Hence I do not hesitate in regarding the principal figure in the miniature before us as representing either St. Gregory or St. Benedict. I think there can be equally little doubt that it is the lower left-hand figure which is intended for St. Dunstan; the low, cap-like mitre and pallium bespeaking his high dignity, whilst the form of the former proves the early date of the drawing, as the mitre is seen of a conical form, or centrally depressed, in the drawings of the latter part of the eleventh and twelfth centuries.

The miniature is surrounded by a beautiful arabesque border of branches and foliage, with flowers, animals, and birds introduced into the middle of the whorls, as we have seen in the Lambeth Aldhelm and the Boulogne Psalter. The architectural details of the drawing are very interesting, and carefully treated.

On folio 28 is the figure of a monk or bishop, seated writing beneath a rounded arch, which, with the dome, is architecturally treated in the same manner as in the miniature above described. It is engraved by Strutt (Dresses, i. pl. 27), and is given as that of Walfstan, Bishop of Worcester and Archbishop of York (1062—1023); and Mr. Planché believes that the MS. was written, and the drawing made, during the lifetime of that prelate.

[The miniatures copied from the Harleian MS. 2908, by Strutt (Dresses and Habits, i. pl. 20 and 26), the latter being given as that of the Abbot Elfnoth (who died A.D. 980) presenting his book of prayers to St. Augustine, the founder of the monastery of Canterbury, from the frontispiece of the book itself, are of German execution, written, according to Dr. Waagen, evidently at Augsburg, about A.D. 1000—1010.]

[Another so-called miniature of St. Dunstan is contained in the Royal MS. 10 A. 13 (Brit. Mus.), copied by Strutt (Dresses and Habits, i. pl. 50). It represents an Archbishop, in a low conical mitre (with a gold nimbus), fully robed and wearing the pallium, engaged in writing, holding a pen and a knife, or parchment-scraper, the inkpot fastened at the corner of the desk. The book is inscribed, "OBSCULTA [Ausculta] O FILI PRECEPTA MAGISTRI," being the commencement of the Rule of St. Benedict. The figure is described by Casley, Strutt, and subsequent writers,[*] as representing "Dunstan, Archbishop of Canterbury, from a MS. of the twelfth century." The MS., which is rather of the thirteenth century, contains a copy of "Dunstani Expositio in Regulam Sti. Benedicti," and hence the inaccuracy of the supposition that the drawing was intended for Dunstan, just as, on the same account, Mr. Turner represented him as having introduced the Benedictine Order into England (the fact being that there had existed no other Order in England) from the time of St. Augustine). The words inscribed on the book are the commencement of the "Regula Sti. Benedicti," and prove, therefore, that the portrait is intended for St. Benedict himself.[†]]

THE PONTIFICALE OF ST. DUNSTAN.

A FINE folio volume in the Imperial Library of Paris (MS. Lat. No. 943) is traditionally known as the Pontificale of St. Dunstan. It is of the latter half of the tenth century, and contains a very full ceremonial, including the ordeal of judgment by red-hot irons and boiling water. It formerly belonged to the Bishopric of Sherborn (Ecclesiæ Scyreburnensis), of which the celebrated poet Aldhelm was the first bishop, in 705, and which ultimately, in 1217, was transferred to Salisbury. The Paris MS. contains a list of the twenty-one bishops of Sherborn, commencing with Idhelm (or Aldhelm, 705), and terminating with Æthelric (980): it differs in a few particulars from the printed lists. The volume also contains a list of the books in the library "Seæ Mariæ" at the period of its execution, which is closely written, and extends to a page and a half. There are also two Anglo-Saxon homilies on the dedication of a church; an episcopal decree on the celebration of the Mass; also, "literæ commendititiæ" from the Church of Sherborn to a certain penitent; also a remarkable Anglo-Saxon letter from Bishop Æthelric to Æthelmer respecting certain disputed tributary payments. But it is chiefly interesting in respect to the outline miniatures which it contains. The first of these, occupying the whole page, represents the Crucifixion, excellently drawn. The Saviour is already dead, his eyes closed, and head fallen upon the right shoulder, with a cruciferous nimbus, draped only round the middle of the body; feet apart; and at the foot of the cross beneath the feet is a two-handled vase; at the top of the cross is the outstretched hand of the Father; an angel

---

[*] The figure is partially copied of full size in the "Pictorial History of England," i. p. 343, but is erroneously referred to the Cottonian MS. Claudius A. 3. The Claudius portrait of Dunstan is quite different.

[†] Regarding the translation of the Rule of St. Benedict into Anglo-Saxon, we read in the "Historia Eliensis,"...

[‡] Eadgarus Rex et Alfreth (sive Ælfred) dederunt Seo Æthelwoldo manerium quod dicitur Suthlova et Cynegythiam quod pertinebat, quod Comes qui dicitur Seule dudum possederat : eo pacto ut ille regulam Sci Benedicti in Anglicum idioma de Latino transferret, qui sic fecit."

on either side descends from the clouds, bearing a napkin. The Virgin and St. John (the latter with both hands open and elevated) stand on either side of the cross. All the figures are well-proportioned, and the outlines in red and black ink only. The drapery is of the usual fluttery character. A narrow foliated border forms a slight frame to the drawing. Three other pages are occupied by three full-length figures, 8 inches high, representing, in a most remarkable manner, the three persons of the Trinity, also in outline, each bearing a cruciferous nimbus, and each bearing a book, marked in the first and second drawings with two crosses, but plain in the third. The Father, represented as a man of 50 years old, has a short beard, and wears a crown adorned with pearls and three trefoil leaves. The Son, apparently about 30 years old, has a still shorter beard and bears in his right hand, as does the Father also, a long rod with a small cross at the top. The Holy Ghost, 20 years old, with the slightest trace of a beard, bears in his right hand the book, and in his left either a long red feather, or a twig with small leaves along its whole length, just like the herbage in the miniature of Adam tilling the ground, from Claudius, B. 4. (Palæogr. sacra). The character of the same features at these three different periods of life is well maintained, although the heads are too small. The drapery is fluttery. Each is surrounded by a narrow foliated border. The text commences with a large ornamented A, formed of interlaced ribbons, terminating in dogs' heads, as in the Lambeth Aldhelm.

THE COTTONIAN BOOK OF PRAYERS, &c., TIBERIUS. A. 3.

THIS manuscript, of the latter half of the tenth century, contains the Rule of St. Benedict, and various prayers, &c., written either in Anglo-Saxon, or in Latin with an Anglo-Saxon gloss, containing a contemporary portrait (drawn in outline, and slightly tinted in green and red), of King Edgar and two ecclesiastics, seated under three rounded arches springing from plain capitals, a long roll extending across the drawing, held by the three figures. The King wears a crown, which is represented as if it were square, one of the angles being in front; it is jewelled along the rim, and furnished with an ornamented crest. In his right hand he holds a long curved sceptre resembling a feather (like the object held by the Holy Ghost in the Paris Pontificale of St. Dunstan), but terminating in a fleur-de-lis.* A reduced copy of the figure of the King is given in C. Knight's "Pict. Hist. Engl." i. p. 330.

The ecclesiastic to the left appears to be a bishop, and wears a chasuble terminating in a point in front, and looped up over the arms, which are raised, holding the end of the long scroll. The front of the chasuble is marked with a narrow band down the middle, ornamented with pearls. The figure to the right is that of an Archbishop, seated in a more commanding attitude, looking towards the King, with the right hand elevated, the thumb and two first fingers erect, as if in the act of blessing: he wears the pallium over the chasuble, which has not the band down the middle in front. Both these ecclesiastics are represented with plain nimbi round the head. The figures

* Is this intended for a palm-branch: a peacock or ostrich-feather (subsequently used as a badge by Edward III. and succeeding monarchs): or is it a willow wand, or a branch of the planta genista?

are in outline, slightly shaded with green, purple, and brown. In the lower part of the picture is represented a monk, apparently in the white habit of a Benedictine, with the cowl hanging down the back, the head showing the tonsure, kneeling on the right knee, with the left leg thrown backwards at full length, in a most awkward position. He holds a very long scroll with both outstretched hands, which passes behind his back and extends to the sides of the picture. As the two seated figures of ecclesiastics have the head encircled by the nimbus, it can hardly be considered that either of them represents Dunstan, in which case the kneeling monk must be supposed to be intended for him.

This is prefixed to a Latin article which occupies 50 pages, and is described in the Cottonian "Catalogus tractatum in isto volumine," as "Regularis Concordia Anglicæ nationis monachorum sanctimonialium sub Edgaro Rege, *procurante Dunstano* ['monente Dunstano' in the printed Catalogue], interlineatim inseritur etiam versio Saxonica tempore ejusdem Regis scripta." *

On fol. 114 v. (prefixed to the Latin Rule of St. Benedict, with an Anglo-Saxon interlineary gloss) is a drawing, executed in thick body-colours, but much damaged, of St. Benedict, seated in the act of expounding his Rule to three monks, the book of the Rule lying on a tripod table. The Saint wears a green chasuble fastened upon the breast by a large oblong brooch, or rationale, with the four angles terminating in a sort of fleur-de-lis. He appears to wear a skullcap-shaped mitre, with a band across the forehead, inscribed " Pater," with two large infulæ with triangular ends, on which was evidently inscribed BENE   TUS. The lower garment is red, with a yellow jewelled
                       DIC
border. The monks, who are drawn of a very disproportionate length, wear pale blue (or white), dark green, and flesh-coloured gowns. At the foot of St. Benedict kneels a monk, clasping his foot with one hand and holding a book with the other; whilst in front of the latter monk kneels an extravagantly thin figure of a monk, in a pale green gown, holding a very long label, of which the inscription is also nearly effaced.

The green and red groundwork of this miniature is shaded all round the figures with deeper washes of the same colours, exactly as in the large miniature of St. Mark, copied in my Plate 15, from the singular MS. Reg. I.E. 6, with which it also agrees in the long attenuated figure, exaggerated movements of the limbs, treatment of the outlines, and shading of the flesh, so completely, that I have but little doubt that both were executed by the same artist.

Edward the Elder, and consecrated in 903, in which year Grimbald died. In the year 965, Æthelgar, the reputed possessor of the Rouen Benedictional, was Abbot of New Minster. The Benedictional of St. Æthelwold was executed at Winchester, about the year 970. The volume which has supplied the materials for my 47th Plate is another striking instance, not only of the interest taken by the ruling monarchs in the newly-founded monastery, but also in the arts of design as practised in this part of the kingdom during the latter half of the tenth century, when so many magnificent MSS. were executed. It is a volume preserved in the Cottonian Library, Vespasian, A. VIII, containing the various grants or donations made to New Minster by King Edgar, and bears the date of 966. The King himself was a great reformer both in State and Church, although he sided with the monks against the regular clergy, of which the book before us affords sufficient evidence. The whole of the text is written in letters of gold in the same Caroline minuscule hand as most of the books having the same origin.

The date of the volume is expressly stated in the passage copied in the lower part of the two side-pages in my plate (written in the ordinary characters of the volume): "Anno incarnationis dominicæ DCCCCLXVI scripta est hujus privilegii singrapha;" and the act of donation itself is indicated in the right-hand page: " + Eadgar rex hoc privilegium novo edidit monasterio ac omnipotenti Dūo ejusque genetrici Mariæ ejus laudans magnalia concessit." The opposite page contains the opening of the text itself, commencing with the monogram of Christ used ordinarily in charters for the Invocation. "In nomine Dñi nostri Iħu Xp̄i Omnipotens totius machinæ conditor," written in fine golden capitals. The book itself is evidently referred to in the "Annals of Hyde Abbey":—"Nong' lxvi. Edgar' rex cont'lit novo monas'tio Wy'ton libru' p'uilegior' aureis l'ris se'ptu'."

The miniature forming the frontispiece of the volume is copied in the centre compartment of my plate. It formed also (with the omission of the ornamental border) the first plate of Strutt's "Regal Antiquities," and is described by him as having been taken from a book of grants given by King Edgar himself to Winchester Cathedral (1), and to be written in the old Saxon character (2). Mr. Strutt's description continues:—
" Edgar is here delineated as piously adoring our blessed Saviour, who appears above seated on a globe (3), to show his empire, and supported by four Angels, emblems of the four Gospels (4): under his feet are two folding-doors (5), intended perhaps to represent the entrance into the bottomless pit, which is so placed to convey the idea of his triumph over Death and Hell: in his left hand he holds the Book of Judgment (6), which is to be opened at the last day. The figure on the right hand of the King, I fancy may be done for Cuthbert, the saint of Durham, whose holy life is recorded by the Venerable Bede (7). The woman, not unlikely, is the famous Etheldreda, Abbess of Ely, who, though she were twice married, yet lived and died a pure virgin (8)."

On this description it is to be observed,—1st. That the donation of King Edgar was made to New Minster, not to the Old Minster or Cathedral of Winchester. Relying on Strutt, I introduced the latter name on the title of my 47th Plate. 2nd. That the writing of the volume is especially free from the Anglo-Saxon peculiarities, and, as above stated, is written in a Caroline minuscule hand. 3rd. The Saviour is seated on the conventional rainbow, the green portion indicating a lower division of the Vesica piscis. 4th. The four Gospels are never represented by four angels. It would be contrary to all the rules of Christian iconography to represent the Saviour as supported by the Gospels, which are emanations from himself. 5th. The feet of the Saviour simply rest upon a footstool, various instances of which may be pointed out in the

J x

plates of this work.   6th. The Saviour is always represented as holding in his left hand the book of the Gospels, and generally, as here, with his right hand extended, or elevated in the act of benediction.   7th. It is extraordinary that Strutt should have overlooked the keys, the tonsure, and the shaven features of St. Peter.   There were no local reasons for introducing St. Cuthbert into the picture.   And 8th, Mr. W. Young Ottley, in his notice of this miniature addressed to Mr. Gage (Rookwood), "Archæologia," xxiv. p. 33, considers the female figure to represent the Madonna, overlooking the palm-branch and cross, which she holds in her hands—emblems of a female martyr.   Strutt, it will be seen, thinks the figure intended for St. Etheldreda, without giving any reason for such an opinion.   She was, it is true, one of the most famous female Saints among the Anglo-Saxons, and hence, as well as from the fact that she was one of the patron Saints of St. Æthelwold (having been Abbess of the monastery of Ely, which he refounded), we find her introduced as one of the two English Saints represented in his grand Benedictional, the other being St. Swithin, to whom the Cathedral, or Old Minster, of Winchester had been dedicated.   It is not therefore improbable that, as Æthelwold had been raised to the see of Winchester in 963, she should be represented in this New Minster miniature in 966.   St. Etheldreda, however, died quietly in her bed, as shown on one of the capitals of Ely Cathedral ; and if we search among the other Anglo-Saxon Saints who were martyred, we might possibly not be wrong in selecting St. Ebba, slaughtered, with her nuns, by the Danes, who burnt their nunnery over their heads.   Mrs. Jameson says respecting her, " St. Ebba should bear the palm, and, being of royal lineage, she would have a double right to the crown as princess and as martyr." (Legends Mon. Ord., p. 60.)   St. Etheldreda received the veil at the hands of St. Ebba.

"The style of this miniature," says Mr. Ottley, "with its surrounding ornaments, though the figures are smaller, is so much like that of St. Æthelwold's Benedictional, that I will not undertake to say it is not by the same hand.   The Angels appear decidedly of the selfsame family as those in that volume."

On the page opposite to the miniature is inscribed the verses :—

SIC CELSO RESIDET SOLIO QUI CONDIDIT ASTRA
REX VENERANS EADGAR PRON' ADORAT EŬ.

THE BENEDICTIONAL OF ST. ÆTHELWOLD.

Plate XLV.

THIS magnificent volume, the noblest of all the surviving productions of later Anglo-Saxon art, belongs to the Duke of Devonshire.   It consists of 119 leaves, 11½ by 8½ inches in size, and is written in large Caroline minuscule characters, nearly a quarter of an inch high, the capital initials sometimes of large size, being formed of gold-leaf laid upon size, and afterwards burnished, and which is in general solid and bright.   The origin of the volume is due to the great Æthelwold, who having received the monastic habit from St. Dunstan at Glastonbury, was, at the recommendation of the latter, appointed Abbot of the newly-erected royal monastery of Abingdon in A.D. 948, and was subsequently, in 963, made Bishop of Winchester, where he died in 984, and who, after his death, was enrolled in the calendar of English Saints.

The volume from which the accompanying drawing has been copied contains the Ancient Benedictional of the See of Winchester, as we learn from the prefixed series of verses written in letters of gold, commencing:—

> PRESENTEM BIBLŪ JUSSIT PSCRIDERE PRESUL
> UUINTONIAE DNS QUI FECERAT ESSE PATRONŪ
> MAGNUS APELLUUOLDUS VERE GNARUS BENE XPI
> AGNOS UELLIGEROS AB DEMONIS ARTE MALIGNA
> CONSERVARE DŌ FRUCTŪ QUOQ REDDERE PLENŪ
> ICONOMOS CLARUS UENERABILIS ATQ BENIGNUS
> HIC CUPIT, ARBITER UT UENERIT QUI DISCUTIT ORBIS
> TOTIUS FACTŪ QUID QUILIBET EGERIT ATQUE
> MERCEDĒ REDDET QUALEM TUNC FORTE MERENTUR
> AETERNĀ IUSTIS UITAM, INIUSTIS QUOQ POENĀ
> QUENDA SUBIECTŪ MONACHU. CIRCOS QUOQ MULTOS
> IN HOC PRECEPIT FIERI LIBRO BENE COMPTOS
> COMPLETOS QUOQ AGALMATIB UARIIS DECORATIS
> MULTIGENIS MINIIS PULCHRIS NECNON SIMUL AURO
> CRAXARE HUNC SIBI PRESCRIPTUS FECIT BOANARGES.

The verses proceed to set forth the uses of the book for the edification of the lambs of the fold, with prayers for their spiritual welfare, terminating with a prayer for the scribe himself:—

> OMNES CERNENTES BIBLU HUNC SEMP ROGITENT HOC
> POST META CARNIS UALEAM CAELIS INHERERE.
> OBNIXE HOC ROGITAT SCRIPTOR SUPPLEX GODEMANN

Now we know from the Red Book of Thorney Abbey, quoted in Harl. MS. 6978, that Godemann, who was a monk of Winchester and chaplain of Æthelwold, was appointed, at the instance of the latter, Abbot of the monastery of Thorney, which he (Æthelwold) had then recently founded. This is stated in one of the early records to have taken place in 970; so that the volume before us must, in all probability, have been executed between 963 and the latter year.

The volume, in its present state, is a grand pictorial repository, containing thirty illuminated miniatures and thirteen other ornamental pages, generally surrounded by rectangular borders, with beautiful rosettes at the angles composed of conventional foliage and flowers, or of arches resting on similarly ornamented columns, each page where the opening of some particular benediction occurs being in capital letters of gold; and where a miniature or painting fronts a decorated page, the arches or borders of both pages are made to correspond, leading to the probable conclusion that the open volume was placed on the altar within sight of the people on high festivals. It is certain, however, that several of the original illuminations have been cut out of the volume, such as the Massacre of the Innocents, St. Michael, one of the groups of Confessors, and probably the two groups of the "Noble Army of Martyrs."

As the whole of the existing miniatures have been beautifully engraved in Mr. Gage (Rockwood's) Dissertation in the 24th volume of the "Archæologia," I shall here simply indicate the subjects of each.

1. A group of seven Confessors, crowned, and with the hair cut short, standing under

3 Y

a triple arch, the three foremost having their names, " + Scē Gregorius presul͞" [not 'papa']; " + Scs Benedictus abbas;" and " + Scs Cuthberhtus antistes," inscribed on their palliums. This drawing is copied in colours in Mr. Humphreys' " Illuminated Books of the Middle Ages."

2 and 3. Two groups of female Saints, forming the Chorus Virginum, all of whom are crowned except the two principal figures in the third drawing, representing St. Ætheldrytha and St. Mary Magdalen, each of whom has the head surrounded with a pearl-edged nimbus. These figures, especially the latter two, are beautifully drawn in excellent proportions. The small Angels, filling in the open arcades of these and the adjacent drawings, are also charmingly designed.

4. 5. 6, and 7. The Twelve Apostles, three in each drawing, standing under conical or rounded arches, St. Paul distinguished only by his head partially bald, and St. Peter by being the only Apostle with the tonsure and clean-shaved, holding a small cross in his extended right hand, from which hang the two keys.

8. The Salutation.—The Archangel standing to the left before the Virgin, who is seated between columns supporting a rounded dome.

9. A grand drawing representing the Saviour (of large size, bearded, within the Vesica piscis) coming in the Clouds to Judgment. He bears a book and a long staff, with a small cross at the top; the words " Rex regum et Dn͞s dominantiū " on his garment. Above is a host of Angels, some of whom bear the cross, spear, and sponge.

10. The Birth of Christ.—The Virgin, on a large bed, occupies nearly the whole of the drawing. A female attendant arranges her pillows. Joseph is seated to the right; below, to the left, is the Infant in swaddling-clothes, lying, with the heads of an ox and ass.

11. The Stoning of St. Stephen (represented tonsured, and with a plain gold nimbus). —In the clouds a beautiful figure of the youthful Saviour, standing in a Vesica piscis, supported by two Angels.

12. A fine figure of St. John the Evangelist, seated, writing his Gospel: his Eagle, blowing a trumpet, hovers over the writing-desk. — Mr. Gage (Arch., xxiv. p. 37) thinks this trumpet is a large golden inkhorn, failing to observe that the inkhorn, small and black, is fixed at the top of the arm of the chair. (In the Gospels of Lindisfarne the Ox of St. Luke blows a horn.)

13. The Consultation of the Magi.—Above is the Virgin resting on a bed, holding the Infant; and below are three old men, sitting, engaged in conversation.

14. The Offerings of the Magi.—The Virgin, seated under an arch, with the Infant sitting in her lap and a large star over her head, welcomes, with outstretched hand, the three Kings, who come forward, in stooping attitude, bearing gifts, with their hands covered and their legs bandage

15. The Baptism of Christ.—A curious composition. The river Jordan is discharged from a reversed pitcher held by an aged figure, with two golden horns, with what I presume to be intended for a paddle, visible behind his head. The water flows upwards most unnaturally, hiding the lower half of the figure of the Saviour, who is enveloped in the Vesica piscis, half-hidden in the water. The Holy Ghost as a dove descends from above, holding in its beak what appears to be a penannular ring with dilated ends.

16. The Presentation in the Temple.—The hand of God descends from the clouds over the young Child, who is held aloft by his Mother with naked hands, and received by Zachariah with covered hands.

17. The Entry of Christ on an ass into Jerusalem.

18. The Visit of the Three Marys to the Sepulchre.—The sepulchre itself, with the Angel seated on the great stone, occupies the whole of the centre of the picture; the three females on the right side, and the four guards on the other, being driven into the marginal framework.

19. Christ standing within the Vesica piscis, holding a long staff in his left hand, surmounted by a cross, and his right hand open and elevated, appears to the Apostles. St. Thomas stretches forth his finger to thrust it into the wound in the side of the Saviour. St. Peter, who alone is tonsured, holds up the two keys, surmounted by a cross.

20. The Ascension (copied in my 45th Plate).—Here the Virgin and St. Peter, tonsured and shaved, occupy the foremost place amongst the *eleven* Apostles. The framework, generally more than an inch wide in these pictures, is nearly absorbed by this drawing.

21. The Descent of the Holy Ghost (accompanied by two Angels) upon the Twelve Apostles.—The Dove is inclosed within a Vesica piscis, and emits copious flames from its mouth upon the heads of the chosen twelve; the Virgin being absent.

22. A grand figure of the Deity as an aged man (holding up the right hand in the act of benediction, with a cruciferous nimbus, having a golden circlet round the head, and seated on a rainbow within the Vesica piscis) is introduced in the middle of a large initial O, opposite to the now wanting figure of the Trinity, the loss of which is greatly to be regretted, as the pictorial treatment of this subject in manuscripts of this early date is exceedingly rare.

23. A fine female figure, with a gemmed nimbus, holding a lily in her left hand and a book in her right hand, representing St. Æthelrytha, one of the two patron saints of St. Æthelwold himself.

24. The bust of the Saviour, with a gemmed and cruciferous nimbus, and the right hand elevated in the act of benediction, enclosed within a golden O.

25. The Birth of St. John the Baptist.—The Mother in a bed, and the Child in a cradle, occupy the upper part of the drawing; below, Zachariah seated, writing with a style on a tablet, "Iohannes est no(men ejus)," with four seated figures looking on.

26. Above is represented the Crucifixion of St. Peter, head downwards; two soldiers, armed with swords, fasten the feet with ropes to the cross. Below, a soldier, with uplifted sword, is about to cut off the head of the aged St. Paul.

27. A full-length figure of St. Swithun, the other patron of St. Æthelwold, tonsured, shaved, and with the right hand elevated in the act of benediction.

28. St. Benedict, aged, with a golden circlet round the tonsured head, seated below a rounded arch, holding a crown in his left and a book in his right hand.

29. The Death of the Virgin.—Here the hand of God holds a crown at the top of the picture, with four attendant Angels; below are some of the Apostles standing engaged in conversation. The figures of the Virgin and her female attendants are treated as in the Benedictional of Æthelgar.

30. A Monk, or Bishop, standing under a rounded arch, delivers a book to a number of priests and other attendants, who, together with the surrounding architectural details, are only slightly sketched in red chalk.

THE MISSAL OF ARCHBISHOP ROBERT OF CANTERBURY, or OF ST. GUTHLAC.

Plate XL.

THIS famous volume, now in the public library in the Hôtel de Ville of Rouen, formerly belonged to the Abbey of Jumièges (where Edward the Confessor passed many of the years of his youth), as is evident from the following coeval anathema in the handwriting of Robert, Bishop of London, afterwards Archbishop of Canterbury, who was formerly head of that monastery, and who died there in 1053, and by whom the volume was presented to that abbey:—"Quem si quis vi vel dolo, seu quoquo modo isti boo subtraxerit animæ suæ propter quod fecerit detrimentum patiatur atque de libro viventium deleatur et cum justis non scribatur." The Dominical tables extend from A.D. 1000 to 1095. The volume has also been termed the Book of St. Guthlac, the first sentence containing an orison for the protection of that saint. It is of a large quarto size, measuring about 13 inches by 9, and is illuminated precisely in the style of the Benedictional of St. Æthelwold, written in the latter half of the tenth century. At the commencement of the volume is a copious calendar, followed by a short poem on the lunar revolutions, the days of the week, and months of the year. The illuminations, chiefly consisting of scenes of the life of the Saviour, occupy entire pages, and are surrounded with framework designs with large rosettes at the corners, ornamented with conventional foliage interlacing in a curious manner, as in the Æthelwold Benedictional, the Gospels of Canute and of Trinity College, Cambridge, &c.: the framework is considerably heightened with gold leaf, which has occasionally become tarnished. Many of the pages are also entirely written in fine golden capitals inscribed in similar borders. The following is a list of all the illuminations in this interesting book:—

Fol. 25 v. A fine framework of gold and colours enclosing the words "Per omnia sæcula sæculorum" in large golden letters.

Fol. 26 r. The commencement of the Canon of the Mass, VERE DIGNUM (in its contracted form as a grand capital), ET JUSTUM EST in a border.

Fol. 26 v. The TE IGITUR of the Mass in a similar frame.

Fol. 32 v. The Birth of Christ.—Here the Virgin is lying on a short-legged bed, which extends across the drawing, with the head supported by cushions, which are being arranged by a female attendant. An Angel descends from above towards the Virgin. Below, to the right, Joseph, of diminished size, is seated, regarding the Holy Child lying in the manger to the left, with an ass and the head of an ox.

Fol. 33 r. The Angel appearing to the Shepherds, in the upper part.—At the top of the drawing six Angels are enclosed within a semicircular space, to represent the heavenly Host. The Angel, just alighted on the earth, announces the glad tidings to two shepherds, who are surrounded by their flocks. Below, the Flight into Egypt is represented in a homely manner. The Virgin, seated on an ass, holds the Child in her lap, who stretches out its hands to Joseph leading the ass, and carrying the Virgin's distaff on his shoulder. This part of the picture is engraved in Dibdin's "Bibl. Tour," i. p. 167. Its quaintness has always rendered it a great favourite with me; forty-five years ago I made a copy of Dr. Dibdin's engraving of it.

Fol. 37. r. Herod with his attendants alarmed at the appearance of the Star.—The king, wearing a Phrygian cap, and holding a rod in his left hand, is seated on a high-backed chair or throne. Before him stand a number of the inhabitants of Jerusalem, some pointing to the star with great spirit. This is one of the best-designed groups in the volume. Below, the three kings, of small size, on horseback, with Phrygian caps and long spears, journey towards Jerusalem, represented by a house surrounded by walls and towers.

Fol. 37 v. The three kings, wearing Phrygian golden caps, approach with naked legs and feet, but with the hands covered, bearing gifts to the Holy Child sitting in the lap of the Virgin, who is seated on a chair with a cushion, placed in an architecturally-designed alcove. Below, the Angel, with outstretched wings and hands, appears to the sleeping kings, lying side by side, and enveloped in a claret-brown cover. This is one of the most pleasing compositions in the entire volume; it is enclosed within an elegant trefoil arch, resting upon golden columns ornamented with small green rosettes in a very unusual manner.

Fol. 71 r. The Betrayal of Christ is copied in my 40th Plate. It is by far the most effective drawing in the work, many of the figures exhibiting considerable energy. The curious manner in which the background is treated, which also occurs in some of the other drawings, can scarcely be intended to represent clouds. The banded legs of the soldiers, the form of their weapons, as well as of the lantern, merit notice, as does also the elegant treatment of the framework.

Fol. 72 v. The Crucifixion.—The Saviour, with a cruciferous nimbus, has a napkin fastened round the middle of the body; the two feet are spread out, but no nails are visible; the beard is short and round; the eyes are directed towards the Virgin, who stands weeping with her face covered, to the left; St. John, standing to the right, also partially covers his face with his right hand, his left hand holding a book.

Fol. 71 r. The Descent from the Cross.—I unfortunately made no tracing from this drawing. The figure of the Virgin Mother is, however, touchingly expressed.

Fol. 72 v. The three Marys and the Angel at the Tomb.—Here the Angel, holding a sceptre in his left hand, and with the right hand extended, is seated at the door of a Byzantine temple with a rounded dome, upon the great stone forming the mouth of the tomb; the napkin, rolled up, lies at his side; to the left, the three Marys approach the tomb, one bearing a censer, another a large basin with spices. The features of the females are essentially of the late Anglo-Saxon pattern, with the chin square and the mouth long and straight. M. Langlois has given a fac-simile of this drawing in his "Essai sur la Calligraphie."

The treatment of this group in the "Missal," as compared with the same subject in the Benedictional of St. Æthelwold (Archæol. xxiv. pl. 20), or in that of Æthelgar (ibid. pl. 34), is very tame. It needs only to compare the two engravings from the Rouen volumes, to acquiesce in the opinion of the Abbé Gourdin, of the superiority of the artist of the Benedictional of Æthelgar, from which, however, Dr. Dibdin "ventured to differ entirely in such conclusion" (Bibl. Tour, i. 170). There is a boldness and freedom, for example, in the drawing of the Angel, which Dr. Dibdin has himself published (*ibid.* p. 171) from the Rouen Benedictional, which contrasts very satisfactorily with the constrained and spiritless angel in the Missal as published by M. Langlois.

Fol. 81 v. The Ascension.—Here only the bottom of the dress of the Saviour, with his feet and the lower part of the oval Vesica piscis, is seen mounting into the clouds in the upper part of the drawing. Two Angels floating below, direct the attention of the group of disciples to their rising Lord. St. Peter, holding the keys, stands to the right, and the Virgin, enclosed within a blue Vesica piscis, stands rather to the left of the group.

Fol. 84 v. The Descent of the Holy Ghost is singularly treated. The Dove, seen sideways, is enclosed within an oval Vesica piscis, supported by two Angels from above. The twelve Apostles, with St. Peter bearing the keys, and tonsured, in the middle, are seated in the lower part of the picture, and on their heads descends a torrent of flames from the mouth of the Dove. The Virgin is absent.

Fol. 132 v. St. Peter, in a fine square frame, copied by Dibdin, "Bibl. Tour," i. 168.—The Saint is represented of large size, seated on a cushion upon a square seat, without back or sides. He is beardless, with the top of the head shaved; he holds the two keys dangling from the second finger of his right hand, and an open book in his left. His hair is light blue, the upper garment green, the lower garment orange; the plain nimbus, book and footstool are gold.

Fol. 158. A golden circle, containing the Lamb of God, is supported by two standing Angels, with a company of Saints in the lower part of the picture. The head of the Lamb is surrounded by a cruciferous nimbus; the right fore leg is raised, and holds a book marked with a cross. It stands upon an arched bar of gold, on which a curtain is thrown.

Fol. 57 r., 82 r., 85 r., 113 r., 114 r., 159 r., 165 r., and 174 r., contain headings of various portions of the text, mostly written in fine golden capitals within frames or borders, generally square, and agreeing in character with that of my plate, except that the angles are generally arranged so as to form large beautiful rosettes of varied design.

The miniatures in this volume, as compared with the three in the Benedictional of Æthelgar, are smaller and much more constrained in the drawing of the figures; the colours are also not laid on so thickly, nor are they so brilliant. Although evidently emanating from the same school (New Minster) as the Æthelwold Benedictional, it is by no means so carefully or splendidly executed as that volume. Much body-white is used for relief at the edges of the folds of the drapery, as well as to mark the lights of the features, especially above the eyebrows and along the nose.

Some of the prayers at the end of the volume have Anglo-Saxon rubries; one amongst them I found of considerable interest, from its mention of King Edward the Martyr, who was killed in 978; it commences as follows :—" Ds qui beatum Eaduueardū regem Anglorum iniustæ occisum præjustificas, et miris signis mundanis declaras," &c.

THE BENEDICTIONAL OF ÆTHELGAR.

THIS fine volume, also preserved in the Public Library of Rouen, is a fitting companion to the Missal of St. Guthlac, described in the preceding article. It is, like it, a folio in a wooden binding, measuring 12½ by 9½ inches, and consists of 191 leaves. It is illuminated with miniatures (but much more sparingly than its companion volume), having foliated and architectural borders and capitals and letters of gold. It contains not only a Benedictional, but also a Pontificale, and includes, among other ceremonials, the form of " Consecratio Regis Anglorum vel Saxonum," also the " Consecratio Reginæ."

It is written in a fine bold minuscule character, larger than that of the Missal, and it cannot be doubted that it is coeval with the Benedictional of St. Æthelwold and is a production of the monks of New Minster at Winchester; moreover, that it was executed during the life of Æthelgar, who, in 965, was Abbot of New Minster, in 977 was made Bishop of Selsey, and in 989 translated to the See of Canterbury. It is probable also that it was carried over to Normandy by Robert, the Norman Archbishop of Canterbury, who was obliged to fly the kingdom in 1052, and who ended his days in 1056, in the Abbey of Jumièges, of which he was Abbot at the time that Edward the Confessor promoted him to the See of London. Hence, in a catalogue of the books of the Cathedral of Rouen drawn up in A.D. 1111, this Benedictional is expressly mentioned as the " Benedictionarius Roberti Archiepiscopi;" and hence the same title, with the addition of " Cantuariensis " written on an erasure on the first leaf of the volume. There has been considerable controversy as to the propriety of this latter addition, as there was an Archbishop of Rouen named Robert, who died in 1037; but the internal evidence supplied by the volume, and the historical facts connected with it,* are in favour of the Canterbury prelate. See various articles in which this controversy is carried on by Father Morin, of the Oratoire; the Abbé Saas ("Notices des Manuscrits de la Bibliothèque de l'Eglise Metropolitaine de Rouen," 1746, in which, following Morin and Montfaucon, the volume was ascribed to the eighth century"); Dom Tassin, one of the authors of the " Nouveau Traité de Diplomatique," who opposed the views of Saas; also M. Gourdin, " Notices des deux Manuscrits de la Bibliothèque de Rouen," in " Mém. Acad. Rouen," 1812; and a careful descriptive memoir by John Gage, in " Archæologia," vol. xxiv., with a fac-simile of the writing and of one of the illuminations. An entire page of this MS., as well as one from the " Missal," is given by Silvestre.

There are only three miniatures in the present volume. The first represents the scene of the three Marys at the Sepulchre, of which an outline fac-simile is given in the " Archæologia," vol. xxiv., as mentioned in the preceding article.

The second miniature represents the Descent of the Holy Ghost, who, in the form of a dove, descends from above, pouring forth from his beak streams of fire upon

---

* Thus the only two Saints in the English calendar for whom there are benedictions in this volume are Saints Grimbald and Judoc, who were the two Saints whose bodies were subsequently translated from New Minster to Hyde Abbey on the erection of the latter monastery.

the eleven Apostles, who are sitting with heads uplifted in a circle beneath, St. Peter, with the tonsure and without a beard, holding the two keys. Here the Dove is unattended by Angels, the sky is red and streaky, and between the Dove and the Apostles two blue arches are introduced, resting on a central column, round which the Serpent is entwined. A hand in a circle within the upper border of the ornamental frame points to the Dove below. St. Peter and St. Paul wear a green wreath upon their heads.

The third miniature represents the Death of the Virgin. Here only the Virgin is represented reclining on a couch, with four female attendants; no Angels occupy the upper part of the picture, but over the head of the Virgin is suspended a crown,* by ribbons held by a hand in the centre of the upper border of the ornamental frame.

The page opposite each of these three miniatures is ornamented with an equally beautiful framework, within which the commencement of the corresponding text is inscribed in golden letters.

THE GOSPELS OF TRINITY COLLEGE, CAMBRIDGE (No. B. 10, 4).

Plate XLII.

THIS fine copy of the Latin Gospels is so entirely in the style of the Benedictional of St. Æthelwold and the Rouen books above described, that we can only consider that it is contemporary with them. In addition to the Eusebian Canons—which occupy a number of ornamental pages at the commencement of the volume, and are enclosed between columns with bases and capitals of classical foliage, supporting rounded or conical arches, decorated with fantastical animals and leaves painted in unnatural tints, in strong body-colours—there is a grand figure of the Saviour, seated within a blue Vesica piscis, introduced beneath a rounded arch resting on short capitals ornamented with foliage entirely in the St. Æthelwold style, and of which a fac-simile is given in my 42nd Plate. The Saviour is here represented with white flowing hair and short beard; the head covered with a napkin, and wearing a golden crown surrounded by a green nimbus. In his left hand he holds a very narrow book, marked with a ✚; whilst his right hand is extended upwards in the act of benediction. His upper robe is of gold, relieved with pale buff lines, indicating the folds; his under-garment is pale pinkish salmon-coloured, and above his feet appears the lower portion of a third inner garment or shirt. The drapery is here much folded and very fluttering. The naked feet rest on a golden footstool. The ornamental foliage is very conventional in its elegant treatment, and is greatly relieved with opaque white.

The pages opposite the commencement of the several Gospels are occupied with square ornamental frames, within which the Evangelists, of smaller size than usual, are

---

* The crown is formed of a golden circlet, with three strawberry leaves, or rather, three trefoils, a peculiarity which Mr. Gage (Arch., xxiv. p. 130) comments upon, stating that in the Cottonian MS. Tiberius, B. v., executed between 989 and 903, the same form of crown appears on the head of Alexander the Great. On looking over the series of coins of sole Anglo-Saxon monarchs, I observe that Canute is the only king who is represented with such a crown (Ruding, Coins, pl. 23). He commenced his reign in 1016.

seated writing their Gospels. St. Mark, who is seated on a golden chair or throne, with a diapered cushion, dips his pen, held in the right hand, into a small inkpot at the side of his seat, looking upwards towards his symbol, which occupies the upper part of the design, being in the form of the upper part of the body of a man with wings, and with the head of a lion. The framework is quadrangular, the angles formed into large rosettes, with broad gold bars and interlacing foliage, narrow and poor in design, as contrasted with the St. Æthelwold borders; the middle part of the top, bottom, and two sides of the frame enclosing the Evangelist are also ornamented with quatrefoils, in each of which is represented a Saint, with a blue or red nimbus, and holding a book. The nimbus of the Evangelist is red, his upper garment gold, and the lower yellow.

THE LATIN GOSPELS OF KING CANUTE.

AMONGST the old Royal MSS. in the British Museum is preserved a fine copy of the Latin Gospels (No. 1 D, ix.), written and ornamented precisely in the style of the Benedictional of St. Æthelwold, and which would appear by an entry, apparently of the eleventh century, to have probably belonged to King Canute himself, and to have been bestowed by him upon the Cathedral of Canterbury. The volume is fully described in my "Palæographia sacra," and it need only here be noticed that the Eusebian Canons are wanting; that the volume has no miniatures properly so called; that each Gospel commences with a beautiful initial letter, entirely in the late Anglo-Saxon style (that of St. Mark's Gospel is given by Shaw in his "Dresses and Decorations," and that of St. Luke in my "Palæographia"), each followed by a few words of the text written in fine golden capitals, and enclosed in beautiful rectangular borders, with the angles forming large and splendid quatrefoil rosettes, with interlacing foliage of various colours strongly relieved at the edges with opaque white paint; the broad bands of the frame, as well as those of the great initials, are covered with gold leaf highly burnished, which has here and there become tarnished. The volume will scarcely bear comparison with the Gospels of Trinity College, Cambridge, although it exceeds it in interest, in consequence of the entry respecting King Canute above alluded to. A satisfactory fac-simile of portion of one of the borders and two of the initials is given in Wyatt and Tymm's "Art of Illuminating." The connexion of King Canute and his wife Emma with the Abbey of New Minster, the probable place of origin of the Gospels in question, is fully proved by the Hyde Abbey book, in the old Stow collection, which contains portraits of the royal pair, which have been repeatedly engraved, and are described in the following page.

THE monastery of New Minster, commenced by King Alfred, was erected in the immediate precincts of the Old Minster of Winchester, now the Cathedral, in the cemetery on its northern side. The close proximity of the two establishments led, however, to constant quarrels, whilst the ringing of the bells at different hours interfered with the performance of divine services in each, until, in the beginning of the twelfth century, it became necessary to remove New Minster to Hyde Meadow, at some distance, and hence the name of the Abbey became changed to Hyde Abbey. During the reign of King Canute a register was drawn up of the possessions of the Abbey, formerly in the possession of Mr. Astle, then at Stow, and now at Ashburnham House, of which the MS. is of the small folio or large octavo size, and from which Strutt (Horda, i. pl. 28) engraved the frontispiece, in a manner, however, much inferior to the original for truth and expression. Above is represented the Saviour, seated, in the act of benediction, within the Vesica piscis, attended on either side by the Blessed Virgin, holding a book, and with her head so much bent forward as to appear humpbacked, and by St. Peter holding a gigantic pair of keys.

Below are portraits of Canute and his queen Elfgiva, in rather elegant whole-length attitudes, with their names inscribed—"CNUT REX" and "ÆLFGYVU REGINA." The monarch, with cross-gartered legs, and holding a regular Danish sword in his left hand, lays hold of a cross placed upon an altar in the centre of the drawing with his right hand, towards which also the Queen stretches forth her open right hand, holding up the skirt of her gown with her left hand.

Two Angels are drawn above the heads of the royal pair, and direct their attention towards the Saviour, with uplifted forefingers of one hand; whilst, with the other hand, one places a crown on the head of the King and the other holds a garment above the head of the Queen. The crown is a circlet of gold, adorned with three trefoil leaves, as seen for the first time on the coins of Cnut. Below, in a semicircle under a series of arches, are the monks of New Minster assembled.

A good deal of difficulty has been mastered in accomplishing the attitudes of these figures, with almost complete success.

On the reverse of the first leaf are two groups of martyrs and saints, each led by an Angel, carefully engraved by Dibdin in the first volume of the "Bibliographical Decameron." Opposite, on the recto of the following leaf, is a representation of St. Peter, with attendant Angels, opening the gates of Paradise. A bishop and a priest from this group are engraved by Strutt (Horda, pl. 27, f. 4). Below this latter is a contention between Devils and Angels for the souls of the departed. The original outlines are in a bistre tint, with some of the parts purposely retouched for the sake of effect. The figures are disproportionately tall, the draperies flowing and rather fluttery, elongated hands and feet, and a general delicacy of expression throughout, both in the faces and figures. The volume has been described in detail in O'Conor's "Bibl. Stowensis."

THE GOSPELS OF BISHOP ETHELSTAN. A.D. 1012—1056.

THIS is one of the most beautiful little copies of the Gospels executed in the later Anglo-Saxon period, and is preserved in the Library of Pembroke College, Cambridge. It is rendered additionally interesting from the fact of its origin being attested by an Anglo-Saxon entry on the first page, containing the boundaries of the See of Hereford, inscribed: "Hanc discrtione [descriptionem] fecit Æthestan Episcop', written on the same kind of vellum as the text of the volume, which it also closely resembles, although evidently by a different scribe. It is of a narrow 8vo. form, measuring 7¼ inches by 4, and contains the four figures of the Evangelists, with illuminated initials of the several Gospels. These four figures are executed with very great skill, and are painted in gold and various colours with great delicacy, opaque white being used with great effect in the lights. All the four Saints are engaged in the work of writing their Gospels in different attitudes, and all wear a large outer robe of gold, on which the folds and ornaments are indicated by lines scored with a hard point. St. Matthew is a fine figure engaged in dipping a feather pen into a golden inkpot, holding a scraper in the left hand upon his book. St. Mark is busy mending his pen, which he holds up to the light, and cuts the point with a large knife. This figure is drawn with wonderful freedom, and is one of the cleverest productions of the later Anglo-Saxon artists. St. Luke is seated at a table, with his body bent, and ill-drawn, holding an open book, with his pen stuck behind his ear, and with a knife in his right hand. St. John is seated writing with a golden pen. He and St. Matthew wear a red under-garment, St. Luke a lilac one, and St. Mark a pale blue one; and all have the head encircled with a golden nimbus, with a margin of pearls.

The initials of the Gospels are large, and somewhat in the style of those of the Gospels of King Canute, but neat and less elaborately ornamented.

THE PONTIFICALE OF JUMIÈGES.

A PONTIFICALE, which formerly belonged to the Abbey of Jumièges, is now contained in the Public Library at Rouen. It is of Anglo-Saxon origin, as appears by Anglo-Saxon glosses and the introduction of Anglo-Saxon saints, and is evidently contemporary with the Missal of St. Guthlac and the Benedictional of Æthelgar, above described. There are only two miniatures in the manuscript, which were carefully figured, and the manuscript described, by Mr. Gage, in the 25th vol. of the "Archæologia." [*] The first miniature represents a Priest in his stole, holding the book before a Bishop, who

---

[*] A reduced copy of the first drawing is given in C. Knight's "Old England," fig 222; and of the second in the "Pictorial History of England," i 236 incorrectly referred to the Cottonian MS of Cædmon), and also in "Old England" fig 215

is in the attitude of prayer, with his arms and hands extended, the maniple being held by the left hand. The figure of the Bishop is eight inches high, entirely drawn in red outlines, that of the Priest being in red and black. The other miniature faces the "Ordo qualiter domus Dei consecranda est," with which the manuscript commences, and represents the ceremony of the dedication of a church by a bishop, with a crowd of attendant clergy and another of the people. The church has two towers, capped by large-sized weathercocks, in the proper shape of the birds, and the door guarded with ornamental iron-work. The Prelate is without the mitre, and is habited in his cope, which is fastened by the pectorale: in his left hand he holds the maniple, and in his right the pastoral staff, called, both in this and Archbishop Robert's manuscript, Cambatta, the head of which is round like a ball. In what appears to be an interpolated leaf, is introduced a form of malediction, used by the "Lamaletensis monasterii eps," which is considered to refer to the Abbey of Alet (Llan alet), in Brittany.

THE GOSPELS OF ABBOT RAINALDUS.

AMONGST the 800 MSS. in the Public Library of Rouen is preserved a fine copy of the Latin Gospels, written in the latter half of the eleventh century in this country, which was sent as a gift by Rainaldus, the Abbot of Abingdon, to the Bishop of Jumièges. Rainaldus had himself formerly being a monk of the latter monastery, and afterwards one of the chaplains of William the Conqueror, by whom, in 1084, he was appointed Abbot of the former monastery, where he died in 1097. The donation is thus inscribed within the volume :—

Rainaldus non proprii electione meriti, sed Dei gratia preveniente indignus Abbas Abbendonensis hunc ʃc̄̄ evangelii textū sic auro argentoque ac gemmis ornatum beate Dei genetrici ac scm̄p virgini Marie beatoque Petro Gemmeticensis cenobii mittit cunctis, fribs inibi D̄O servientibs ad honore Dei atq̄ cjus matris perpetualiter in eode loco servandum Et si quis eu inde aliqua fraude seu ingenio subripuerit abstulerit vel rapuerit D̄ni n̄i ac eis ipʃi beati Petri apħori principis maledictione subjaceat atq̄ in sempiternū anathema (the first initial R alone being enlarged and in red ink).

The ornamental arrangement of the first page, containing the beginning of the Gospel of St. Matthew, is different to any which we have above described, showing the commencement of the fashion for side borders, terminating in long flourishes across the bottom of the page, which afterwards became so much in vogue. The words INITIUM SCI EVANGELII SECUNDUM MATHM are arranged in four lines at the top of the page, and written in large Roman capitals; the great initial L(iber generationis) entirely occupies the left side and lower portion of the page, the upright and horizontal bars divided into compartments, and terminating in flourishes and dragons' heads. In the middle of the upright stroke is a circular medallion, in which is represented either an abbot or bishop, wearing a low mitre, which seems rather intended for a quadrangular crown, from which on each side depend the two infulæ. The lower angle of the letter is filled in by a combat between a warrior and a dragon, the tail of which is of great length, and branching into a regular arabesque ; the warrior has the head unarmed, but bears a sword and large round shield. The whole is drawn in red outlines.

ÆLFRIC'S ANGLO-SAXON HEPTATEUCH.

THE Cottonian MS. Claudius, B. IV., is the finest known copy of this work of Ælfric, and is profusely ornamented with 397 drawings illustrative of the text of the early books of the Bible, which, from their being drawn entirely in the costume, and according with the habits of our Anglo-Saxon forefathers, are of the highest interest. These drawings generally extend across the page, many of which have two, or even three, of them. Towards the end of the volume many of them are simply sketched in slightly, in outlines of different colours; but in the greater portion of the volume they are painted in thick body-colours. I have given a careful description of the manuscript in my "Palæographia," together with a copy of one of the miniatures representing the Expulsion from Paradise and Adam and Eve tilling the ground, the trees treated in the same conventional manner as in the Arundel Psalter, No. 60 (see my Plate 49). The largest miniature is that of the Building of the Tower of Babel (copied in Strutt's "Horda," pl. vi.). Many other of the drawings were also copied by Strutt, Knight (Hist. of England), Fairholt (British Costume), Wright (Domestic Manners), &c., as illustrations of Anglo-Saxon dresses, armour, architecture, manners, and customs, &c.; so that I have not thought it necessary to give any further copy from it in this work, although I had prepared several for it.

HARLEIAN PSALTER, No. 603.

THIS very fine volume, of the latter part of the tenth century, has been already alluded to in the description of the Utrecht Psalter, from which it was evidently copied. Like that volume, it is written in triple columns, and illustrated with a great number of drawings extending across the page, consisting of outlines in different coloured inks, drawn with great freedom, the figures being of small size and often crowded together, with the limbs greatly attenuated and the garments fluttery. In no part of the volume are the drawings coloured: they are by several hands, some being very rude and stiff, and others wonderfully free; in some they are only slightly indicated in pencil; and many blanks, beyond the middle of the volume, are left for drawings.

In most instances the drawings are exactly copied from those of the Utrecht Psalter, comparison therewith now being easy, in consequence of the British Museum having recently obtained a complete and careful set of copies of the drawings in the latter volume (MSS. Add., 22, 291).

The MS. has very been extensively used by Strutt, C. Knight, Fairholt, Shaw, T. Wright, and others, in the illustrations of the dresses, armour, architecture, manners, and customs of the Anglo-Saxons.

The drawings of the Harleian volume have, in their turn, been copied in the Psalter of Eadwine, of the first half of the twelfth century, in the Library of Trinity College, Cambridge, which is also written in triple columns, with the outline drawings partially tinted with red, blue, and green. The initials of each Psalm are highly illuminated in gold and colours, in a style quite unlike that of any of the Anglo-Saxon volumes which we have passed in review. The first page is entirely occupied with a large drawing, in two compartments, in the upper of which two buildings of handsome elevation are represented; one inscribed "Sancta eccla," in which the "Beatus vir" is seated; whilst in the opposite one "Superbia" is seated. Between these two buildings is a contest between a Man and an Angel, the latter endeavouring to draw the mortal to the former edifice. Beneath is a representation of the infernal regions. At the end of the volume is a large bird's-eye view of the Monastery of Christ Church, Canterbury, and a portrait of Eadwine, the writer of the volume, more than a foot in height, both of which have been engraved in the "Vetusta Monumenta."

The volume is expressly entered under the title "tripartitum Psalterium Edwini," in a catalogue of the books of Canterbury Cathedral drawn up in 1305. In addition to the fac-similes from this MS. published in my "Palæographia," several others will be found in T. Wright's "Domestic Manners," &c.

The Bibliothèque Impériale of Paris also contains a tripartite Psalter, agreeing closely, in the style of its writing and initials, with that of Eadwine. It is numbered MS. Suppl. Lat., formerly 1194, now 8846. A fac-simile of the text and fine initials is given by Silvestre, and it is referred to the middle of the thirteenth century. Some of the drawings, however, are precisely similar to those of the Eadwine and Harleian Psalters, such as the roundabout, copied by Cahier and Martin (Mél. d'Arch., i. pl. 45, p. 252); but the drawings are by various hands and at successive periods, during at least two hundred years, and some spaces are still left blank. A few of the small groups, or detached figures, are given in Sere's fine work. At the commencement of the volume are 84 miniatures of Biblical history, arranged in rows, occupying seven pages.

By way of comparison with the miniature of the roundabout in the Utrecht Psalter, I add a description of the entire drawing in which the Paris roundabout is contained. Christ, in the clouds to the left of the top of the drawing, gives a spear to an Angel; to the right, a smith is at work at a fire, with an attendant. In the middle of the picture, to the left, small figures extend their hands towards Christ: David holding a scroll in each hand, sits in the centre. At the bottom is a group of figures revolving round circles of different coloured concentric rings. In the middle is the roundabout or turnstile, turned by four figures, and to the right, an Angel gives a scroll to a group of figures. The entire drawing is intended as an illustration of the 11th Psalm: "Salvum me fac Dne. &c."

THE HARLEIAN RULE OF ST. BENEDICT

THIS MSS. (numbered 5431), although not containing any miniature, is especially interesting for the beautiful series of initial letters which it contains, executed in the same style, and evidently contemporary with the Lambeth Aldhelm and Bodleian Cadmon, drawn with great precision; the flourishes and strokes terminating in birds' heads and leaves.

THE VATICAN MS. OF MARIANUS SCOTUS.

THIS is a large 4to. volume, written throughout in a strong Hiberno-Saxon hand, with rather rudely-designed interlaced capitals of the later Irish character, written in the twelfth or thirteenth century. On the verso of the 15th leaf is a list of Irish kings, 48 in number, commencing with Conn. ast Cormac an. lx., and ending with Flann McMoil Leehnaill. The initial D on fol. 31 is similar in form to that of the Psalter of St. John's College, Cambridge, figured in this work, the first line being written in fine characters, almost like those of the Gospels of Lindisfarne. The initial D of the 2nd book is square in form, and made of a strange two-legged animal. Fol. 103 is occupied by a drawing of the Descent from the Cross, in an excellent style of art, drawn in outline and slightly touched with red lines in the dresses. The falling body of the Saviour is held by Joseph of Arimathea, the Virgin holding the right hand of her Son to the left, whilst an attendant kneeling, on the right side, knocks out the nail from the foot with a hammer.

THE RAWLINSONIAN LIFE OF ST. COLUMBA.

AMONGST the Rawlinson MSS. now in the Bodleian Library, Oxford, is a large folio Irish volume, probably written as late as the fifteenth century, remarkable for containing a large and full-length portrait of St. Columba, habited as a bishop of the period when the MS. was written : as such, I believe it is quite unique. The Saint wears a splendid high mitre, decorated with foliage along the edges, and bears in his left hand a pastoral staff, the wheel terminating in a dragon's head, from the open mouth of which spring two large leaves, one filling the open central space, and the other extending downwards; the open right hand is held upwards.

4 1

ADDENDA ET CORRIGENDA.

Page 6, line 43, read "*where* the heathen."

P. 33, line 23. The group of cats and mice here referred to, occurs at the foot of p. 34 (not 134), in the lower part of the grand illuminated page of the XPI (Matth. i. 18). This page has been reproduced in chromolithographic fac-simile from the drawings of Miss Stokes, by Mr. Gruner, for the forthcoming part of the "Vetusta Monumenta" of the Society of Antiquaries of London.

P. 41. The suggestion made in this page, that the miniature of St. Mark, copied in my 15th Plate from the so-called Biblia Gregoriana, was a subsequent addition possibly of the tenth century, has received strong confirmation by my discovery, during the progress of this work through the press, of a miniature apparently by the same artist, in the Cottonian MS. Tiberius, A. 3, of the tenth century, described above in p. 130.

P. 46. The Garland of Howth.—The two large rude and much defaced illuminated pages remaining in this volume, described above in p. 47, have also been reproduced in fac-simile by Mr. Gruner, from the drawings of Miss Stokes, for the Society of Antiquaries of London.

P. 56. During the progress of this work through the press, my attention has been directed by the Rev. W. Macray, one of the librarians of the Bodleian Library, to the remains of a fine large 4to. volume of the Gospels, written entirely in the style of those of Mac Regol, containing, however, only the Gospels of Saints Luke and John. The grand initial page of St. Luke only now remains, and it unfortunately is much injured from having been pasted down to the cover of the book ; it is ornamented entirely in the style of the Gospels of Mac Regol and St. Chad. The initials of the verses throughout are surrounded by rows of red dots. Its press-mark is Rawlinson B. N. 167.

P. 80, line 4. For stories, read *stones*.

P. 87. In my "Palæographia sacra" I devoted an article and a plate to the Psalters of St. Ouen and Bishop Ricemarchus, giving a fac-simile of the commencement of the 51st Psalm from the latter MS. The two other illuminated pages of the same volume, containing the beginning of the 1st and 101st Psalms,* have been reproduced in fac-simile by Mr. Gruner, from the drawings of Miss Stokes, for the Society of Antiquaries of London.

Plate 1, line 3 of the text, for CSAIA, read *ESAIA*; the cross-bar of the C having been omitted in some copies of the Plates.

Pl. 15. For seventh century, read *tenth* century. See p. 41, and note in the present page.

Pl. 17. For menu, read *manu*.

Pl. 22. For Durnon, read *Durnan*.

Pl. 28. For Penetential, read *Penitentiale*.

Pl. 47. For Winchester Cathedral, read *New Minster*.

---

* The numeration of the Psalms differs in the English Prayer-book from that of the Roman use ; the 51st and 101st in the latter being numbered 52 and 102 in the former, as in the Hebrew. I have given the Roman numbers as in the MSS.

APPENDIX.

THE various ancient Art-relics executed in these islands during the period over which the production of the copy-scripts which form the subject of this work extended, and which have survived to our days, exhibit so complete an identity, both in general design and detail, with the miniatures and ornaments of the MSS. themselves, as to lead to the conviction that the painters of the latter were evidently the artists and designers of the former, and that consequently the different classes of remains illustrate each other; that, if the age of any particular manuscript be determined, we are able approximately to determine the age of stone, or ivory carving, or metal chasing, of which the art is so completely identical with the designs in the MSS.

SCULPTURED STONE MEMORIALS

This identity of design is carried indeed sometimes to a singular extent; thus, many of the great stone crosses, measuring from 10 to 20 feet in height, are divided into compartments, each filled in with designs precisely similar to those in the compartments of the great initial letters of the MSS.; so that we might suppose the former to be only immensely magnified strokes of the letters.

These great sculptured stone memorials exist in most parts of these islands, those in each great district presenting features of their own. In Cornwall these stones are comparatively simple, and generally chiselled into the form of a Greek or Latin cross. In Wales they vary in form, but are generally inscribed with the name either of the maker, or, if memorial stones, the names of the deceased and his father, expressed in a peculiar formula of which the Roman notations admit no instance. The Welsh stones are, moreover, ornamented with sculptured patterns, in which the interlacing ribbons and dragons, and also the diagonal Z-like patterns occur; but I have nowhere met with the spiral patterns in Wales, and there are very few instances in Wales of the human figure being introduced upon the stones. In the Isle of Man the contrary is the case, as a great variety of human figures are introduced in connection with the ornamental details, and in most instances accompanied by a Runic inscription. In Ireland the crosses are of a gigantic size, generally surmounted by a wheel cross, the stem sculptured with all the Celtic ornamental patterns, and also with various chiefly religious scenes, but rarely with inscriptions; whilst in Scotland we find domestic as well as sacred subjects sculptured, inscriptions are of the greatest rarity, but, on the other hand, a great number of the stones bear certain symbolical figures to which the usual names of the Spectacle, Sceptre, and Elephant patterns have been applied. I must refer to Mr. Stuart's great work on the Sculptured Stones of Scotland (2 vols. folio, published by the Spalding Club), Mr. H. O'Neill's beautiful work on the Irish Crosses, Mr. Cumming's "Runic Remains of the Isle of Man," and Mr. Blight's work on the Cornish Remains. The Welsh crosses and inscribed stones have formed the subject of an extensive series of papers by myself in the "Archæologia Cambrensis." These I propose shortly to collect

together in one volume, and complete by the addition of a considerable number which still remain unpublished.

Want of space has prevented me from giving in the present work any drawings of these stone memorials, of which I possess a most extensive series of rubbings.

In my paper in the "Journal of the Archæological Institute," on the Characteristic Ornamentation of the Irish and Anglo-Saxon Artists, alluded to in the Preface to this work, I have spoken of the font of Deerhurst Church, figured in the "Journal Brit. Arch. Assoc." i. p. 65, as probably the oldest ornamented font in England, from the fact that it is there represented as covered with the spiral pattern, which, as we have seen in the course of this work, was not used in MSS. in England after the 9th or early part of the 10th century, and of which in stonework I know no other English example. The ancient will, however, in vain search for the font at Deerhurst —where, indeed, it had long lain neglected,—as it was some years ago removed by the Canons of Christ Church, Oxford (to whom both churches belong), to the church of Longdon, in Worcestershire, where I at length found it, and am able to state that, although the body of the font is entirely covered with a series of spiral lines (four of which spring from a central point, and go off to as many adjoining whorls, all the whorls being of equal size), the top and bottom of the font have a foliated border, unlike any Hiberno-Saxon work, and which leads me to refer its date to the 11th or 12th century.

BOOK-COVERS AND CUMHDACHS.

The magnificent Book-covers, "auro argento gemmisque ornata," which are repeatedly mentioned in connection with the fine early copies of the Gospels—such, for instance, as the Gospels of Lindisfarne, have, for the most part, long disappeared; but there still exist a number of metal cases, which have served to hold some of the smaller Irish manuscripts, and which generally exhibit restorations at various periods, indicated by a diversity in the art of the different overlying pieces of metal. These are also generally ornamented with large crystals or other gems, and are known under the name of Cumhdachs. Of several of these mention has been already made in the articles on the Book of Armagh, p. 80; the Psalter of St. Columba, p. 82; the Book of Dimma, pp. 83, 84; and the Gospels of St. Mulling, p. 93.

My Plate 52, fig. 9, represents a small group of ecclesiastics from the Cumhdach of the Stow Missal above described (p. 88). It is evidently of a very early date; other portions of the cover, as represented by O'Conor, being more recent.

In Plate 53, fig 6, I have given a representation of the greater part of the front of the Cumhdach of the Gospels of St. Moliase (or Molash), which measures 5¾ inches by 4½, and 3½ inches deep. In this figure I have omitted the sixteen small outer compartments at the sides, top, and bottom of the front, as the chased metal plates in ten of them are wanting, whilst the others are filled with sockets for jewellery, which has also disappeared, or with interlaced filigree-work, like some of the small compartments in my

4 G

plate. It is of bronze bound with silver, overlaid with open-work riveted on white metal silvered. The interstices of the open-work pattern at the back are filled in with thin copper plates, engraved with interlaced ornament. The front will be seen to form a cruciform, or rather a wheel-cross design, with the emblems of the four Evangelists occupying the angles, designed in a most barbarous manner, each being intended to be represented with four wings, two of which are angulated and cross each other on the breast. These figures are inscribed "✠ Math(eus). ✠ ho(mo). ✠ Marc(us). ✠ leo. ✠ Lucas. ✠ vitulus. and ✠ Iohan(nes). ✠ aquila." Portions of gold filigree and interlaced ornaments, with sockets for jewels, occupy some of the remaining compartments of the open work, one ruby remaining in its setting. An inscription, commencing "✠ or do ifailad doch," runs round the edge of one side; whilst one of the ends has in one of its compartments a figure of an ecclesiastic (?), holding a small book and another object, quite in the style of the Evangelists in the Gospels of MacDurnan, with a forked beard. The lid is wanting, but the bronze enamelled hinge remains, with sockets, one of which retains a portion of blue glass. This very interesting relic, together with its enclosed Book of the Gospels, belongs to the Royal Irish Academy, and has been very carefully and fully illustrated by drawings and photographs, and described by Miss Stokes, in a communication made to the Society of Antiquaries of London on the 21st November, 1867.

Here must be described the very curious ivory diptych of the 8th or 9th century, belonging to the church of St. Martin, Genoels-Elderen, Limbourg, exhibited at Mechlin in 1864. On the front leaf (*see* Plate 52, fig. 4) is represented the Saviour, young and beardless, with a cruciferous nimbus inscribed with the letters REX, holding a book and a cross, trampling on the lion and dragon, and attended by two angels, and inscribed (in capital letters, often conjoined or enclosed within each other) "✠ UBI DNS AMBULABIT SUPER ASPIDEM ET BASILISCUM CONCULCABIT LEONE ET DRACONEM;" the whole surrounded by a border composed of the Z-like pattern (of which latter I have only represented the left side); the whole having the background open-cut. The back leaf is divided into two compartments; the upper representing the Annunciation, inscribed "UBI GABRIEL VENIT AD MARIAM," and the latter the Salutation of the Virgin and St. Elizabeth (with Zachariah and Joseph), inscribed "✠ UBI MARIA SALUTAVIT ELIZABETH." The whole is open-cut, and surrounded by an open-cut interlaced ribbon pattern, of which a portion is represented in my Plate 52, on the left-hand side of fig. 3. I am acquainted with no other instance of such a treatment in ivory-work.

The only other carved ivory with which I am acquainted, which can satisfactorily be ascribed to an Anglo-Saxon artist, is a small plaque, with a representation of the Saviour seated in glory, within the Vesica piscis, with the Virgin Mary and St. Peter standing on either side. Below, two Angels support a cross, having eight small figures standing at its sides. It bears an inscription in angulated Anglo-Saxon capitals, and belongs to the Cambridge Antiquarian Society. It is very much defaced.

Here also may be incidentally mentioned the curious embossed LEATHER SATCHELS or BOOK-COVERS, to which allusion has been made (p. 80) in the description of that in which the Book of Armagh is preserved, as likewise to one in Mr. Petrie's collection; I found a third, in the library of the Irish Monastery of St. Isidore at Rome, and one is preserved in the library of Corpus Christi College, Oxford, containing the Irish Missal.

METAL SHRINES AND CASKETS.

Of ANCIENT SHRINES, the most important now in existence is that of St. Manchan, or St. Monaghan, belonging to the Irish Bishop Kilduff. It is a coffer of yew, the sides sloping together from the base upwards, to form a roof-like ridge; it is mounted in gilt brass or bronze, and stands on four legs, from three of which project strong brass rings 3 inches in diameter, through which staves to carry the shrine may have been passed; the fourth ring is wanting. On each of the sloping wooden sides is riveted a bronze ornament in form of a Greek cross, 19¾ inches by 18½ inches, with hollow hemispherical bosses at the ends of the limbs, 3⅞ inches in diameter, engraved with interlaced patterns; a similar large boss in the centre of each cross seems to have been ornamented with silver-gilt *repoussé* plaques, one of which, showing a leaf ornament, remains. Beneath the arms of one of the crosses are riveted ten bronze figures, probably intended for saints, gradually diminishing in size from 6½ to 5 inches. These figures are very curious, having the upper part of the body either naked or covered with a tight fitting garment, which shows the indentations of the ribs; the arms are, however, seen to have a puckered covering. Most of them have short beards, but three have the beard long and forked, the ninth figure holding the two ends of his beard with his hands. Several hold small books; and two hold a short hooked stick, which does not appear of sufficient size for one of the short pastoral staves, or cambutta. Round the waist, reaching nearly to the knees, each wears an apron, philibeg, or kilt, ornamented longitudinally with various patterns, the remainder of the legs being naked. One of these figures is engraved in the "Dublin Penny Journal," i. p. 57. The angles are bound with brass, supported by grotesque animals' heads, with eyes formed of dark enamel or glass. Along the base of the shrine the interstices are filled with oblong pieces of enamel, 1⅓ inch long by ¾ inch deep, yellow and red, *in remarkable angular patterns*. Four pieces of similar enamel ornament the limbs of each of the crosses. The triangular ends are fitted with brass plates, with interlaced lacertine patterns in relief, framed in an edging, 1 inch wide, of brass, similarly chased. It is destitute of any inscription; but it is asserted that it was made at the expense of Turlogh O'Connor's son Roderick, in the 12th century; and is not unjustly described by the annalists as the most beautiful piece of art—"opus pulcherrimum quod fecit opifex in Hibernia."

In Mr. Petrie's collection of Irish antiquities is contained a small shrine with sloping sides, coming to a sharp ridge at the top; it measures 9 inches by 7 inches. The front side has affixed to it *four* small bronze plates, about 2 inches high, and varying in breadth from 1⅝ to 3 inches. Two of these respectively contain three, and the third two figures of ecclesiastics, whilst the fourth contains three figures of females. Seven of these curious figures are represented of the full size in my Plate 52, figs. 5, 6, and 8; fig. 5 being a precise copy of one of the pieces. In fig. 6 I have represented, in one group, three of the most striking of the four remaining male figures; but have only given a single female, as the three are identical. The dresses, as well as the objects in the hands of these little figures, are exceedingly interesting; whilst the long plaited hair of the females seems copied from the fashion of the Norman ladies of the 12th century. The bottom of the shrine is ornamented with a diaper formed of small Greek crosses, with marginal borders formed of ribbons interlaced with enamel, and with small square enamelled bosses. This relic is traditionally known as the "Shrine of St. Moedoc," of Ferns, and has been very carefully illustrated and described by Miss Stokes, in a memoir read before the Society of Antiquaries of London on the 21st November, 1867.

There remain also various specimens of metal-work, generally chased with the representations of the Crucifixion, which have most probably been affixed to shrines or other similar objects of religious use. Of these the most remarkable is the bronze plate of the Crucifixion now in the Museum of the Royal Irish Academy, carefully represented, from a photograph by Mr. Stuart, in the Illustrations to the 2nd vol. of his "Sculptured Stone of Scotland, plate 16, originating from Chia-sionuno, the central seat of art in Ireland, and brought to the Academy from Athlone, and which Dr. Petrie considered to be a thousand years old. The general design of this relic is as rude as the same subject is represented in the Psalter of St. John's College, Cambridge (Palæogr. sacr.); although nothing can be more beautiful than the chased spiral and interlaced ornaments with which the different figures are covered. The principal figure is 7 inches high, the head disproportionately large, the body covered with a long garment reaching from the neck to the feet, and furnished with sleeves reaching to the wrists. Two extraordinary angels hover over the arms of the cross, and Longinus and the spear-bearer (wearing large triangular cloaks) occupy the sides below the arms of the cross. The plaque measures 9 in. by 6 in.

In Plate 51, figs. 7 and 8, I have represented, of the size of the originals, two smaller bronze chasings of the Crucifixion, almost as archaic in their design as the one above described; they are in low relief and open-cut in the back parts of the design. No. 7 is, I believe, in the collection of the Royal Irish Academy and No. 8 was exhibited by Matth. J. Anketell, Esq., in the great Dublin Exhibition of 1853. My figures are made from electrotypes. It will also be noticed that in all these early representation of the Crucifixion the Virgin Mary and St. John are never introduced.

Of RELIQUARY CASKETS several still exist, exhibiting entirely the system of ornamentation of our ancient MSS. One of these, of wood covered with chased and elegantly incised metal plates, is contained in the Royal Museum for "Nordiske Oldsager" in Copenhagen (see Wornsaae's "Afbildninger," fig. 363). It measures 5¼ in. wide by 4 in. high, and is in the shape of a house, with the cover forming a ridge-like roof. In the front are three raised circles, within which are introduced three dragons' heads, forming the terminations of spiral lines; the whole of the remaining surface ornamented with interlaced ribbons, so slightly incised and so much worn that I was not able to take a satisfactory cast of it.

A somewhat similar casket, both in use and workmanship, preserved in Monymusk House, Aberdeenshire) erected on the ruins of an early Culdean monastery), is described and figured in all its details, in colours, by Mr. Stuart, "Sculp. Stones," vol. ii., Illustr. pl. 11.

A third casket of the same form, and measuring about 4 in. long by 3½ in. high, was exhibited by the Royal Irish Academy in the great Dublin Exhibition of 1853. The three circular ornaments in front are enamelled in pale yellow and dark green colours, and the ground surface is incised with the step pattern. The ridge terminates at each end in a duck's head.

The Grand-Ducal Museum of Brunswick also contains an ivory casket nearly of the same form as the three preceding of the back of which a representation is given in Plate 52, fig. 1. It is divided into small compartments, on which are sculptured, in low relief, fantastic but not inelegant dragons and birds with long interlaced tails; except in the lower central compartment, in which the spiral pattern is introduced and in the middle compartment of the lid, in which the animals are spotted, as in the branches of a central tree. A long description of the casket, supposed to have been made for the reception of a copy of the Scriptures rather than for a reliquary, is given, with figures of all the four sides, by Professor George Stephens in the "Journal of the Kilkenny Archæological Society," vol. ii., new series, 1859. The bottom of the casket is plain, but is surrounded by a narrow border, on which is inscribed (twice repeated) the Runic inscription seen beneath the reclined figure 53rd Plate. Several readings have been given of this inscription in the same journal, one of which would refer the casket to the 6th century and to a Northumbrian origin. On comparing the Runic letters, however, with the various alphabets

given in Professor Stephens' great work on Runic inscriptions, I find them to accord best with a MS. of the 9th century. The ornaments on the other sides of the box resemble those of the back, except that the spiral pattern does not appear on either of these.

The STAVES or the AXE of ST. LACHTIN (belonging to A. Forrester, Esq., described and figured in the "Vetusta Monumenta," vol. vi. pl. 10), the FETTER POTHEEN, or Shrine of St. Patrick's Tooth, belonging to Dr. Stokes (a work of the 13th or 14th century, with Gothic arches and lettering); the SHRINE or ST. PATRICK'S BELL, placed in Down Abbey in 1186, carried off by Edward Bruce in 1315, and now belonging to the Roman Catholic Bishop of Down and Connor; the CINT NAOMH (or Holy Body), formerly belonging to the chapel of Temple Cross, in Westmeath (at Valdancey's Coll., i. p. 73), bearing on its front a figure of the crucified Saviour, of a very rude and early type, and a large oval crystal the mensural upper part with a rude figure of a priest (the head in relief) and two figures on horseback, and large birds, the interstices filled in with early interlaced work now belonging to Geo. Smith, Esq., of Dublin; and the splendid Cross or Cong, in the museum of the Royal Irish Academy (of which there is an admirable coloured drawing in the South Kensington Museum—may all be referred to in this place.

PASTORAL STAVES.

Allusion has already been made, in the description of the Gospels of MacDurnan, to the ancient PASTORAL STAVES or Cambuttæ of the Anglo-Saxon and Irish bishops, which are quite unlike those of any other country, and of which no example is described or figured either by Messrs. Barraud and Martin ("Le Bâton Pastoral," 1856), or the Comte Bastard (in the "Bulletin Com. Hist. et Arts de France," tome iv., 1860). One of the most important of these, as a work of art, is that belonging to the Duke of Devonshire, supposed to have been used by St. Curthag, first Bishop of Lismore. It is made of wood over-laid with bronze, and is very similar to my figure 2 in Plate 53. The head is partly gilt and set with bosses of glass or vitreous mosaic, and surmounted by a crest formed of four lacertine animals in open-work, terminating below in a monster's head with blue glass eyes. An ornamental boss, much worn, is fixed in the middle of the stem, formed of no fewer than thirty small compartments, filled in with figures of monstrous animals and men interlaced together; one of which (formed of four men kneeling but without arms) is represented in Plate 53, fig. 3. This portion, as well as the ornamented base of the staff, is niellioed and inlaid with silver. There is an Irish inscription on the staff, stating it to have been made for Nial Mac Meic Æducain (Bishop of Lismore, who died in 1113) by Nechtan. It is most probable that the wooden portion of the staff is much more ancient, and that the inscription refers only to the metal cover. Careful figures of this staff, with its details, are given by Mr. H. O'Neill (" The Fine Arts and Civilization of Ancient Ireland," 1863). It is 3 ft. 9½ in. long.

The pastoral staff of Clonmacnoise, represented in Plate 53, fig. 2, resembles the preceding in general form, but the head is inlaid with silver and niellioed in an interlaced pattern, surmounted by a row of grotesque animals biting each other's tails, in bronze, of which only five remain; the end of the crook bears a large head, and beneath it is a full-length figure of a bishop treading on a dragon; a projecting band of ornament at the top of the stem is formed of grotesque monsters with tails interlaced and set with studs of blue glass. In the centre of the stem is a boss inlaid with silver and niellioed ashed or greatly worn. It is evident from the worn state of this central band that these staves must have been carried resting upon the shoulder of the bishop. Another boss with inserted plaques of interlaced ornaments, and with sockets for studs, surrounds the bottom of the staff above the hand spike. It is 3 ft. 7 in. long, and belongs to the Royal Irish Academy.

The pastoral staff of St. Melis, belonging to the Right Rev. Bishop Kilduff, is represented in my Plate 53. fig. 3. It is of yew, covered with plates of bronze riveted on the surface of the crook, and three knaves covered with small interlaced ornament in *repoussé* work; bands and rows of studs, two of which, of coral and glass respectively, remain, seem to have ornamented the head and other parts of the staff, the figure of a bishop, in a niche edged with silver, is fixed at the front of the crook. Although apparently of 12th century work, some portions of the ornament may be older. It is 3 ft. 1 in. long.

The pastoral staff of MacInnis, in the same style, which belonged to Cardinal Wiseman, was exhibited in the great Dublin Exhibition of 1853, and bears an Irish inscription on the under part of the crook, the crest of which is formed of twenty-two birds arranged in pairs. It has recently been acquired by the British Museum, which also possesses the upper part of another staff, having a number of small compartments filled with golden interlaced filigree-work. Several others, also more or less entire, are in the Museum of the Royal Irish Academy; and another, highly ornamented and enamelled, with portions of six others, of plainer design, are in the collection of Mr. Petrie.

The head of the highly ornamented Quigrich or Crozier of St. Fillan has been engraved, with its details, from my drawings, in the "Journal of the Archæological Institute," vol. xvi. p. 42, accompanied by curious notices of its supposed miraculous powers; and in the same work are engraved portions of what appears to have been an Irish Tau cross, having a boat-shaped head, with the ends recurved, and terminating in dragons' heads, and with knaves in the style of the Lismore crosier. It is in the Museum of the Kilkenny Archæological Society, and is quite unique.

In the Treasury of the Cathedral of St. Gall is preserved the reputed pastoral staff of St. Gall. I regret that I am unable to give any account of its form or material.

In Plate 53. fig. 1, I have represented, of full size, the head of another unique pastoral staff curved in walrus-tooth, found in the ruins of Aghadoe Cathedral, in Ireland. (*See* "Gent. Mag." April, 1864, p. 413.) The whorl terminates in a large dragon's head biting the leg of a man trying to escape, whilst the crown of the head of the dragon is seized by the mouth of a smaller nondescript animal, whose neck, body, and legs form portion of the interlaced work of the stem of the staff. The crest of the crook is formed by a series of pierced step-like crockets. (*See* further on Early Celtic Caulmlite, Stuart, "Sculp. Stones of Scotland," ii. liv., and Robertson, "Proc. Soc. Antiq. Scotland," ii. 14 and 123.)

SACRED BELLS.

Another class of relics held, like the Combdachs and Cambattx, in great veneration, and often used for the purpose of administering oaths, consists of the HAND BELLS of the early saints, which have from time to time been covered with precious metals and gems, and which consequently often exhibit successive stages of art-work. Of these the most highly decorated is the Bell of St. Patrick, now belonging to the Rev. Dr. Todd, of Trinity College, Dublin. This bell, which is frequently referred to in the Irish annals, was known under the name of the "Clog an-eadhachta Phatraic," or "the Bell of St. Patrick's Will," given by St. Columba to the church of Armagh. At the commencement of the 12th century it had a special keeper: its subsequent custody remained in the same family for several centuries, proving a source of considerable emolument. In A.D. 1044 its desecration cost the inhabitants of the barony of Lower Dundalk, co. Louth, and of Cremorne, co. Monaghan, an enormous penalty; Niall, son of MacFlachlain, having carried off twelve hundred cows and a number of prisoners, in revenge of the perjury committed in taking a false oath on this bell. The bell itself is of the usual square form, diminishing upwards, formed of thick sheet iron greatly corroded, with a

loop at the top for the hand. It is 6 in. high, 5 in. wide, and 4 in. deep, at the mouth. It is enclosed in a splendidly ornamented case, of which my Plate 52. fig. 1, represents the side view, whilst fig. 2 represents the upper part of the back, showing portion of the Irish inscription. The entire height of the cover with its handle is 10½ inches. The boldness of the interlaced filigree ribbon design, the ribbons terminating in the heads of strange lizard-like animals, is very striking; whilst the manner in which the birds are introduced in the branches of a tree (in fig. 2), recalls the treatment of the Brunswick ivory casket. To the square knot in the middle of the ornamental circle on each side is affixed a chain. The ornaments of the circle and top are chased, but the remainder are cut out in open-work and fixed by pins to the copper plate of the sides. Originally it appears to have been covered with ornaments of gold and silver and coloured pastes. Cornelians and crystals mounted in silver and gold have, however, been added by way of reparation. The front of the lower portion of the cover is arranged so as to form a cross with a great crystal at the intersection of the arms, which are formed of bars divided into compartments with smaller interlaced patterns, the whole surrounded by borders divided into oblong compartments, alternately filled with precious stones and ornamental metal-work; as are also the four spaces above and below the arms of the cross.

The inscription, which extends round the four sides of the back of the bell, is to be read (in English characters):—

Or do donnall o Lachtind lu i ndem-
ad in chru oru do Donnall chomarba phatrac ie u ule
mad oru dunij Cathalm u uecchulain do mair es eh
bor oru do Chondmig o Inmaem cona marnib ro comung

Of which the following is a literal translation:—"A prayer for Donnell O'Lochlain, through whom this bell [or bell shrine] was made; and for Donnall, the successor of Patrick, with whom it was made: and for Cahalan O'Mulhollan, the keeper of the bell and for Cudulig O'Inmainen with his sons, who covered it."

Donnell O'Loehlain or MacLochlain, as he is called by the Four Masters, was monarch of Ireland A.D. 1083—1121. The "successor of Patrick" here spoken of was Donnell MacAmhalgadha or MacAulay, who was Archbishop and Abbot of Armagh, A.D. 1091—1105: so that the cover of the bell must have been executed between the two latter dates.

A folio volume descriptive of the bell, with five chromo-lithographic plates, was published by Messrs. Ward & Co. Belfast, 1850, from the pen of the Rev. Dr. Reeves. (*See* also Reeves' "Eccles. Antiquities of Down, Connor, and Dromore," pp. 369—375; and Stuart's "Historical Memoirs of the History of Armagh," Newry, 1819.) My figures are taken from a very careful series of drawings made by Mr. Henry O'Neill.

Another bell, about 8 in. high, of bronze, also ascribed to St. Patrick, being simply inscribed with the name PATRICI, and destitute of ornament, is in the collection of Mr. Petrie.

The Bell of St. Gall is also preserved in the Treasury of the Cathedral of St. Gall. It is of the usual quadrangular form. (*See* "Irish Eccles. Journal," vol. v. p. 137.)

The Barnan Cuslawn or Cellsin, or Bell of St. Columb's, brother of Cormac M'Cullenan, king, bishop, and lexicographer of Cashel, killed in A.D. 908, was exhibited by T. L. Cooke, Esq. together with the Bell of St. Ruadhan of Lorrha, that of St. Cuanna of Kilshanny, that of St. Molua of Clonfert Molua, that of St. Camin of Kilcamin, and several others, in the great Dublin Exhibition of 1853, and has, with the whole of his collection, been purchased by the trustees of the British Museum. The first of these is 11½ in. high and 8 in. broad at the bottom; the upper part is beautifully inlaid with gold and silver, and nielloed; a figure of it is given in the "Archæologia Cambrensis," iv. p. 23.

The Clog Meguc, or Bell of St. Meguc, with its shrine or cover, and an ancient bell called the Barre Garreaghan, are in the collection of Archdeacon Beresford, of Ardagh; the golden bell

OTHER EARLY METAL RELICS

THE FLABELLUM

THE HOLY KNIFE

in Russia, there are usually placed five loaves of oblation, but in Greece generally only one, upon the credence-table, and where it is blessed and divided during a preparatory office of the Credence, at which the public are rarely present. These loaves are flat cakes, having in the middle a small square projection, stamped on the top with a cross and the letters IC. XC. NI. KA (i. e., Jesus Christ conquers) in the four angles. This middle piece is called the Holy Lamb (*amnos*); and, after a benediction, each side of it is pierced by the priest at the recital of the words, "He was led as a lamb to the slaughter, and as a blameless lamb before his shearers, so opened he not his mouth." The holy spear is then thrust obliquely into the right side of the Holy Lamb, and at the words, "For his life was taken away from the earth," the latter is lifted from the loaf, which, in like manner, is blessed, cut and stabbed at its right side, at the words, "One of the soldiers, with a spear, pierced his side," &c. The several loaves are then cut into many small pieces, each in honour and memory of the Virgin Mary, or some special saint, the bishop and clergy of the diocese, the founder of the church, the living, or the dead. When thus blessed and divided, it is covered with the star-cover, the veil, and the pall, and left at the credence-table until the second grand procession during the Mass, when it is carried with as much pomp as possible from the Credence Chapel through the church to the High Altar within the Iconostasis, the gates of which are closed during the most solemn portion of the service of the Mass. Such is the ceremonial use of the knife in the Eastern Church, but in the Romish Church, the host being only a thin wafer, is broken, not cut, by the priest; but it is still the custom in some churches, after the Mass is ended, to bless and cut into small pieces a loaf of bread (Eulogia), which is then distributed among the people; and the Anglo-Saxons followed this custom of giving the holy wafer, which was cut into small slices with a knife, very likely set apart for the purpose, for distribution among the people, who went up and received it from the priest, whose hand they kissed; and Dr. Rock informs us ("Church of our Fathers," i. p. 136) that at Vercelli, in the sacristy of St. Andrew's, is kept a very curious knife, said to have once belonged to St. Thomas of Canterbury, and is supposed to have been used by him in England in cutting the holy loaf. It is most likely of Anglo-Saxon workmanship, and was given to this church by Cardinal Guala, or Walo, who came as legate to England in 1216. The blade is of an unusual shape, and its handle of box-wood, carved with the occupations of each month throughout the year, somewhat resembling the same subjects in Shaw's 'Dresses and Decorations,' from the Anglo-Saxon MS. Julius, A. VI. This knife is figured in Allegranza's 'Opuscoli eruditi,' p. 35. 410.: Cremona, 1781. Among the sacred ornaments belonging, in the early part of the ninth century, to the church of St. Riquier, in France, was 'cultellus auro et margaritis paratus' (De Altarioum Ornatu,' Chron. Centol., ed. D'Achery, Spicil, ii. p. 306.) There can be little doubt but such a richly ornamented knife must have been for cutting the holy loaf." The miniatures which I have published, consequently, seem to me to go far to prove that both the knife and fan were employed in the Anglo-Saxon Church.

RELICS OF ST. CUTHBERT.

As the Gospels of Lindisfarne, written in honour of St. Cuthbert, constitute so important an element in the early history of the arts of this country, I cannot close this Appendix without noticing the remarkable series of relics of that Saint still preserved in the Cathedral of Durham. These consist of the fragments of his coffin, portable silver altar, comb, burse, and robes. The body of the Saint was enclosed in three coffins, the innermost of which, not only on the testimony of Reginald and the anonymous monk, both his-

torians of St. Cuthbert, but also from that of the coffin itself, was doubtless the identical coffin in which the remains of the Saint were placed in A.D. 698, eleven years after his death. The entire surface of this coffin was covered with figures of saints and inscriptions, cut in grooved lines, agreeing exactly with the style of the drawings and the form of the letters (and even the spelling of the name *Iohannes*, in the nominative case) with the undoubted earliest Hiberno-Saxon figures of the Evangelists.

Mr. Raine, in his "Saint Cuthbert," has given a fac-simile of the upper part of the figure of St. John, of the full size the head, with the nimbus, is 4 inches high; the right hand is laid open upon the breast, and the left hand, covered, holds a book. Unfortunately, the whole of this coffin is broken into small fragments, so that no entire figure exists but those of St. Thomas, St. Peter (holding in his right hand the keys), St. Andrew, St. Matthew, St. Michael, and St. Paul, with another figure, with a Latin inscription in Runic characters, which Mr. Raine thinks may be intended for IHSUS SANCTUS, a suggestion which does not appear to me tenable, as the Saviour is never so designated. Figures with wings, apparently angels; another figure, holding a sceptre; portions of drapery; St. Luke with a bull, with a nimbus; the Virgin and Child, the fore feet of a lion, and the head and neck of an eagle, with a nimbus, occur on various fragments. With respect to the letters of the inscriptions, Mr. Raine observes that "it is marvellous how perfectly they resemble the capitals in the Gospels of Lindisfarne given by Astle, and thus prove themselves to be coeval with that book."

The various accounts of the enveloping the body of the Saint attribute the use of gorgeous robes account for the fact that Mr. Raine was able to discover, amongst the fragments, not fewer than five different silken embroidered coverings, of two of which he gives engravings. One of these represents a knight on horseback, with hawk and hound, enclosed in an elaborate eight-lobed rosette, surrounded by detached leaves, below which is a border of ornaments which Mr. Raine fancied represented the .... of Jesse; below which is a row of rabbits, which Mr. Raine supposed had especial allusion to Lindisfarne, where that animal abounded. The other robe represents in an ornamented circle, a fantastic ship sailing on the sea, surrounded by fishes and ducks; the latter again supposed by Mr. Raine to represent the "eider ducks," in which St. Cuthbert took such great delight that they have ever since been called by his name, and consequently prove that the splendid robe was expressly made for the Saint just as Dr. Rock supposes that the ornamental birds represented in the MSS are also intended for St. Cuthbert's ducks. The many specimens which have lately been figured of Byzantine fabrics enable us to determine that these robes were certainly brought from the East; and when we refer to the royal donations made to St. Cuthbert's tomb, we find King Athelstan in person visiting the shrine of the Saint, and presenting to it a great number of valuable objects, including two patens, one made of gold and the other fabricated of Grecian workmanship (*Greca opera*), seven robes, three curtains, three pieces of tapestry, &c.; whilst King Edmund is expressly said to have turned aside on his march against the Scots, to visit the shrine of St. Cuthbert and invoke his aid, when, upon bended knee, he placed two bracelets taken from his own arms, together with two robes of Grecian workmanship, upon the holy body—"duo pallia græca supra sanctum corpus posuit." There can be little doubt that these are the two robes figured by Mr. Raine.

A large ivory comb (one of the usual episcopal *insignia*)

...bound, across its ornaments, as apparently full of interest with a large sort of cover beads and with a large hole in the middle between the rows. It is connected here in connection with the legend that the body of the Saint was incorruptible, which appears to have been evidenced by the few golden threads with which the head was girt having been confided to the faithful as the hair of the Saint, which were of course not displaced when placed in a frame. Mr. Raine, however, considers this comb merely contemporary with St. Cuthbert.

The small square portable altar, measuring 6 inches by 5½, covered with a silver plate, is unquestionably of the time of the Saint himself. In the centre, within a circle, is a cross with crystal limbs, terminating in scrolls, the spaces between the limbs filled in with raised interlaced narrow ribbons, surrounding this was a circular border, inscribed with Roman capital letters half an inch high, but the few remaining are of doubtful interpretation, the angles of the square are filled in with a foliated ornament. The tablet of wood thus covered was also found to be inscribed "IN HONOR . . . . S PETRI," with two crosses; the letters precisely resembling the capitals employed in the Durham MS., A. D. 17, coeval with St. Cuthbert.

The stole and maniple found on the body of the Saint are not less interesting, as the date of their execution is fixed by the period between 905 and 916 by the inscriptions of each, show-ing that they were made by Queen Ælflæd, the wife of King Edward the Elder, "PIO EPISCOPO FRITHESTANO" of Winchester, and there seems no reason to doubt that they were taken by King Athelstan, in 934, two years after Frithestan's death, from Winchester, and deposited at the shrine of St. Cuthbert amongst his other gifts, which, with a maniple being expressly mentioned amongst them. The groundwork of the stole is cloth of gold thread, as brilliant as when first made. In the middle of its length was embroidered the Agnus Dei, followed by full-length figures of all the Prophets, whose names were inscribed at the sides. The maniple contained in the middle the Dextra Dei, and at each of St. Gregory, Peter the Deacon, St. John Baptist, St. Sixtus Episcop. Laurence the Deacon, and St. James. These figures are by no means ill drawn, and are beautifully embroidered. Many of them hold branches, and foliage is freely introduced.

A girdle of scarlet and gold thread, two bracelets of gold tissue, apparently also portions of the donations of King Athelstan, a second maniple of more recent date, a linen bag for holding the sacramental elements, doubtless used by St. Cuthbert, together with his pectoral cross of gold (Raine pl. 1, fig. 3, "Old England," fig. 233), and portions of the fine gold wire found about the head, which has been supposed to be the material exhibited as the indestructible hair of the Saint when held in the flame (Raine, pp. 59, 212), are still preserved at Durham.

On a former examination of the tomb of the Saint in 1104, there was found a small copy of the Gospel of St. John, of which an account and fac-simile are given by Dr. Milner, to the "Archaeologia," vol. xvi. which is written in small Roman uncials of a very ancient character. (See "Pal. sacr. pict. Congr. SS. Augustine and Cuthbert," fig. 3.)

Thus the tomb of St. Cuthbert formed a veritable museum of mediæval art.

XP AUTEM
GENERATI
SIC ERAT CUM ESSET DIS
PONSATA MATER EIUS
MARIA IOSEPH ANTEQ̄A
CONVENIRENT INVENTA
EST IN UTERO HABENS

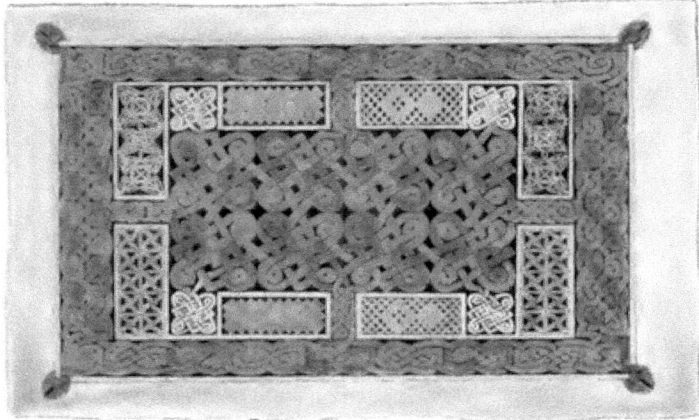

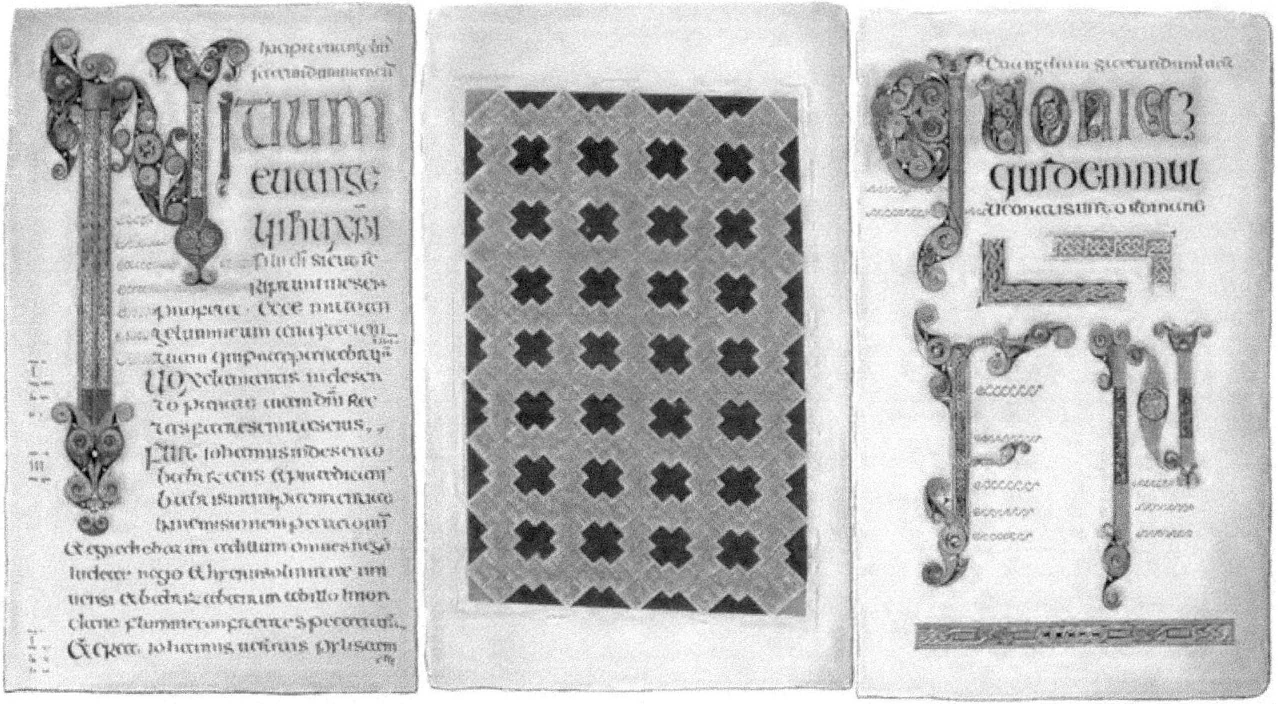

	ioseph	
VI	fuit	heli
VI	fuit	macchat
VI	fuit	leui
VI	fuit	melchi
VI	fuit	iauue
VI	fuit	ioseph
VI	fuit	macchat inc
VI	fuit	amos
VI	fuit	uacuum
VI	fuit	esli
VI	fuit	uagge
VI	fuit	maadh

Canon primus inquo iiii·

matĥ   marc   lucas   iohan

scs mĩchaͤl   scs cabriͤl

matt
the
us.
euang

lu
cas.
euang

mar
cus.
euang

ioh
an
nis.
euang

thomas scribsit.

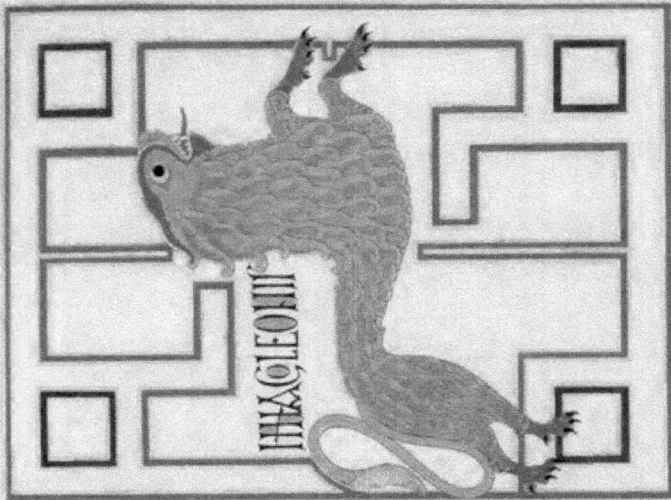

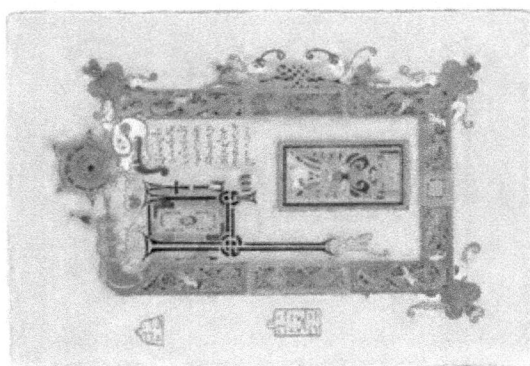

VITA CARET FINE ITA

cum constupuisset ihs

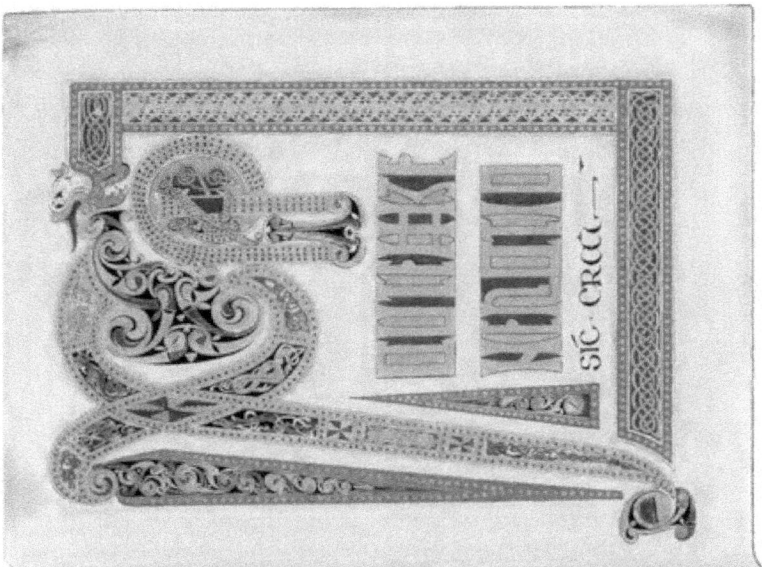

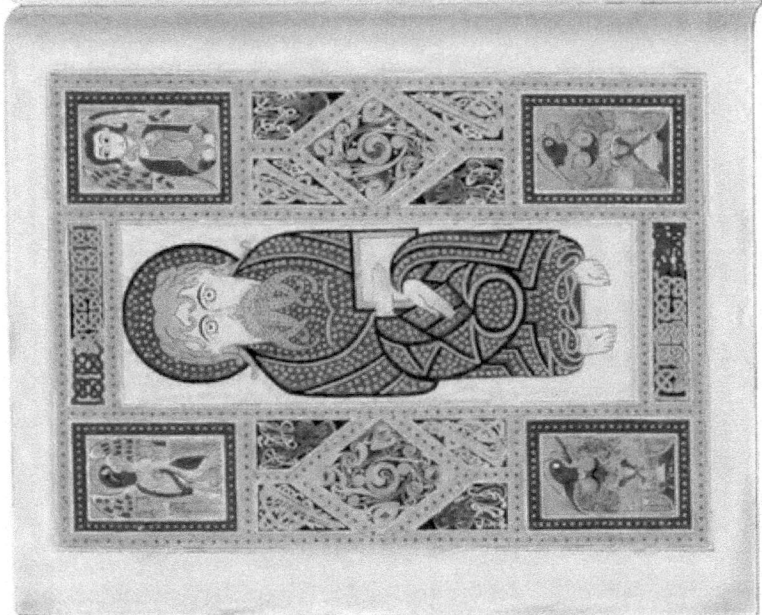

BEATUSVIR
QUINON
ABIIT
INCONSILIO
IMPIORUM
ETINVIACAROSSINONSTETIT
ETINCATHEDRA PESTIH
LENTIAENONSEDIT

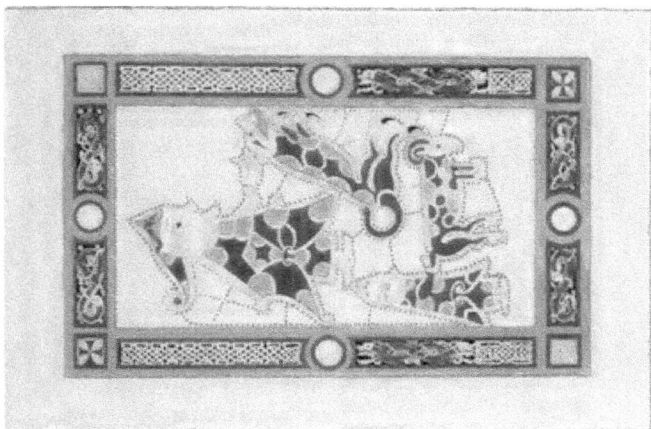
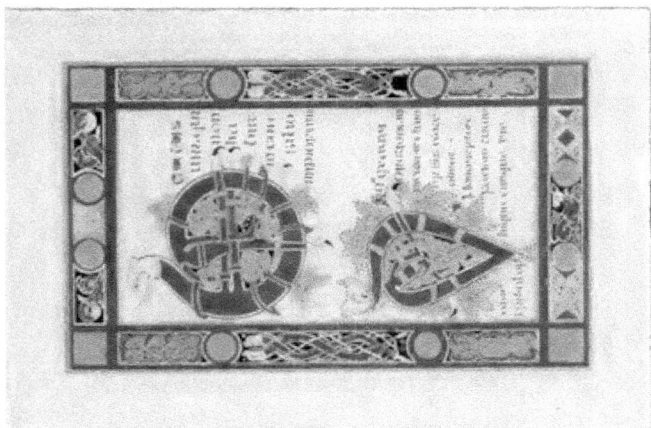

AMIDVDVM
ADPONTIFICALE
PROFICISCENSEON
TILIABVLVM FRA
TERNISSODALIVM
LATERVISEOMITAT⅁
ALMITATISVRE
SCRIPTA ME EMDI
OERITATIALLATA

XXXX

TVRONENSIVM VRBANA MINIMVS DORI EVANGELICVM

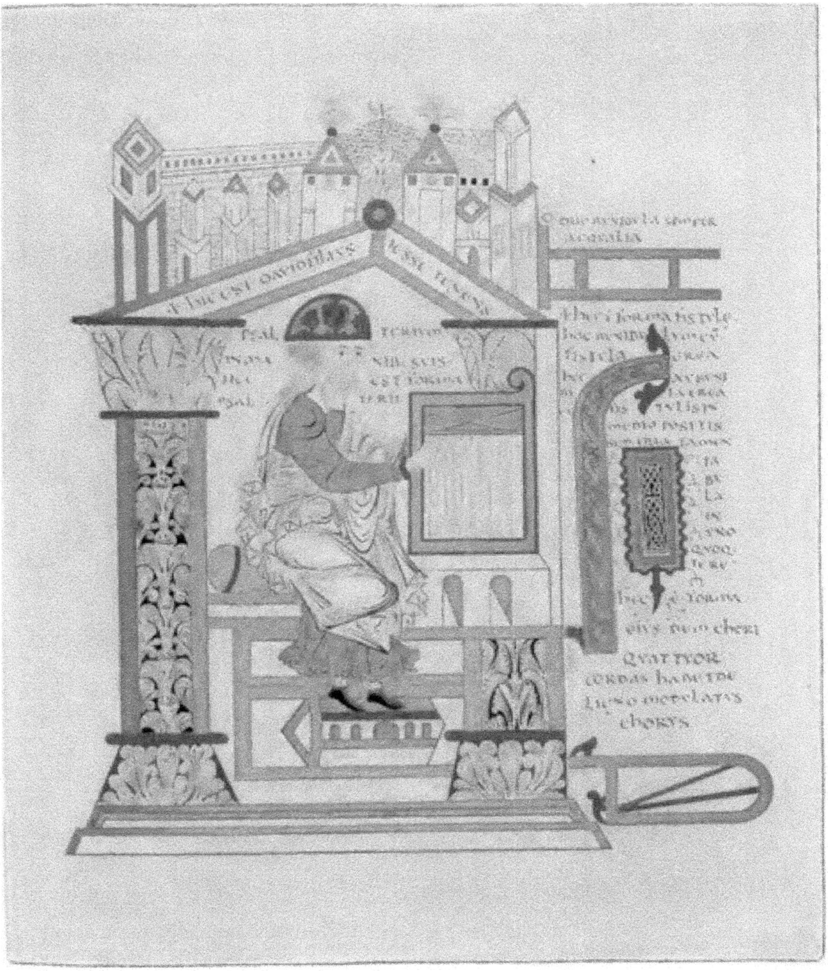

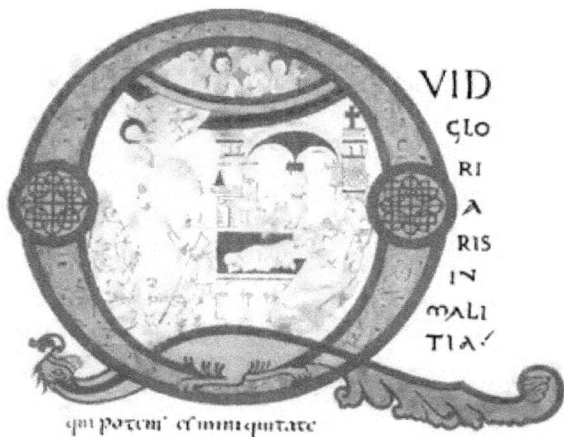

VID
GLO
RI
A
RIS
IN
MALI
TIA!

qui potens es in iniquitate

N͂E
EX
AV
DI
O
RA
TIO
NEM
MEAM.

& clamor meus ad te veniat ·

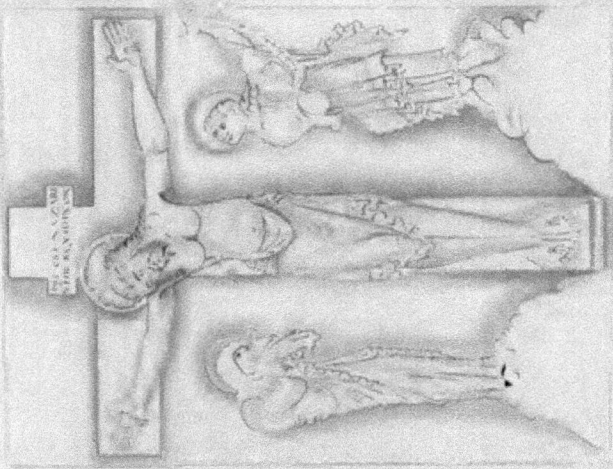

BE A TVS

VIR QVI NON
ABIIT IN CON
SILIO IMPIORVM
& inuia peccatorum nonstetit:

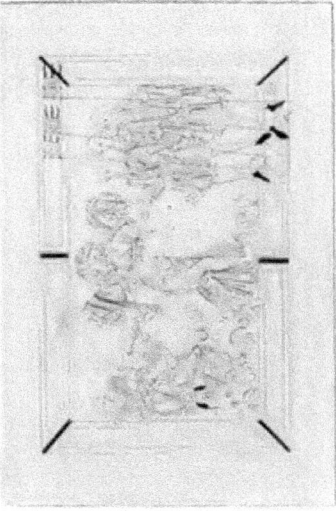

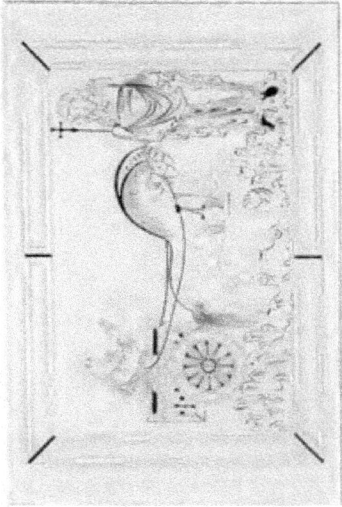

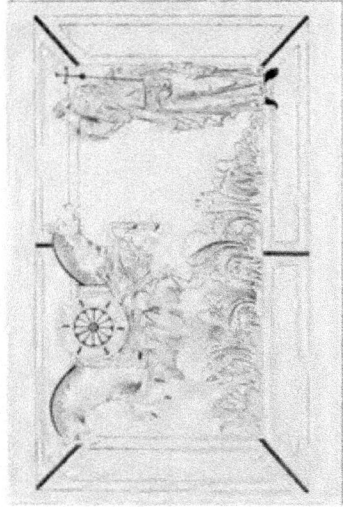

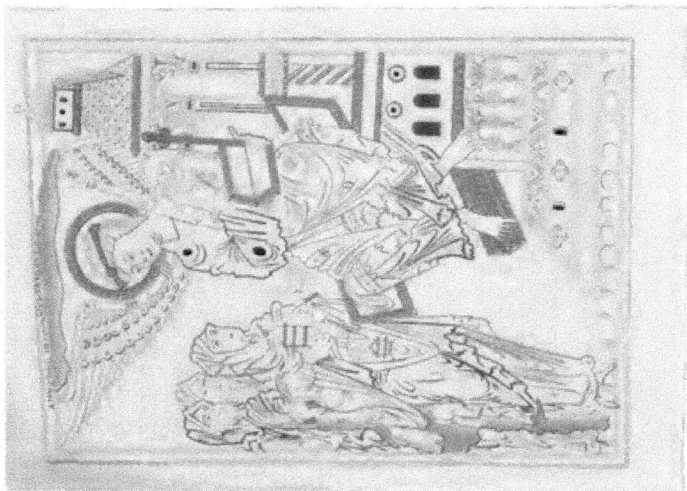

☩ EADO
GAR REX
hocpriuilegi
umnouodoi
OTIMONASTERI
OACOMNPOTEN
TIOÑOEIUSQUE
çenThiciohii
feiuslaudans
macnaliacon
sxxii

scripsit Biufprauilegi
fingrophu

DOM
NI
POTENS
TOTIVS
MACHI
NAEⒸNDIⒶ

A uno incarnationis
domini ꝺcccclxxvi.

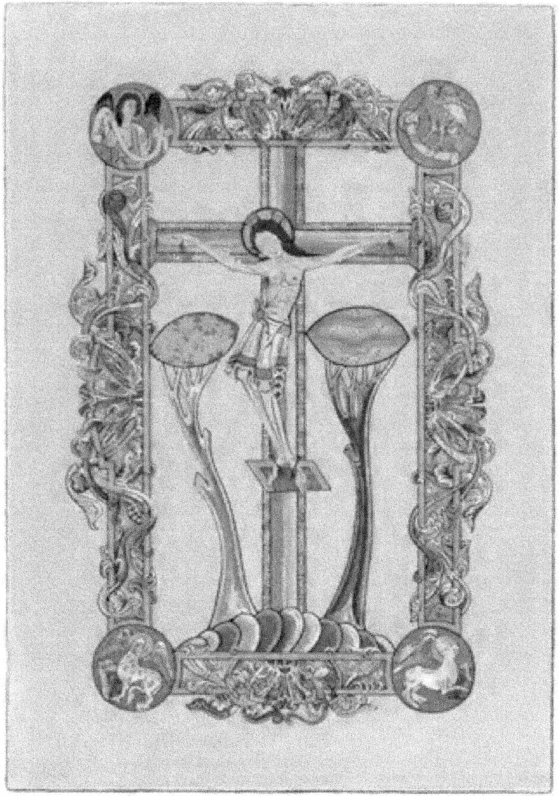

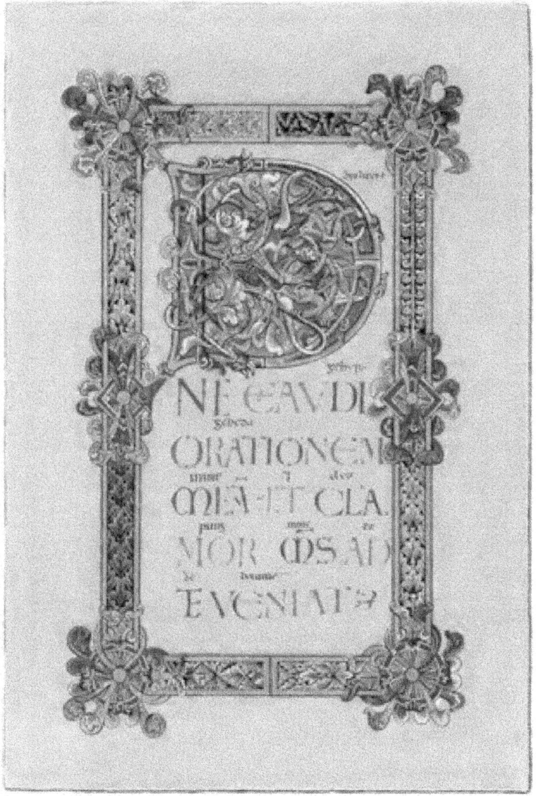

www.ingramcontent.com/pod-product-compliance
Lightning Source LLC
Chambersburg PA
CBHW030901270326
41929CB00008B/519